PRAISE FOR RED HOT & HOLY

"*Red Hot & Holy* is stunning on so many levels. This, ladies and gentlemen, is what the Divine Feminine looks and feels like—embodied, immediate, down-to-earth, and completely accessible. Bravo, Sera Beak!"

> CHRISTIANE NORTHRUP, MD, author of the *New York Times* bestsellers *Women's Bodies, Women's Wisdom* and *The Wisdom of Menopause*

"Sera Beak's memoir will take you on a passionate, provocative, and revealing journey through one woman's soulful sojourn into her true self. Red Hot & Holy makes no apologies, bares all, and crosses boundaries into uncharted mystical and emotional lands. If you're looking for a spiritual page-turner, you don't wanna miss this phenomenal book. I couldn't put it down!"

> KRIS CARR, bestselling author of *Crazy Sexy Cancer*

"*Red Hot & Holy* is wildly original, hilariously funny, and deeply wise. I think it can start a movement of the great and good and maenadic ladies of the Red persuasions. It is truly cataclysmic and magnificently dangerous! I would join up even in my now-76th year. It is what life is all about . . .'"

> JEAN HOUSTON, author of *The Wizard of Us: Transformational Lessons from Oz*

"Sera Beak blazes with bold and flowing passion for the direct mystic transmission and primal creative power of the sacred feminine. *Red Hot & Holy* is juicy, funny, raw, and a wonderful contribution for modern-day soul adventurers."

> SHIVA REA, yogini and author of *Tending the Heart Fire*

"'Red Night of the Soul!' Only Sera Beak could approach the classic spiritual emergency as an occasion for make-up sex with the Holy One. Sera embraces the whole of soul-life with fearless and often hilarious directness, from the most harrowing plunges into the depths of emptiness to the most intimate reunion with the Sacred Self."

> MIRABAI STARR, author of *God of Love* and translator of *Dark Night of the Soul* and *The Interior Castle*

"I heard that once a young person came to Hafiz, asking for permission to use some of his poems in another language. And after permission was granted, said, 'What is the most important quality in the translation I need to make the poems . . . true? And Hafiz replied, 'My poems—like great art—lift the corners of the mouth, the soul's mouth, the heart's mouth—and affect any opening that can make love.' I think there is some grand art in the work of Sera Beak. Go for it; grab hold, dance, fly, applaud life."

DANIEL LADINSKY, international bestselling author

"Sera Beak's *Red Hot & Holy* is a permission slip to bring your most soulful self to the spiritual table without limiting restrictions. In a world full of spiritual self-help teachers who are either feeding your ego, nourishing their own, or asking you to be less of Who You Really Are, Sera Beak is a refreshingly disruptive breath of light. Don't read this book if you're not willing to get out of your comfort zone. But if you're ready to unleash the full potential of your true self, dive in. This book will ignite fireworks in the heart of your soul and leave your spirit dancing a red hot tango."

LISSA RANKIN, MD, *New York Times* bestselling author of *Mind Over Medicine*

"If you're looking for a spiritual book filled with raw passion, brutal honesty, and uncompromising integrity look no further; Sera Beak's *Red Hot & Holy* is it. Sera's heart fans the flames of Divine Grace and fierce wisdom. Read this book and let it burn baby burn."

CHRIS GROSSO, bestselling author of *Indie Spiritualist: A No Bullshit Exploration of Spirituality*

"Sera Beak is the real raw deal. She is a direct hotline to the divine feminine. The consequence of encountering her—in person or through her glorious book—is that the intensity of your connection to your own divinity turns on and turns up to a luscious new volume. A blast of Sera is as good as dancing naked in the moonlight."

REGENA THOMASHAUER, creatrix of Mama Gena's School of Womanly Arts

"What do you get when you combine a weird, hip angel of a thirty-something woman, advanced training in the study of religion, laugh-out-loud writing, God as Girl, and a direct encounter with a cosmic soul no longer 'tricked into a tradition'? You get Sera Beak. You get this book. Which is really not a book at all, but a living revelation and American Gnostic gospel posing as a spiritual memoir."

JEFFREY J. KRIPAL, author of *Authors of the Impossible:*
The Paranormal and the Sacred

"This is a brave, untamed, and yes, holy and hot book. Sera Beak describes a spirituality unfettered by dogma (traditional or new age). Like all true mystics, Sera's words compel us to fearlessly confront whatever stands in the way of our awakening. Sera Beak is pioneering new pathways."

GAIL STRAUB, teacher, activist, and author of *Returning to My Mother's House:*
Taking Back the Wisdom of the Feminine

"Sera Beak is the real deal, and her fearless, fabulous book is on the must-read list for all of my soul sisters!"

KATHLEEN MCGOWAN, bestselling author of *The Expected One*

"Finally, a book *both* my mother-in-law and I can enjoy!"   MARY MAGDALENE

"Holy. Shit."   SERA'S SHADOW

RED HOT & HOLY

RED HOT & HOLY

A HERETIC'S LOVE STORY

SERA BEAK

sounds true
BOULDER, COLORADO

Sounds True, Inc.
Boulder, CO 80306

Copyright © 2013, 2015 Sera Beak

Sounds True is a trademark of Sounds True, Inc.

Published 2015

Cover photo © Karina Marie Diaz

For permissions information, see page 263.

Printed in the United States of America

Library of Congress Cataloging-in-Publication Data
Beak, Sera, 1975–
  Red hot and holy : a heretic's love story / Sera Beak.
    pages cm
Includes bibliographical references.
ISBN 978-1-62203-053-8
1. Beak, Sera, 1975– 2. Spiritual biography. 3. Spirituality. I. Title.
BL73.B43A3 2013
204.092—dc23
[B]
                                    2013000542

Ebook ISBN: 978-1-62203-111-5

10 9 8 7 6 5 4 3 2 1

Stay as Close as you can to your own experience; don't stray too far off course. Stay with Us. Give people a front row seat to Our Relationship — that's where the real action is . . . that's Love's Real Reminder.

THE RED LADY

CONTENTS

To God's Wife, Buddha's Buddhette, Shiva's Shakti, Mohammad's Missus, J.C.'s Magdalene, El's Asherah, Great Spirit's Snuggle Bunny, Our Mother Who Isn't Only in Heaven, The Great SheBang, Yo Mama, She She Powa, Madame Mojo, Soul Sista, The Original Redvolutionary, The Secret Lineage Hopper, The Holy Grail Grinner, The Ecstatic Exclamation Point after All That Is!, The Forecast of Fire, The Numinous Naughty, The Freak Flagger, The Licking Life Force, The Everlasting Embrace, The Casual Fridays of Spiritual Life, The Engagement Ringer, The Red Thread, The Cornucopia of Compassion, The Creative Cause (and Effect), The Constant Offering, The Loudest Inner Ruption, The Cardinal Rule Breaker, The Queen Bee, The Snake Charmer, The Mama Bear Hug, The One Who Plays Powerfully, The One Who Shakes Certainty, Bakes Boldness, and Wakes Wisdom, The Influx of Inspiration, The Flood of Freedom, The Ultimate Blasphemy, The Heretic's Heart Pump, Your Name in Scarlet Letters, The Embodiment of Embodiment, The Post Partum Passion Flower, The Popped Cosmic Cherry, Profundity's Panty Raider, The Red Light District of Divinity, Ass Consciousness, Laughter's Lubricant, Lightning's Lingerie, Creation's Centerfold, Beauty's Compass, Salvation's Strip Tease, Duality's Smooch, Nonduality's Life Coach, Orthodoxy's Heart Attack, All Creatures' Comfort, The Dispenser of Delight, The Grace Smuggler, The Center of the Rose, The Prophetess's Present, The Seductress of the Senses, The Skin Saver, The Flesh Frisker, The Spine Waver, The Tail Blazer, The Dark Dame, The Shady Lady, Your Guttural Instinct, The Earth's Perfume, The Sassy Sound Biter, The Seventh Veil Dropper, The Ultimate Groin Grabber, The Wonder from Down Under, Our Lady of Horny Holiness, The Pioneer of Pussy Power, The Dominatrix of Doubt, The Most Experienced Lover of Us All, The North and South Pole Dancer, Star Light, Star Bright, The Very First Super Star Who Knew Her Might, The Sound of Your Music, The Red Hot Chili Pepper, The Booty Shaker,

The Ever-Coming Reminder of Raw Reality, The Silent Roar, The Sacred Rager, The Deviant Destructress of Anything That Keeps You Small, The Cosmic Permission Slip to Be Your All, The Ripest, Juiciest, Forbidden Fruit, The Angel Who Wears Prada, The Devil Who Wears Paradox, The Virgin of Las Vegas and the Whore of the Vatican, The One Who Makes Love for a Living, The One Who Turns Tricks for Transformation, The One Who Makes Dogma Faint, The One Who Makes Fire Sweat, The One Who Longs to Touch and Be Touched, The Queen of Hearts, Your Absolute Adoration, The One Who Laughs Inappropriately, The One Who Has Nothing to Hide (but has always been hidden), The One Who Scares All Major (and most minor) Religions, The One You Were Taught to Mistrust, The One Who Alters Every Altar, The One Who Understands the Power of Adornment, The One Who Boogies in Your Body, The One Who Decorates Your Dreams, The One Who Turns Your Shadows into Puppets, The One Who Mud-Wrestles Spirit (and wins), The One Who Feels . . . Everything, The One Who Is Furious at What We Have Done to Her Planet, The One Who Begs Your Breath into Your Belly, The One You Never Have to Clean Yourself Up For, The One Who Wants ALL of You

on Her Dance Floor.

The One Who Demands Your Entire Heart to Live in and Your Entire Life
to Love In,
The One Who Misses You,
The One Who Aches for You,
The One Who Knows You,
The One Who Embraces You,
The One Who Unleashes You,
The One Who Lives for You and in You and through You and as You,
The One Who Can Be Found in the Next Closest Mirror
If You Wink Just Right . . .

PRELUDE

Imagine that you and I are sitting at a plush wine bar that is draped with Red velvet curtains. We're about to order our second glass of a spicy floral pinot noir,

when you suddenly lean in close,

and ask me to share my love story, and hold nothing back.

A Red-hot blush spreads across my body as I reflect on what it is you are asking.

Because my Love Story is an epic, really — most definitely a saga, for sure a spiritual soap opera. It's dramatic and emotional, personal yet archetypal, mundane yet multidimensional, ancient yet modern, familiar yet foreign, hilarious and even cheesy at times (cheese comes with the whole love-story genre).

It's filled with eccentric characters, such as Mary Magdalene, the Hindu goddess Kali, the Persian poet Rumi, the Zen mystic Ikkyü, the Buddhist teacher Saraha, some of the Hebrew bible bad girls (Eve, Lilith, and the Whore of Babylon), the Swiss psychotherapist Carl Jung, Gnostics, *tantrikas, dakinis,* witches — all mixed together with Red wine, tattoos, past lives, erotic encounters, heretical lineages, and quite a bit of fire, tears, and Red rose petals.

After my initial hesitation, I start talking — not because I especially *want* to talk about myself in this way or because I think my story is so special or unique or deserves the next three hours of your time, but because I know, deep down, past my insecurities and shyness and worries about what you're gonna think of me, that if I actually tell you the truth, it will give you permission to tell *your* truth.

Because I know I'm not alone with All This . . .

and because I know the best way to get to know a Goddess is to listen to a woman tell her story . . .

and because I know She can only roar through our voices when we stop being so goddamned careful, spiritually correct, and hidden . . .

and because I have risked everything, and will continue to risk everything—including your friendship and opinion of me—for Her.

So, I want you to feel my gaze, see my flushed cheeks, smell my breath, and watch my body movements. I want you to witness my nervousness and occasional awkwardness, my openings and my closings, my passion and my pain, which always accompany sharing what's real.

We will laugh our asses off, we will roll our eyes, we will let tears come and go, we will pause for long moments, just 'cause. We will take breaks to stretch our bodies and shake our booties. And, throughout it all, we will hold the space for the Divine to dance between us, massaging extra-tight pieces of us loose, rubbing our bellies, tickling us when we start taking ourselves or our stories too seriously, and grounding us when we are not taking ourselves or our stories seriously enough. We will honor the Divine in this way, and we will allow the Divine to honor us. For it takes a tremendous amount of courage to share our heart's truth.

And there will be Moments,

like right now . . .

when I/She will reach toward you

and press my/Her warm palm against your beautiful Red heart . . .

and Together,

We will Remember what words can never communicate.

FIRE HAZARDS

1. My writing has received comments like this:

    I find your blog totally disgusting and tasteless. You call yourself a woman of God? You should be ashamed of yourself! I can't believe your filthy mouth! NOT funny at all and no class whatsoever.

    —*Concerned*

    I have a dirty mouth and a dirty sense of humor. Kinder commentators have described my writing as "tongue in cheek." *Most* of the time, it's Her Red tongue in my rouged cheek. I recognize and honor the fact that not all of us are used to such candor when it comes to spirituality, but my irreverence arises from a deep reservoir of reverence, respect, and profound love for the Divine.

2. Therefore, this book comes with a three-drink minimum. Red wine is my suggestion. Or rose tea. Or angel sweat.

3. On a sober note: I'm a white, middle-class, Western woman who has been gifted with the life circumstances, time, and resources to dive deep into her soul and write about it. It is a privilege and a responsibility that I take very seriously. When any woman reveals her soul publicly and dares to act from this inner source of Divine authority, it is a private-turned-public revolution—for me, it happens to be a Redvolution. Writing my Love Story is an act of service to all women and this planet.

    My hope is that this book ignites your own revolution and reminds you to live *your* Love Story, within and without the fire.

4. On a lusher note: This book shares what happened when I fell in love with a Red hot and holy Goddess and later received a series of

Rouge Awakenings—highly uncomfortable, hugely humbling soul spankings from said Red Goddess, which turned my life upside down and set it on fire. (Being Redvolutionary does not make me very cool, but it does make me hot.)

5. I call this Red hot and holy Goddess "the Red Lady" or "my Lady." She might appear in this book a bit like my imaginary Friend, but you should know right away that She's more Real than I am. Who the hell is She? That's the ultimate question and answer that inspires this entire book. Read on to find out.

6. This book is not a treatise on the Divine Feminine or on the *color* red. Nor is this my autobiography—otherwise I would have included falling in love with that Turkish mobster while writing for the travel guide *Let's Go: Turkey,* or getting worms in my feet at a yoga retreat in Mexico, or running from a pack of rabid dogs in Kathmandu, or getting blessed by a young Catholic mystic priest in Croatia who had the stigmata and then gaining twenty pounds in two weeks. Not exactly the blessing I was hoping for. Point is, the focus of this book is less on my external voyages and more on my internal journeys with Red.

7. In fact, I wrote this book from the inside out. My methodology: I have an intuition/personal experience/vision/dream that resonates as truth. Afterward, an external quote or piece of wisdom shows up that supports or comes close to describing my own experience (and says it much better than I ever could). So I use it. I do not allow the quotes or external sources of wisdom to use me. Therefore, many of the quotes and research I use in this book are completely taken out of their original context and are made to fit my Red context. My apologies to those who wrote the excellent quotes and offered the wonderful wisdom—I mean no disrespect.

8. Therefore, it's best to read this book while wearing Red rose–colored glasses. If you *only* use a lens of scholarship, psychology, history, mythology, religion, philosophy, feminism, anthropology, sociology, Jungian analysis, integral theory, New Age, or pop spirituality to understand this book, I shall fail you, repeatedly. Sometimes even on purpose. My gentle request is that you not analyze the information in this book *too much.* Pay more

attention to how this book makes you *feel* rather than just how it makes you think.

9. Although Red rose–colored glasses are encouraged and my personal Love Story forms the backbone of this book, enough impersonal information is included to inspire and support your own unique vision and soul journey. However, if you prefer a less personal Red book, please check out my first book, *The Red Book: A Deliciously Unorthodox Approach to Igniting Your Divine Spark.*

10. *Artistically,* this book is a mashup. If you're not familiar with this term, a mashup happens when a DJ mixes two or more songs together, overlaying beats, underlying melodies, and mixing vocals. At first a mashup sounds a little dissonant, but if you relax into it, a wider movement of sound happens, communicating a much bigger Message than any of the songs could have done alone.

This book is part spiritual memoir, part self-help, and part Shout-Out from my soul to yours.

Sometimes I sound like a girlfriend. Sometimes I sound like a professor. Sometimes I stop speaking in English and start speaking in my native Red tongue.

11. *Structurally,* the book is split into B.M. (Before Marion) and A.M. (After Marion), which refers to the time in my life before and after I interviewed the eighty-something-year-old Jungian analyst extraordinaire Marion Woodman.

The first five chapters in B.M. are foundational and read *relatively* normally (well, for a love-drunk, slightly risqué religion scholar). My story heats up after I leave Harvard (chapters 6–9).

In A.M. (chapters 10–22), everything changes. Abruptly. My story gets more raw, more personal, and definitely more freaky. In fact, the last five chapters could give you heartburn . . . or a heart attack. I might even lose you.

(This is *not* one of those books where it's okay to skip ahead. Divine winks—synchronicities, symbols, dreams, poems, guidance, heavy-breathing holy hints—flirt off every page, and only the direct encounter with all of them allows the full Redvelation to happen.)

12. *Energetically,* this book resembles a Red rose—outer lighter petals first, then the inner darker petals, and finally, the center.

13. *Spiritually,* this book is an Offering to and from Red.

   During an American tour in 1922, forty-five-year-old modern dancer Isadora Duncan received a lot of saucy press about her passionate performances in Boston. In fact, one paper said, "She looked pink, talked red, and acted scarlet."[1]

   At her second concert, Isadora told the audience: "Thank God the Boston critics don't like me. If they did, I should feel I was hopeless . . . I give you something from the heart. I bring you something real."[2] The audience supposedly consisted of quite a few students from Harvard. At the end of her performance to Tchaikovsky's *Pathétique,* she held up a red scarf and shouted,

This is red! So am I! . . . You were once wild here! Don't let them tame you![3]

   And the Boston audience caught sight of Isadora's naked breasts, (about which she later remarked, "For am I not striving to fuse soul and body in one unified image of beauty?"[4]). The mayor of Boston proceeded to ban her from all future performances in the city, and her tour manager warned her if she made one more speech like that or "mismanaged" her garments again, the tour was dead. Isadora ended the tour rather than cap her self-expression.

   This book is a Red scarf that reveals part of my Body.

This is red! So am I! . . . You were once wild here! Don't let them tame you!

(BEFORE MARION)

Red is the color of blood, and I will seek it:
I have sought it in the grass.
It is the color of steep sun seen through eyelids.

It is hidden under the suave flesh of women,
Flows there, quietly flows.
It mounts from the heart to the temples, the singing
mouth—
As cold sap climbs to the rose.

I am confused in webs and knots of scarlet
Spun from the darkness;
Or shuttled from the mouths of thirsty spiders.

Madness for red! I devour the leaves of autumn.
I tire of the green of the world.
I am myself a mouth for blood . . .

CONRAD AIKEN
"Red Is the Color of Blood"

I

DIVINE WILD CHILD

I want us to envision that what children go through has to do with finding a place in the world for their specific calling. They are trying to live two lives at once, the one they were born with and the one of the place and among the people they were born into. The entire image of a destiny is packed into a tiny acorn, the seed of a huge oak on small shoulders. And its call rings loud and persistent and is as demanding as any scolding voice from the surroundings. The call shows in the tantrums and obstinacies, in the shyness and retreats, that seem to set the child against our world but that may be protections of the world it comes with and comes from.

JAMES HILLMAN
The Soul's Code

As a child, I was madly in love with God. Gaga for God. In grade school, I used to write "I (heart) God" at the top of all my homework assignments and in the margins of the notes I passed to my girlfriends about which boys we thought were cute. Next to *The Little Princess,* a children's bible was kept on my bedside table for nightly reading. Miracles? Prophetic dreams? Angels? Healing the sick? Sign me up for those gigs! And every Thursday I believed J.C. dropped by my bedroom so I could ask him personal questions and tell him which sister was annoying me the most. I was magnetized to rosaries, prayers, and pyramids the way other kids were to doughnuts, MTV, and Cabbage Patch Kids, and every time I saw a religious figure (priest, nun, Buddhist monk, Hare Krishna) out in public, it would take an enormous amount of willpower not to *stalk* them.

When Career Days at school would come around, my questionnaire would look a little something like this:

Favorite subject? God
Favorite hobby? God
What do you want to be when you grow up? God

(Okay, there was a brief time when I was six years old when the answer to that last question was "an albino." I thought albinism would make me glow in the dark.)

When I was a child, God was not a belief or a magical Santa Claus type. He was as real as my heart. I *felt* Him (inside me). I *recognized* Him (everywhere). I *knew* Him (personally). We hung out together, and I never wanted our rendezvous to stop. I only wanted us to draw even closer. I assumed I was experiencing what many Catholics refer to as "the call" to be a priest, so I matter-of-factly informed my parish priests and Sunday school teachers of my future vocation. They laughed, patted my head, and told me I couldn't have heard the call to be a priest because I had a vagina.

Okay, they didn't say that last part, but believe me, it was implied.

They did tell me that only men were allowed to be priests because Jesus only had male disciples (to which Mary Magdalene juts out her left hip and slaps her round cheek with *The Gospel of Mary Magdalene*). But, of course, I could always be a nun.

Every time I was told I couldn't be a priest, it felt like a silver bullet was being shot through my Red heart, because when I told those religious authorities I was being called, I *really* meant it. God called to me not only through my Red heart but also through the trees, the stones, the birds, my parents' Oldsmobile station wagon, grocery carts, and shiny Red apples. I remember walking all ninja-like behind my family on summer-night strolls so they wouldn't catch me kissing the trunks of trees, lovingly caressing the warm stones, and affectionately patting the dirty sidewalk. What was clear to me when I was a wee one (and probably to you when you were that young) was that I was here to Love, and that everything in this world was *aching* to Love and Be Loved in return. That's right, *everything*. Even grocery carts.

The whole
World is secretly on fire. The stones
Burn, even the stones
They burn me. How can a [wo]man be still or

Listen to all things burning? How can [s]he dare
To sit with them when
All their silence
Is on fire?[1]

— *Thomas Merton,* "In Silence"

As you might've ascertained, despite (or because of) my unfettered giddiness for God, I wasn't exactly a traditional Catholic. I was bored out of my mind during Mass. I openly questioned the hell out of almost everything my poor Sunday school teachers taught that did not resonate with my experience of the Big G. I wanted a pink Trans Am as my future nun-mobile. I dramatically swiveled my young hips when I walked up and down church aisles . . . *for* God. I thought Jesus was hot. Seriously hot. And I thought we should celebrate his holy hotness each Sunday with rockin' music and ecstatic dancing.

Before I overdose you with my spiritual sass, I should share a few of my many personal paradoxes: In my early years, I often acted like a divine wild child. But when I was ten years old, my family moved from the Red-hot clays of Georgia to the green, cool plains north of Chicago, where I became painfully shy, desperate to fit in, a "good girl," and a devout people-pleaser. Like many children, I learned to hide what was most true for me, and I became terrified of speaking publicly, especially when what I wanted to say didn't match the spiritual or social status quos surrounding me. As Gaston Bachelard teaches, "What is the source of our first suffering? It lies in the fact that we hesitated to speak. It was born in the moment when we accumulated silent things within us."[2]

By sixth grade, I started exploring everything from astrology to reincarnation, astral dreaming to auras — basically the New Age aisle in any bookstore became my second home. I quickly found out that the Catholic Church did not readily accept these metaphysical subjects. Trusting my honest curiosity for the ever-expanding realms of "Spirit" that I was experiencing over the set beliefs of the beloved tradition I came from, I quite respectfully, but with utter certainty, left the Church.

By the time I reached high school, I was the girl you would go to if you had a peculiar dream or you thought your dead grandmother was trying to contact you or you felt a weird vibe in your basement. I wore purple Doc Martens with my school uniform, danced at all-night raves, had a serious boyfriend, was vice president of my class, laughed at the right jokes, said the right things, and continued to keep my passion for the Divine on the down low. I stuck out just enough to be thought of as special and cool, but not enough to be thought of as weird or (gasp) *uncool.*

It was exhausting.

I remember one much-needed spring break my family spent on Kiawah Island, outside Charleston, South Carolina. Almost every night, I would wander past the shifting sand dunes, plop down on the beach, play Peter Gabriel's "Mercy Street" on my CDman ("She pictures a soul, with no leak at the seam"), and bawl my eyes out. Everything in me reached out, aching to go "home." While I knew God was just as much here as elsewhere, I also knew that places and spaces existed where I felt *much* closer to the Divine than I did in high school, than I did on the North Shore of Chicago, than I did on planet Earth. Lying heartbroken on the still-warm sand, gazing up at the starry night, I would forward the CD to Gabriel's "Red Rain" ("Red rain is coming down all over me"), and sometimes I could feel Something indescribably loving reaching toward *me.*

My senior year in high school, I found a mentor—a wonderful religion teacher who introduced me to the fascinating work of Swiss psychotherapist Carl Jung, mythologist Joseph Campbell (who coined the oh-so-popular phrase "follow your bliss"), and spiritual-lite book classics such as Hermann Hesse's *Siddhartha.* I realized that I didn't have to drop-kick divinity every time I entered a classroom. Instead, I could actually *feed* my hunger for divinity *in* school. This was a breakthrough.

When I got to college, I created a "self-determined major" in religious studies (my small liberal arts school did not offer a religion major at the time), which was the perfect cover for my fetish for all things spiritual. Now I could talk about God or angels or reincarnation anytime I wanted, without sounding like a total freak, 'cause I was *studying* it *for* school. That's right, I became a *religion scholar.* (You need to give that last line a badass attitude and vocal inflection or it just won't read right.)

While studying the world's religions with excellent professors in a liberal arts environment, I couldn't help but develop a genuine appreciation for the diverse beliefs that support our wisdom traditions, for the profundity of *all* the holy texts, and for the sacred splendor that *all* religions can't help but reflect at their core. So, I became a Hoover for the Holy during my first two years of college. I sucked up every religious book, practice, and teaching I could get ahold of. But alas, my passion for my studies began to wane at the end of my sophomore year of college. (I realize that was sort of soon to become dissatisfied with my favorite academic subject, but when it comes to divinity, if I'm not feelin' It, I have a difficult time paying attention.) I started to fall asleep in my sociology/psychology/anthropology of religion lectures, rolled my eyes in my Jewish/Islamic/Hindu studies classes, and wanted to tear off my clothes and run around screaming in my Christian theology courses.

As an empathetic, open-minded, and politically correct student, I was alarmed by my spiritually *incorrect* feelings. You see, at that point in my life, I had nothing external to point to in my studies of religion—or in my personal explorations of New Age spirituality—to validate my chronic internal cravings for more *heat,* movement, aliveness, wildness, and okay, yes, sexiness when it came to spirituality. As British poet Colin Oliver moans, "What a sad thing to be part of institutions which wind up dousing the very thing that began them: Fire."[3] Thinking, or rather *hoping,* that my spiritual frustration was simply due to too much class time, I decided to go abroad.

I spent part of my junior year studying the Tibetan religion, culture, and language in Nepal, Tibet, and Dharamsala, India (the seat of the Tibetan government in exile). Vajrayana Buddhism is a vibrant mixture of the religious philosophy that originated with Siddhartha Gautama (aka the Buddha) in India around the sixth century BCE and the animistic/shamanistic tradition, called Bon, that was alive in Tibet way before Buddhism crossed the Himalayas. This form of Buddhism is pretty "far out"—chock-full of colorful deities, guiding oracles, unsolved mysteries, and local magic. It sounded like the perfect religious tradition to reignite my scholarly passion.

During this intensive program, my classmates and I had the privilege of learning from many well-respected *rinpoches,* monks, and nuns (all varieties of Tibetan Buddhist teachers and practitioners), including the Dalai Lama himself, whom I got to meet, auspiciously enough, on my twenty-first birthday. My classmates earnestly studied all the Buddhist texts they could get translated; bought all the sandalwood incense, *malas* (prayer beads), and *thankas* (sacred Buddhist paintings) they could fit into their dusty backpacks; meditated their asses off; hopped from one teacher to the next to receive Buddhist transmissions (sacred teachings); took the bodhisattva vow (a vow to become enlightened in order to help all beings); and started shaving their heads like the monastics (yep, even some of the girls).

And where was I during this Buddhapalooza? I was there, front row and center (with my long hair) . . . for a few months anyway. And then the all-too-familiar feelings of spiritual discontent and frustration returned. So, I started ditching meditation practice so I could dance in my room to English

7

trip-hop, cutting morning circumambulations around the Dalai Lama's temple in order to wander around the colorful Indian bazaars, and passing on megawatt spiritual transmissions from important teachers in order to cruise the backpackers' English book swaps.

One day, while digging through worn-out copies of *Siddhartha,* I came across Tom Robbins's *Skinny Legs and All* and devoured that fine piece of luscious literature in one long, sweaty sitting over refills of *po cha* (Tibetan yak-butter tea). In case you haven't had the honor, *Skinny Legs and All* is full of charmingly chatty inanimate objects, messy intimate human relationships, frisky deities, passionate sex, rowdy humor, and Salome's dance of the seven veils. While reading this dusty book at the base of the Himalayas, something inside me started to

Come Back to *Life.*

The next day, I self-consciously raised my hand in my Buddhist studies class and, with a shaky voice, said that while I respected everything I was learning, "enlightenment" sounded (gulp) kind of *boring* to me. The class fell silent. The Buddhist teacher shrugged his shoulders. I turned a deep shade of Red.

Was I egotistical, rebellious, ignorant, and materialistic? A bit. But when I was living and studying in India, Nepal, and Tibet, even though I was around astute spiritual wisdom, time-honored sacred practices, and oceans of compassion, I began to feel like a part of me was dying, or at least drying up like some sort of creepy desert image from Al Gore's *An Inconvenient Truth.* So what gives?

Follow the Red brick road . . .

One day, not long after my classroom confession, a rough-looking, long-haired Buddhist teacher I met in a tea shop told me a story about a Buddhist monk named Saraha, who lived in the eighth century in Bengal. Like all monks, Saraha was a renunciant. He lived in a monastery, shut away from work, family, sex, chocolate, and so on. He couldn't talk, touch, or even look at women, because women were seen as distractions on the path. In fact, at this time in Buddhism's history, women were thought to be incapable of achieving enlightenment; they had to wait to be reincarnated as men in order to go for the gold.

The story goes that one day, spiritually studious, always-on-time, robes-always-ironed, mind-always-clean Saraha was outside the monastery, running some errands for his fellow monks, when suddenly a group of wild women surrounded him and started teasing him about his Buddhist practice, touching him, calling him pet names, giggling, rubbing themselves up against him, and getting all sorts of close encounters with him.

Saraha was horrified. He realized this event not only made him "impure" but also could get him kicked out of his monastery. He begged the crazy women to stop harassing him and said he would do anything if they would go away and let him go back to his monastic life in peace. The sexy troublemakers told him they would leave him alone for good *if* he spent one night with them in the jungle. Saraha agreed, probably thinking: "Hey, this can't be so bad. One night in a jungle teaching the Buddhist dharma [path] to these strange, undisciplined, unspiritual women, and then I can go back to my life as a simple Buddhist monk." Yeah. Uh-huh. 'Cause that's what makes for a good story.

So, off Saraha went into the deep, dark jungle with the seductive women who were actually dakinis—female beings who manifest enlightened activity, free from conventional perceptions, attitudes, and beliefs. Interestingly enough, dakinis often appear to practitioners in Red. According to many Buddhist beliefs, these enlightened feminine beings usually pay a visit to a man (or someone too immersed in their masculine consciousness) when he (or she) has become too rigid with his (or her) spiritual reality.

Welcome to the Jungle

In the jungle, Saraha soon found himself drinking wine and dancing and getting it on with the ladies in a manner he never, *ever* expected of himself. He felt honey-soaked, electric, intoxicated, like he was in some sort of alternate reality where he got to participate in some very unorthodox "spiritual" practices. At one point in the hot, tangly evening, Saraha had a powerful vision of a Red Feminine Being who told him where his next spiritual teacher would be found. The following morning, Saraha left his passionate playmates and went to the place he had seen in his vision. But when he arrived, there was no temple or monastery or even house with the usual ornaments or pomp that announced a great spiritual teacher lived there. There was nuthin' but a rambly old hut with a lower-caste woman sitting outside, making arrows.

Saraha assumed the Red Goddess who had danced through his visions had been wrong, dead wrong, so he asked the poor, lowly woman where he could find an esteemed teacher of the dharma who lived nearby. The woman's enlightened answer caused Saraha to fall on the floor at her feet and beg to be her disciple. The woman agreed to take him on as her student, and later she took him on as her consort (tantric sexual partner). While these two were *quite* heretical and even considered dangerous by the Buddhist traditionalists and local wine merchants, they are known today as two of the greatest teachers of Tantric Buddhism.

I resonated with that story. A lot.

But after my studies in Tibet and subsequent travels through several other countries, studying different religions, I began to feel incredibly alone, spiritually speaking. I had left the Church because I couldn't be a priest and because they weren't open to my spiritual explorations in the "other realms." And although I learned wonderful things from my New Age adventures in high school, they didn't offer me much solid ground to stand on. I had then assumed (and desperately hoped) that by studying the world religions and traveling around the world to experience their lived reality, I would find my true Home—a tradition, community, practice, lineage, perhaps even a teacher that resonated with my heart.

But alas, I was finding that the world's religious traditions were teaching an experience and expression of the Divine that, though magnificent and wise, did not fully support *my* personal knowing, passionate feminine yearnings, and authentic self-expression. And this left me with an aching heart and some serious spiritual self-doubt.

The day I returned to the United States after my studies abroad, I spent the entire night covering every inch of my pastel bedroom walls with rich Red fabric. I didn't understand exactly *why* I was redecorating my living space with this vivid color (purple was my favorite color at this time in my life); I assumed it was simply a side effect of hanging around all those vibrant Indian bazaars. But now I know that a deeper part of me intuitively recognized that after all my exciting, but spiritually unfulfilling, studies and travels

I needed to be wrapped in Red.

I needed to be wrapped in Her.

MYSTICAL MISFITS

The only people for me are the mad ones, the ones mad to live, mad to talk, mad to be saved, desirous of everything at the same time, the ones who never yawn or say a commonplace thing but burn, burn, burn like fabulous roman candles exploding.

JACK KEROUAC

The first day of my senior year in college, as I was nodding off in the corner of my philosophy of religion class, a woman giving a presentation read this phrase out loud:

Keep walking, though there's no place to get to.
Don't try to see through the distances.
Move within. But don't move the way fear makes you move.[1]
— *Rumi*

My body jolted awake. In one quick, forceful motion, my torso bent forward, touching my knees, and then slammed back into the seat, not unlike the movement you would make if you drove your car into a tree while wearing a seatbelt. Call it "Divine whiplash." My classmates looked at me curiously.

My professor raised his eyebrows. I acted like I had dropped my pen. During the next few weeks, my professor introduced us to a few of the world's mystics, and my passion for religious studies returned. It was like receiving a

Spiritual Blood Transfusion

What was so hot about many of these mystics, especially for a college student, was that in their day, not only were they getting drunk, dancing, wandering around naked, creating art, poetry, music (as the great psychoanalyst Carl Jung said: "Only the mystics bring what is creative to religion itself"[2]), but much to my delight, they also had senses of humor. As Daniel Ladinsky translates the sixteenth-century mystic Teresa of Ávila: "How did those priests ever get so serious and preach all that gloom? I don't think God tickled them yet. Beloved—hurry!"[3] Many mystics were revolutionaries and had a remarkable knack for inspiring thousands with their wisdom and actions. Some even went rogue, religiously speaking. Truth is, when you study the mystics, you find that no one ever got close to the Divine—really close; I'm talking nose to Nose, tongue to Tongue, heart to Heart, hip to Hip—by strictly following the rules. Therefore, in their day, many were deemed heretical, unorthodox, and transgressive.

But what *really* lit me up like a pagan Christmas tree at the Vatican was that these mystics were madly in love with the Divine, and it was this ecstatic love that determined and shaped their lives.

Here's a heated handful of those mystics . . .

FALLING OFF THE HIGH HORSE

Let's start with the man who shook me out of my seat, Jalal ad-Din Rumi, a Persian mystic from the thirteenth century whose poetry peppers many modern bookshelves, not to mention greeting cards at Whole Foods. Why does Rumi turn us on like very few others? Because he reminds us how to be a true lover of another, our self, this world, the Divine—all at the same time—via rapturous prose that makes every angel want to become human (or at least want to wine and dine one).

> If anyone wants to know what "spirit" is,
> or what "God's fragrance" means,
> lean your head toward him or her.
> Keep your face there close.
> *Like this.*

When someone quotes the old poetic image
about clouds gradually uncovering the moon,
slowly loosen knot by knot the strings
of your robe.
   Like this?

If anyone wonders how Jesus raised the dead,
Don't try to explain the miracle.
Kiss me on the lips.
   Like this. Like this.[4]
—*Rumi*

Bottom line: When Rumi's knocking, every pore becomes a doorway.

How did he get so spiritually sexy? Not easily. Rumi was a well-respected Islamic scholar and spiritual teacher who had thousands of followers and a sweet and stable life of privilege and fame, until he had a Rouge Awakening.

One fine day, Rumi was riding a horse through town, when he came upon a rascally, disheveled, wandering dervish named Shams (a dervish is a practitioner of Sufism, a mystical branch of Islam). Shams asked Rumi a question (we're not quite sure *exactly* what it was), and Rumi gave a common spiritual answer that would have pleased his scholarly colleagues and conventional devotees and probably his mom, but not this wild man. Shams retorted with his own unfiltered answer, which caused Rumi to promptly fall off his horse in stunned surprise. He literally "fell off his high horse"—his paradigm popped, his perspective shifted, and his ass was awakened and grounded . . . by Red.

Last year, I admired wines.
This, I'm wandering inside the red world.[5]
—*Rumi*

Shams is believed to have shown up in Rumi's life wearing Red. In fact, if you ever get a chance to see the traveling whirling dervishes (those who practice a Sufi moving meditation that was created by Rumi after he met Shams), you'll notice that when the dervishes enter the sacred space (or move onto the stage), before they begin to whirl, each bows to a hunk of red wool, which represents Shams. Rumi explained once that in dream symbolism, to be dressed in a red garment means ecstasy and joy, green denotes asceticism, white indicates the fear of God, and blue and black signify mourning and grief.

Anyway, after that fateful fall, Rumi and Shams became inseparable, secluding themselves so they could enter into *sohbet*, mystical communion, a space of learning and sharing that stems from the heart, not just the mind. Rumi's relationship with Shams reflected and intensified his intimate relationship with the Divine.

> There's nothing left of me.
> I'm like a ruby held up to the sunrise.
> Is it still a stone, or a world
> made of redness? It has no
> resistance to sunlight.[6]
> —*Rumi*

As you can probably imagine, this drastic change of lifestyle of their beloved teacher distressed Rumi's students and family. So they asked Shams to skedaddle. He did. Briefly. What you can probably *not* imagine is that when Shams returned, someone close to Rumi actually had Shams murdered.

Shams' abrupt presence and then brutal absence destroyed Rumi. Well, the old Rumi—what some might call his "false self," the part of him that was more personality driven and people pleasin' and always trying to "fit in," the part that held him back from his soul's purpose, which was to live Divine Love out loud. But Rumi's epic love and loss, and the resulting recognition of his true self, created one of the greatest mystical poets this world has ever known. In honor of their divine relationship, Rumi wrote a book professionally titled the *Divani Shamsi Tabriz (The Works of Shams Tabriz)*, but which Rumi personally called his "big red book."[7]

> I am a naked man standing inside a mine of rubies,
> clothed in red silk.
> I absorb the shining and now I see the ocean,
> billions of simultaneous motions
> moving in me.[8]

Rumi ripped my Red heart back open to shamelessly loving the Divine (in private). He was the first human I had ever encountered who expressed through words what I experienced through feelings. This is what *most* of Rumi's readers feel because he fearlessly expresses that innate yearning we all share deep down, where the fires of truth burn brightest:

To Love

to *really* Love

Something that includes but is Bigger than us . . .

and to Be-loved by that Divine Presence

in Return.

THE RED THREAD OF PASSION

The fifteenth-century Japanese Zen Buddhist master Ikkyū Sojun was quite scandalous and a total renegade in his day. His unorthodox philosophy influenced Japanese art, literature, and religion. What made Ikkyū such a rebel? He blatantly believed that his honest human passion (often referred to in his spiritual tradition as the "Red Thread") didn't compromise his enlightenment. He exclaimed: "If one avoids giving pain, if one abides by what is virtually Buddhism's golden rule, to live inoffensively, why not live passionately!"[9] Ikkyū enjoyed *sake* (Japanese liquor) and women and was not a fan of temples and meditation halls. He preferred to hang out in alternative haunts:

> Ten days in this temple and my mind is
> reeling!
> Between my legs the red thread stretches and
> stretches.
> If you come some other day and ask for me,
> Better look in a fish stall, a sake shop, or a
> brothel.[10]

Despite his heretical ways, Ikkyū was kind and conscientious with his students. When he would manage to stay in temples, he took his duties very seriously . . . until he felt the internal nudge to get his groove on or he felt that those around him were not living in alignment with the true Zen path, getting too caught up in the ritual instead of living from the heart. Then he would take off for the hills.

Ikkyū railed against overzealous ideals of self-conduct and any beliefs or traditions that he felt stagnated authentic spiritual experience. At one time, he even burnt his *inka,* a written statement from his previous teacher confirming Ikkyū's enlightenment—a shocking and risky move because Zen masters needed this statement to be recognized as teachers and to attract students. After Ikkyū burnt his "proof of enlightenment," he sauntered off to the nearest bar. (Belch.)

Ikkyū fascinated the hell outta me, not only because of his radical ways, but also because he was a holy man *having sex with women.* He knew the vagina, intimately. Most mystics I had studied, while definitely prone to mystico-erotic experiences with the Divine, still made a point *not* to rub their hot and holy hands all over another human's private parts. What really got me curious was that some scholars even believed that it was through Ikkyü's carnal encounters with women that much of his poetry and spiritual realization came into full fruition. In fact, at age seventy-seven, Ikkyü fell in love with a young blind woman, and they spent many happy years together. He wrote, "A woman is enlightenment when you're with her, and the red thread /of both your passions flares inside you and you see."[11]

I'll leave you with one of his most famous koans (a parable, question, or statement that cannot be figured out or accessed with the rational mind) to whisper to your lover tonight, or to the mailperson, or to your hair stylist — because really, now, what are they gonna be more affected by: "Thank you" or this?

> When, just as they are,
> White dewdrops gather
> On scarlet maple leaves,
> Regard the scarlet beads![12]

Regard the Scarlet Beads!

LADIES WHO LAUNCH

You might be wondering just about now — okay, where are zee ladies? Well, here are a few fiery female mystics who caught my Red eye.

Let's start our spiritual engines with Catherine of Siena, a fourteenth-century eccentric Italian Catholic mystic, visionary, and healer who, according to Carol Lee Flinders in her book *Enduring Grace,* had a spiritual intensity that was said to be "like the wine of Siena — very red."[13] One of Catherine's spiritual "guardians" (a religious figure from history whom one prays to for guidance) was Mary Magdalene. In one of Catherine's many visions, Jesus appeared, pulled a scarlet cloak out of the wound at his side, and wrapped it around her; from that day forth she was never bothered by external temperature again (now, that's being energy efficient). Catherine experienced a divinity that not only loved the priests and the starving children in Africa and the entire world and yadda yadda yadda, but that also loved her funky female self, personally.

Personally.

Before we go any further, let's take a quick perspective shift. According to integral philosopher Ken Wilber, there are three perspectives of divinity: first person (I), second person (we), and third person (it). The first-person perspective is an inner experience of divinity, when we recognize that we are made up of the same stuff as the Divine—I Am That. This first-person perspective is most commonly used in Eastern traditions like Buddhism. The second-person perspective is a personal relationship with the Divine—I and Thou are relating. This second-person perspective is most common in Western Abrahamic traditions (Judaism, Christianity, Islam). And the third-person perspective is of an impersonal Divine force that we often experience through science, nature, the cosmos—Everything. Just. Is. It. Einstein's awe-inspiring perspective on the universe via physics comes to mind. All three perspectives of divinity are true and equally valid, and all three flow through each other. However, there's most likely one perspective that each of us finds ourself using more than the others, one way of recognizing and engaging and encountering the Divine that really gets our own juices flowin'.

You can probably tell by now which perspective gets my Red juices flowin'. The second-person perspective is my fave, *mostly* because the Divine has always rung my inner doorbell and flashed Itself as a deeply relational, distinct *Presence.* When I was in college, I began to realize I wasn't alone with this experience.

Mechthild of Magdeburg, a thirteenth-century female Catholic mystic, describes a moment during one of her visions in which her Beloved (God) reveals his "Divine heart" to her, and she describes it as "red gold burning in a great fire of coals."[14] However, most mystics of the past experienced all three perspectives of divinity. For example, Catherine of Genoa, a fifteenth-century Italian mystic, wrote about God in the first person: "My me of me is god."[15] And Mechthild wrote in the third person: God is "the powerful penetration of all things."[16] But undoubtedly, many mystics were continuously awestruck by the mysteriously precious experience of the *second* perspective: "The special intimacy which ever exists between God and each individual soul[;] . . . a thing so delicate that had I the wisdom of all men and the voice of an angel, I could not describe it."[17] I think Mechthild did a pretty good job. In *Enduring Grace,* Carol Lee Flinders tells us that for Mechthild,

> The paradox enchants her: God is everywhere and surely, therefore
> impersonal; and yet in relation to the individual soul, God is entirely

intimate and surely, therefore, personal. . . . God is there, Mechthild insists, for every one of us, not in a general, impersonal sense, but *there*—so exquisitely right for you it's as if you'd made him up.[18]

HOT AND HOLY BREATHS

Rabi'a was an eighth-century female mystic from ancient Mesopotamia (which is now Iraq). When she was young, she became separated from her parents and was sold into a famous brothel, where she lived and worked for many years.

Now, I'm gonna press "pause" here for just a moment. Although I appreciate Ikkyü's affection for brothels, and while, yes, Red does have a *very* interesting relationship with prostitution and sexuality (we'll dive into that hot pocket later), I want to be clear that Red does not condone any behavior, especially sexual behavior, that abuses or manipulates the will, soul, body, or *energy* of another. OK, I'm pressing "play."

In Daniel Ladinsky's creative translation, Rabi'a said this about her particular line of work: "What a place for trials and transformations did my Lover put me, but never once did he look upon me as if I were impure. Dear sisters, all we do in the world, whatever happens, is bringing us closer to God."[19] You might have noticed something in much of the poetry heating up this chapter: relating to God as Lover or Beloved is an experience shared by a host of heavy-breathing mystics. Rabi'a continued, "I know about love the way the fields know about light, the way the forest shelters, the way an animal's divine raw desire seeks to unite with whatever might please its soul—without a single strange thought of remorse."[20] Not to be outdone, St. Teresa of Ávila wrote, "He spoke to me saying if I do come to you in a dream and satisfy the most intimate of your physical desires, know dear, know it is for the upliftment of all."[21]

Uh, hi there. We need to press "pause" again for a moment and take in that last line . . .

Way In

These mystics experienced a divinity that was *both* immanent and transcendent . . . and horny. Yep, when many mystics felt the Divine, they literally felt turned on, erotically speaking.

Let's slip and slide over to ancient Greece for a moment. The Greek philosopher Plato (400s BCE) described two types of love in his work: *agape* (abstract, impartial love) and *eros* (desiring love). Over the years, many Christian theologians decided agape love was the most "spiritual" type of love. Erotic love, on the other hand, was viewed as uncontrollable, dangerous, fleshy, and even sinful. It therefore was often dismissed as being a viable way to experience and express God. While eros *is* an unrelenting force of Divine Love that *includes* sex and sexual desire (though sex and sexual desire do not always include eros), it is also *so* much more than sticky sheets and scratchy yearnings. Feminist writer Audre Lorde describes eros as:

> The personification of love in all its aspects—born of Chaos, and
> personifying creative power and harmony. When I speak of the erotic,
> then, I speak of it as an assertion of the lifeforce of women; of that
> creative energy empowered, the knowledge and use of which we are now
> reclaiming in our language, our history, our dancing, our work, our lives.[22]

But reclaiming erotic energy wasn't exactly welcomed in the past, especially for spiritual women. In fact, it's fair to say that Christianity (and really most every religious tradition) suffers from *erotophobia*—fear of the erotic. Therefore, many turned-on female mystics did not have easy lives. They lived during times of extreme patriarchy, and many endured life-threatening inquisitions from religious authorities who often deemed their provocative spiritual experiences and ardent Divine Feminine expressions heretical or unenlightened.

In *Enduring Grace,* Flinders tells a spirited story about an encounter between Catherine of Genoa and a priest. The priest told Catherine that he was better able to love God than her because, well, he was a priest and had renounced life, whereas she, who could not become a priest, was still wedded to the lowly world of passion and desire. Catherine immediately responded with "fire in her eye—in fact, fire all over the place,"[23] passionately exclaiming:

> If I believed your habit would add one spark to my love, I would not
> hesitate to tear it from your shoulders piece by piece. . . . Whatever you
> merit more than I, through the renunciation you have made for God's
> sake, and through your religious life. . . . I don't seek to obtain; these
> are yours; but that I cannot love God as much as yourself, you can never
> make me believe.[24]

In other words, Catherine saw Red. And acted like It.

The mystics' cozy relationship with the Divine gave them confidence, illumination, and some *serious* spiritual punch, which did not exactly please those in control. Truth is, when you stop following the herd and start connecting to and trusting in Something much grander, freer, and more Divine *inside yourself,* you can't help but become uncontrollable in the name of Love.

ECSTATIC ACTIVISM

Ecstatic activism is like the wild, tattooed, horny sister of spiritual activism. It emphasizes the *passion* in com*passion*ate action. As Rumi shouted, "With passion pray, with passion make love. With passion eat and drink and dance and play. Why look like a dead fish in this ocean of God?"[25] That's right: for many mystics, experiencing God intimately translated into celebrating life ecstatically.

Lalla was a fourteenth-century female ecstatic activist who sang, "When I became one with the Supreme Word, my body blazed as red hot coal."[26] Lalla felt such Divine ecstasy that she danced naked through the streets, singing love songs:

> Dance, Lalla, with nothing on
> but air. Sing, Lalla,
> wearing the sky.
> Look at this glowing day! What clothes
> Could be so beautiful, or
> more sacred?[27]

(Pause.)

We need to give Lalla some major street cred. A nude woman publicly shaking her stuff for the sacred in the fourteenth century is pretty fucking badass in itself, but if you add into the mix that Lalla lived in Kashmir during a time of massive religious upheaval, things get even more interesting.

Lalla was outright critical of religious ceremonies and religious orthodoxy when they divided people from each other and limited the limitless experience of divinity. Her bold songs and ecstatically moving naked presence revealed a God who existed beyond all human differences, which helped heal serious rifts that were taking place at that time among the Hindus, Buddhists, and Muslims. For most mystics, there is no assumption that their path is the only path or that one religion is the right religion. As Rabi'a said, "In my soul there is a temple, a shrine, a mosque, a church that dissolve, that dissolve in God."[28] This is why so many mystics continue to be the most effective agents of change on this planet. They're not trying to convert; they're trying to commune.

A few years ago, right before I was about to give a workshop on ecstatic activism, I was standing in the checkout line at Whole Foods, trying to open a bottle of kombucha and wondering if I was stretching things too far by making a connection between Red and ecstatic activism. When I raised my eyes from the ridiculously tight bottle cap, they immediately caught the cover of *Smithsonian* magazine, which depicted a photograph of a sweaty, dancing, long-haired man wearing a Red robe with the phrase "Faith and Ecstasy" written across it. My bottle popped open. According to the article, every year, a few hundred thousand Sufis converge in Sehwan, a town in Pakistan near a group of Muslim violent extremists, for a three-day festival marking the death of Lal Shahbaz Qalandar, a thirteenth-century Sufi mystic. *Lal* just so happens to mean "Red" in Arabic. Despite the danger of being so close to the extremists, these Sufis gather every year to douse themselves in rose water, wear Red clothing, chuck flowers and shiny tinsel in the air, and dance ecstatically to drums while repeatedly shouting *"Mast Qalandar!"* or "The ecstasy of Qalandar!"

The author of the article, Nicholas Schmidle, excitedly described this mystical mosh pit: "Enraptured, one woman placed her hands on her knees and threw her head back and forth, another bounced and jiggled as if she were astride a trotting horse. The drumming and dancing never stopped, not even for the call to prayer." Schmidle asked one of the sweaty dancers, "What goes on in your head when you're dancing this way?" The dancer answered, "Nothing, I don't think,"[29] which reminds me of a Jack Kerouac quote, "Everything is ecstasy, inside. We just don't know it because of our thinking-minds,"[30] and of what Teresa of Ávila taught: "The important thing is not to think much but to love much; and so do that which best stirs you to love."[31]

But back to the article. Schmidle asked a Sufi how this celebration could counter the devastating violence of the extremists in the area. The Sufi huffed in reply,

> I can explain to you what love is until I turn blue in the face. But there is no way I can make you feel it until you feel it. Ecstatic dance, this celebration, initiates that emotion in you. And through that process, religious experience becomes totally different: pure and absolutely nonviolent.[32]

At the end of the article, Schmidle described his final day, when he mindlessly moved into the ecstatic crowd. Looking out over "a sea of red," he *finally* cut loose and began to dance with them. He wrote, "If only for a few minutes, it didn't matter whether I was a Christian, Muslim, Hindu, or Atheist. I had forgotten about the dangerous extremists who were searching for me earlier that day. I had entered another realm. I couldn't deny the ecstasy of Qalandar."[33]

Don't Deny the Ecstasy.

MYSTICS "R" US

These mystics felt like long-lost friends to my college self. While no one else around me pointed out, or even seemed to notice, the *Red* winks flirtin' through the mystical traditions, I sure did. And those winks soothed my young Red heart. I didn't feel quite so alone anymore. The writings of the mystics felt like a warm breath of Red wine blown across the cold, tight face of traditional religion. They spoke of a Divine that was much more accessible, relatable, randy, and *familiar* to my own experience.

While most of us have *a lot* of evolving to do before we can meet those mystics third eye to third eye, at our core, we burn just like 'em. As spiritual teacher Caroline Myss so famously said, we're *all* mystics without monasteries. And as Matthew Fox confirms in *Christian Mystics,*

> Deep down, each one of us is a mystic. When we tap into that energy we become alive again and we give birth. From the creativity that we release is born the prophetic vision and work that we all aspire to realize as our gift to the world. . . . Getting in touch with the mystic inside is the beginning of our deep service.[34]

In other words, every single one of us has VIP access to the Awesome—a place and space where the Divine is not just a heady belief or a lovely idea or even a self-helped hopefulness, but an actual *Presence* that craves more intimate one-on-one time *with us.* That's right, It desires us, often *even more* than we desire It. As Rabi'a panted: "God must get hungry for us; why is He not also a lover who wants his lovers near?"[35] And as Teresa of Ávila drooled: "He desired me so I came close."[36]

Come Close.

TRUMPED BY THE
TREE OF LIFE

Life is a woman, a beautiful sorceress seducing our hearts, beguiling our spirits, flooding our being with promises. . . . Life is a woman who with pleasure takes the human heart as a lover but rejects it as a husband. Life is a harlot, but she is beautiful. Whoever sees her harlotry abhors her beauty.

KAHLIL GIBRAN
The Beloved

Due to my mad love for Rumi, I decided to write my senior thesis on Sufism. One sunny autumn day, fifteen new books on Sufism arrived for me at the library, and I excitedly buried myself behind a desk. As I began reading through the first few books, I kept circling back to reread the Sufi definition of humanity's "lower nature," which included the body, sexuality, and desire. And suddenly,

I started to feel strange.

So, I shut those books and opened another book at random, where I immediately read a paragraph about the importance of rising above these "lower elements" at all costs. These "lower elements" were called the *nafs*.

I experienced a catch in my throat, an ache in my belly.

I closed that book and grabbed the next and, again, opened it randomly to the middle, where oddly enough this same point of view continued to be defined: the nafs are related to this world, material reality, and are often regarded as *feminine*.

My heart clamped tight.

Dazed, I looked up from this last book and turned toward the library window, where my gaze met this radiant

Tree.

I responded to this Encounter quite simply . . . by sobbing.

After a few moments (and more than a few concerned looks from fellow students), my body shot out of its chair, and I ran out of the library and across the campus to my adviser's office. I banged like a crazy woman on his door, and he quickly let me in. I was a mess, stuttering and shaking with rage, grief, hopelessness. I sobbed, "Even here, even *here* . . . in Sufism, I'M NOT WELCOME!!!" and proceeded to spill a stormy naf-filled ocean into the room.

Don't forget: I was a *religion scholar* (remember the vocal inflection and badass attitude). I knew intellectually that the Sufi definition and teaching of nafs were much more complex and multilayered than the simplified equation of "material reality = nothin' but badness." And I knew intellectually that most religious teachings directly or indirectly emphasize the spiritual importance of transcending this earth, the flesh, and, well, life, *and* that these elements have most often been called "feminine" and viewed as inferior, illusory, less conscious, and, at times, a trap. Fact was, I had known *for years* that the world religions diss "the feminine." But what I was not expecting was for "the feminine" to be kicked to the cosmic curb even in the mystical sects of these traditions, *especially* the one that my beloved Rumi belonged to—Sufism. And what I really was not expecting was my intensely *visceral* and *emotional* reaction to this fact.

It felt like I was spiritually homeless, once again.

When the tears had run their course, my kind professor gently suggested I come to his next class, titled "The Goddess in India," which just so happened to be starting in a few minutes. I blew my nose one last time and walked with him out the door, leaving all those lifeless books I had specially ordered on Sufism marooned on that desk next to that library window in the

Direct Glowing Presence

of that

Tree

of

Life.

THE GODDESS IS
IN DA HOUSE!

Instead of relating to the word *goddess* or *divine feminine* as statements of
religious belief or as literal representations of a deity, we can use them as
reminders of the infinite forms spirit assumes in our world. We can also
realize how recognizing these images and ideas of a divine feminine are
not meant to enslave us, but to assist us in recognizing our own divinity.

JALAJA BONHEIM
Aphrodite's Daughters

Goddesses—I knew very little and thought very little about
these exotic creatures during my first three years of college. Honestly, Goddesses seemed a wee bit primitive to me, like archaic Barbie dolls
with weird names and bad outfits. Except for spicing up myths, art, and pagan
Earth Day celebrations, Goddesses appeared to have no real spiritual point.

Despite my prejudice—or because of it—*my* Ultimate Reality was about
to get gangbanged by some Goddesses from India. But first, let's get a quick
lay of the Indian land.

Hinduism is the only major world religion that presently worships goddesses as well as gods (and has been actively doing so since 2500 BCE). Some
streams of Hinduism even view Goddess as the End All Be All, the head
Honchette of the Universe. In fact, the first book my professor had us read in
"The Goddess in India" class was an English translation of the *Devi Mahatmya*

(*The Specific Greatness of Goddess*), a popular religious text written about fifteen hundred years ago in northwest India that claims Ultimate Reality is feminine, and a badass feminine at that.

The gist of this ancient spiritual story: One not-so-fine day, demons started wreaking havoc on the planet. Try as they might, the gods were not strong enough to fight them off, so the gods gathered together and prayed for the Great Goddess to come to their aid—the Super She who created the Universe, the gods, and all humans. She appeared gloriously aflame, dressed in *Red,* and wielding weapons in Her many arms. "She bellowed aloud with laughter again and again"[1] and proceeded to kick some major demon ass (while the awestruck gods watched from the sidelines), thus saving the world and causing the gods to fall all over themselves gushing Her praises:

> Hail to the Goddess, hail eternally to the auspicious great Goddess…
> You are the queen of all that does and does not move…
> All and the various knowledges, O Goddess, are portions of you, as is
> each and every woman in the various worlds. By you alone as mother has
> this world been filled up; what praise can suffice for you who are beyond
> praise; the ultimate utterance.[2]

At this point in my life, I had never, *ever* read a sacred text that praised Goddess *over* God. Spiritual shock aside, this idea of a Mega Mom made symbolic and obviously biological sense to me. Females give birth, they are often the primary caregiver, and they become incredibly fierce if they feel their children are threatened in any way (hello, Mama Bear). But as the Divine Leader of the Universe? Well, this was a new theological concept for me.

Yet the Goddess in the *Devi Mahatmya* is not a typical commander in chief, as scholar of Hinduism David Kinsley writes: "She herself is also often pictured as taking an active role in the cosmic process. She is ever attentive to the world, particularly to her devotees, and in various forms she acts to uphold cosmic order and protect her creatures."[3] In other words, this Super She is not simply a feminine form of a masculine deity. She is specifically associated with Shakti—the dynamic and creative feminine power of the universe—and *prakriti,* or primordial matter. These are two elements that male deities are most often *not* associated with . . . on purpose. Why? 'Cuz Shakti and prakriti create our bodies and the material world and—much like the Sufi nafs from chapter 3—are often viewed as hindrances (or even roadblocks) on the more orthodox and transcendent Hindu paths of enlightenment. But here in the *Devi Mahatmya* roared a

Divine Lady who actually appeared to *sanctify* immanence, the earth, our bodies, life. As the gods sing:

> You have become the sole support of the world, for you abide in the form of the earth. Deluded, O Goddess, is this entire universe; you, when resorted to, are the cause of release right here on earth.[4]

Bottom line: The *Devi Mahatmya* was a breakthrough read for me—such a breakthrough read that upon completing the text, I promptly changed my senior thesis from Sufism to the Goddess in India.

MEETING MY SOULMATE

A few weeks after I joined the class, I sat down in my usual seat (front and center), took a notebook and pen from my backpack, and looked up—directly into the gaze of a seriously intense Goddess.

Gotcha!

(Gasp!)

Darshan is a Hindu practice that involves an exchange of sacred energy between Divinity (be it an icon, a holy person, or a poster) and devotee. Darshan means both seeing the Divine and *being seen by* the Divine. In India, it's not enough for you to simply gaze at a holy icon or saint. Nope, you also need to make sure you pop into *their* direct line of sight, because that's a transmission touchdown; that's where the Divine meet-and-greet happens. Gotcha to gasp!

"Who *is* that!?" I exclaimed.

This Goddess was naked except for a necklace of human skulls and a miniskirt of human appendages. She wielded a sharp-looking sword and had a *long* Red tongue sticking out of a mouth dripping with blood. It looked like a Chanel Vamp lipstick application gone wrong. Very, very wrong. This wasn't no sweet and pretty Hindu goddess of prosperity, like Lakshmi, or the brilliant and elegant Hindu goddess of culture and learning, Saraswati, or even the fiercely gorgeous warrior goddess of the *Devi Mahatmya,* Durga. Nope, this Goddess looked like She was from the wrong side of the spiritual tracks. I picked up my things and moved to a seat on the far left of the room . . . out of Her sight.

My professor introduced the garish Goddess in the colorful poster as Kali, a goddess of destruction and creation who predates Hinduism. The down low:

Kali loves to hang out in graveyards, drink the blood of demons, and boogie and howl and stomp and spit and so forth. Unlike many popular Hindu goddesses, She's not married. She does make love with the Hindu god Shiva . . . but only if She can be on top (this seems to be the sexual position of choice for a few sacred ladies; wait until you meet Lilith in chapter 9). Kali is sometimes known as the "'forbidden thing,' or the forbidden par excellence."[5] She reveals the places in our psyches where we have denied our authentic sexuality, rage, killer instincts, animal nature, shadow, and power. These "forbidden" places inside us hold integral elements of our feminine divinity. They are ripe with our promise. Kali wields that sharp sword to slice through illusion and ego and anything that stands in the way of our total liberation: "All the things we are conditioned in a thousand ways to suppress, but that continue to feed our deepest fears and anxieties, confront us in the image of Kali."[6]

Kali has a shocking appearance and engages in unconventional behavior in order to confront us with an alternative to "normal." Kali crashes through our rigid beliefs and micromanaged lives to show us that Something bigger and truer pulses through this world and that we need to respect It. By shaking up one's perceptions of an orderly world, Kali "allows for a clearer perception of how things really are."[7] In other words, this ferocious form of the Feminine Divine is not interested in pacifying our persona or accommodating our life plan or helping us manifest our dream job if these things don't serve our highest truth. She reminds us that we're not as in control as we like to think we are, no matter how many rules we obey or savings accounts we hold or fire alarms we install or vitamins we swallow or positive affirmations we chant.

By facing Kali's terrifying form, we face our deepest fears; once truly faced, the paralyzing terror fades and our life begins to move in its natural divine direction. The power we previously gave to our fears and forbidden shadows is returned to us. Our repression is released. We grow into a spiritual adult—one who is not just looking for the sweet-and-light nurturing side of life, divinity, and our self, but who is also open to and accepting of the rough, stubbly five o'clock shadow of existence. That's right: Through our relationship with Kali, we are asked (and sometimes *forced*) to open to all that life and death offer us—the seemingly positive and the seemingly negative—again and again and again, until we begin to actually merge with Her grand perspective. "The goal . . . is not liberation from the phenomenal world but total illumination, which embraces relative and absolute equally."[8] In other words, this Goddess ain't interested in anybody transcending anything. She wants us *here,* fully engaged, hands muddy.

Although Kali is often depicted having a black form, She is also associated with the color Red. Her priests in India wear Red robes. She has that famously long Red tongue, and She obviously has a thing for blood. Red flowers always adorn Her altars in India, and the heartfelt passion Her devotees have for Her is definitely Red. According to scholar David Frawley, "Kali relates to the physical heart also, which circulates life-force, and to the blood itself which carries the life-force. In this form she is called Rakta-Kali or Red Kali. Kali thus is the pulsing of the heart."[9]

Red? Unconventional? Heart-centered? Erotic? Forbidden? Untamable? A Freedom Fighter? These spiritually unorthodox characteristics sounded familiar to me. Although I knew there was no academic connection between the Hindu Goddess Kali and my Red band of mystics from all over the world, intuitively to me, they *felt* connected. (I could imagine them all getting drunk together on Red wine and playing strip poker.) Obviously, one huge difference between my Redvolutionary mystics and this Red Goddess was that the mystics were devoted *to* a divinity, whereas Kali *was* a divinity to whom others were devoted.

Now, I have just dished out a lot of theory *about* Kali. The practice *of* Kali came later in my life, as you'll read in the A.M. section. Kali was just courting me in college. You see, besides the obvious shocks of Kali's iconographic appearance on the gaudy poster that day and the intuitive links between Her and my Red mystics, I was also experiencing another shock—one of recognition. You know when you meet a guy (or gal) you are immediately repulsed by *and* hugely attracted to at the same time? And you just know, deep down, that you're supposed to experience a close (or even intimate) relationship with this person, even though your ego is totally flipping out, because it knows if you do enter into said relationship, your entire life and sense of self and purpose will get completely hosed, but it also knows that you can't avoid this relationship because it's perfectly necessary for your growth—as a woman and as a soul. I'm talking about what happens when you meet your soul mate(s).

Spiritual teacher Caroline Myss defines a soul mate not as some sort of perfect Prince (or Princess) Charming who chariots your personal fairy tale into the happily ever after, but as the person or people who annoy you the most, push all your buttons, make you face your shit, and even seemingly "hurt" you (or your ideas of who you are) or screw up your life (or your previously set plans for your life), thereby forcing you to grow in new directions, developing and realizing new aspects of your self (positive and negative) that you probably would not have done without their, er, "help."

Meeting Kali was like meeting my soul mate. I was scared to death of Her, *and* I was attracted to life through Her. I knew deep down, where the wild things were trapped inside of me, that we were supposed to hang out and get to know each other in a "more than casual friends" sort of way. But damn It All, I was *not* gonna be the pursuer. After all, I was still a college kid, just trying to get good grades and find the best dance parties and make out with my hunky artist boyfriend and be, well, *cool,* despite my ardor for divinity. (Un)Fortunately, Kali had other plans for me.

THE LICKING

A few weeks before our midyear break, my wonderful religion professor asked me to accompany him to Ladakh (the northernmost state of India) that upcoming summer to study the Tibetan Buddhist festivals and to later present our research findings at the prestigious American Academy of Religion (AAR) conference. I felt grateful for this extraordinary opportunity, as it would build upon my Tibetan studies and language program from the year before, *and* beef up my graduate-school applications, *and* do wonders for my future academic career, not to mention it meant I got to buy a shiny new North Face backpack. And yet . . .

My heart wasn't pumping with excitement.

I felt like I was on hold, waiting for something (or someone).

So, I sheepishly told my surprised professor I would give him my decision after the midyear break. The following nights, I started having dreams filled with blood, lots of blood. In one, someone was sticking two syringes filled with vibrant Red blood into my tongue to "feed me." In another, I was eagerly devouring a sandwich filled with bright-Red blood. As gross as this might sound, it felt like I was Popeye and someone was *finally* feeding me spinach. When I ingested Red in my dreams, health flushed my body, power coursed through my veins, and "smalled" parts of me "grew" bigger. Obviously, some deeper part of me was craving the taste of Redness that Kali now represented, but I had no clear idea what to *do* about this desire.

So Red decided to taste me.

One night, *before* I went to sleep, Kali appeared in a vision:

> She came toward me. Tongue swishing. She started with my left foot. Moving Her tongue slowly and deliberately across the sole of my foot . . .

gently parting my toes . . . one by one. Gliding over the top. Rough yet moist, the way a cat's tongue feels. On fire. Swirling around my ankle and moving firmly up my shin, skimming my knee, and continuing . . . briefly flattening my curves, pushing my skin upward, over the top of my thigh to my hip. Her tongue dipped down again in order to taste the flesh up the back of my leg. The right leg followed. My whole body went through this ritual Red cleanse, every dip and raise, curve and line, each finger . . . deliberately, precisely tasted . . . leaving a trail of fire. A Divine tongue bath. When I thought She was done, She suddenly spread open my thighs and gently sent Her tongue Between.

Inside out

outside In

(Ahem.)

Yeah.

Well, then.

Welcome to my head on a necklace around Kali's neck. I wasn't kidding about the up close and *personal* relationship with divinity we Red ones tend to attract. I'm sharing this intimate experience as a reminder (and a warning) that the Divine Feminine will cross all lines and break all holy hymens in order to bring *all* parts of our self into conscious love. One last lick: although experiencing powerful dreams, visions, and mystical states does not necessarily equate with a growth in consciousness, it does grab our attention and pull it toward our inner wisdom, which can kick-start our evolutionary engines. Vrooooom!

COSMIC CHESS

During the midyear break, my family planned a trip to Costa Rica to visit my older sister, who was volunteering in Central America. En route to our final destination, we were delayed for hours in the Miami airport, along with thousands of disgruntled holiday travelers. Because of my dad's insane amount of frequent-flyer miles, we were eventually ushered to an isolated wing of the Miami airport with only *one* other family. My gregarious dad, Mr. Midwestern-social-guy-who-often-appears-to-strangers-like-he's-running-for-office-but-actually-really-*is*-that-genuinely-interested-in-getting-to-know-other-people, struck up a conversation with the other family's father and soon called me over so he could introduce me to one of the world's top Kali scholars.

(Jaw drops.)

After I picked my jaw up off the floor and gushed about Kali the way a teenager gushes about a first love, the generous scholar gave me not only a rough copy of his soon-to-be-published book on Kali, but also *all* his personal contacts (Indian scholars, translators, research assistants), even living arrangements in Calcutta, *in case* I ever wanted to study this fierce Goddess in Her home environment within the next year.

Needless to say, I got the memo. After the midyear break, I thanked my professor, but told him I had to decline his offer because I was feeling, er, *called* to study Kali in Calcutta the next summer instead.

Before we go on, I want to be clear about something: I'm not sharing this superb synchronicity or future synchronicities (get ready, there's *a lot* more comin') in order to paint some "look how special/connected/chosen/spiritual I am" portrait for you to hang out of reach and admire. I know, with every Red blood cell in my body, that the Universe is constantly conspiring in *all* of our favors, doing whatever It can to help nudge us along our unique paths, often through synchronicities—or what I like to call Divine winks. I hope that by sharing my winks, I make you notice and appreciate the Divine winks that are happening all around you, every day.

Another thing: I didn't want to go to Costa Rica with my family that year. I wanted to hang out with my friends in Chicago for the midyear break instead, and I was being a total brat about it. The point is, I wasn't acting anything close to "spiritual" at that time (my poor parents are nodding their heads vigorously right now), and yet the Universe was still able to scoot my whiney, petulant ass right next to one of Kali's main men (at that time, you could count the number of Kali scholars on one hand). It was seriously like winning the Kali Jackpot (Janepot?), completely unintentionally.

Why am I sharing this with you? Because this is great news for us moody gals who tend to break common New Age-y "laws"—like one must maintain a "high vibe" or be super positive in order to be "in the flow" or to "manifest" your dreams. Yes, healthy emotions and thoughts are important, as are positive vibes, but I'm living proof that the Universe can still work Its magic even when we're spiritually shut down, stressed beyond belief, boiling in a cauldron of negativity, and even being a total bitch. In fact, I think the Universe delights in goosing us when we least expect it. I firmly believe that if at some point in your life, you've sincerely asked the Universe to show you who you are and why you're here, then It can't help but eagerly comply, in sometimes hilarious and often exquisite ways — like playing chess with humans during a stormy layover in the Miami airport.

On that very trip to Costa Rica, I purchased a hand-carved wooden sculpture of a woman on her knees, head bowed, arms thrown over her head, hands together in prayer. What drew me to this small piece of art was how the woman's hair was flowing *upward,* as if she had just thrown herself down that very moment, in spontaneous total gratitude. Although I don't make this physical action every time I receive a Divine wink, it's exactly what I *feel* every time I receive one.

THANK YOU!!!!!

Alrighty then, back to college.

GODDESS GRRRL

Although the Divine Feminine had hijacked my dream world and had begun working Her mojo in my waking world through academic zingers, mystico-erotic encounters, and some truly stunning synchronicities, I had not yet translated Her meaning into my lived reality. So, my day-to-day life didn't change very dramatically after Her initial discovery (recovery?). But my consciousness *was* beginning to expand like a Red balloon with Her possibilities. Perhaps I too could be nurturing and funny ("bellow loudly" like Durga in the *Devi Mahatmya*), as well as ferocious and sexual and badass; and these seemingly paradoxical characteristics did not divorce me from my divinity *or* my femininity. Perhaps my female body held sacred secrets that traditional religions had long ago stopped whispering, and *She* was my way of finally hearing those secrets. Perhaps Goddesses expressed divinity differently than Gods for incredibly important reasons. In other words, perhaps Goddesses *do* have a point — a major fucking point — and it was my duty as a female to know it. Although I had always felt like a very spiritual *person,* I was beginning to understand the distinction of being a spiritual *woman.*

Like the receiver of any spiritual revelation (or, in this case, Redvelation), I was totally on fire. Like the beginning of any new intimate relationship, I was totally engrossed. Like a dedicated student who finally finds her academic purpose, I was one giddy fucking schoolgirl. I had a holy She on my radar, and it honest-to-Goddess felt like I was on Hers. I was falling head over heels in love.

However, because of my sacred swoon, the more I studied the Goddess, the more pissed off and fired up I got. Why have we (I) in the West been so utterly clueless about Her? How the hell have we (I) completely missed Her theological significance, Her biological importance, and Her necessary counterpresence to a mostly masculine expression of the Divine? Why have we (I) accepted Her absence as truth? Why haven't we (I) vetoed the Vatican? Why have we (I) been so complacent about this personal and cosmic imbalance?

I began to feel puffed up, like I needed to prove Her to the entire world and protect Her from all those patriarchal forces that shut Her down. Like many feminist spirituality scholars, I wanted to "bring back the Goddess." To say I became quite passionate about writing my thesis is an understatement. I became consumed, then panicky, and then definitely overwhelmed. My intensity began to freak out my housemates, my mom, and my hunky artist boyfriend. My thesis began to fall apart. One night, before I hit the hay for what was sure to be yet another toss-and-turn-athon, I finally asked Her for help.

That night, I dreamed I was delivering a woman's baby on a table in my college's student center. The baby was so tiny, it could fit in the palm of my hand. I was worried about it surviving, so I frantically ran around the student center trying to find a doctor or someone who could help. But no one would help me. I got into my car, still holding the small baby, and found a hotel. The woman at the front desk told me my room was ready. When I got to my hotel room, the tiny baby transformed into a bee and flew over my head toward a Red glow illuminating a male and female in sexual embrace, exactly like the *yab-yum* ("father-mother") pose—a common Tibetan tantric iconographic posture, depicting a female consort straddling a male deity's lap. But weirdly enough, these two didn't hail from the Far East. "Magdalene? . . . Jesus?" I asked incredulously, and then I opened my eyes.

When I woke up, the intense pressure to "bring back the Goddess" had magically dissipated. I realized that just because the Goddess is a "newborn" to me does not mean She needs my help or protection in order to "survive." She has been alive since the dawn of time (and space), and She will continue to "live" with or without my help. I do not have to prove Her to anyone. She is stronger and more present on (and *as*) this planet than I think She is, and I do not need to cling to Her out of desperation or fear.

And, uh, about that last part of my dream—this was before *The Da Vinci Code* had made its mark, so I had no idea why J.C. and M.M. were Doing It in my hotel room under a Red light. And yet every cell in my body *felt* the Divine truth emanating from this Western tantric version of the Divine Masculine and the Divine Feminine *wrapped together* in Red hot and holy love.

Needless to say, I completed my thesis and, with much trepidation, decided to include my dreams and personal revelations about the Goddess in a final chapter. It was a risky move and provoked a risky response. When I defended my thesis in front of the entire philosophy and religion departments (as well as other curious onlookers), my professor concluded the intensely academic two-hour-long interrogation with this not-so-academic stunner:

"Sera, did you dream of the Goddess? Or did She come to you in a dream?"

Totally caught off-guard (which really is the best way to experience Her), I turned Red. I answered Red:

"The Goddess came to me in a dream as my Self waking back up to Her."

He nodded.

I nodded.

She nodded.

But I had no clue what that sentence I uttered *meant*.

KALI'S CHILD

Education is an admirable thing, but it is well to remember from
time to time that nothing that is worth knowing can be taught.

OSCAR WILDE

hree months and three part-time jobs after my college graduation, I
found myself wandering the crowded streets of Calcutta, interviewing Kali devotees and Indian scholars, participating in various Kali *pujas*
(devotional practices), volunteering at Nirmal Hriday ("The Home of the
Pure Heart," Mother Teresa's Home for the Dying, which is next door to
Kalighat, one of the main Kali temples in Calcutta), *and* trying desperately
to align my Western academic perceptions and personal experiences of this
unruly Indian Goddess with my fieldwork results. They were incongruent, to
say the least.

Although vivacious images of Kali greeted me on almost every Bengali street
corner, Her spiritual presence was shackled with a millennium of orthodoxy
and repressive cultural conditioning. On Kali Puja, the annual festival dedicated to Kali (always held on a new moon), I spent the night wandering

Calcutta's crowded streets, visiting various places of Her worship—from teeming temples to eerie cremation grounds, peaceful private home gatherings to noisy public spectacles. Although I respected each form of worship, finding some of them truly intense and others truly moving and others truly strange, I did not find *my* place to worship Her.

Around 4 a.m., exhausted and sweaty, I walked back to my tiny, bare room at the Ramakrishna Mission and found *my* way to honor Her. I lit some candles, turned on my CD player, and with an aching heart, slowly began to dance to "She makes me wanna die," lyrics in an electronica song by Tricky.

Since we come from different cultures and life circumstances, I expected there to be differences between my personal experiences with Kali and those of the Hindu women I interviewed. However, I simply wasn't prepared to *miss* Kali so much or to feel so alone while I was on Her home turf. Where was my transformative, transgressive, erotic Red Divine Feminine Lady? I had hoped to find more resonance in India than I was finding, as well as something stable on which to place my ever-growing unorthodox experiences of Her. But what was clearer than Evian water was that *their* Kali was not *my* Kali. Finding nothing external to match my internal experiences of Kali, I tucked our strange relationship away and went home three months early, disappointed and confused.

Why had I been guided to study Her in Calcutta?

Here's the skinny on Divine winks: They don't necessarily lead to happiness or a pot of gold or our next date, nor do they necessarily make sense or answer our most burning questions. In fact, they can often seem more like stumbling blocks than signposts. Sometimes, Divine winks validate a budding internal realization or point to the "best" choice to make, but more often than not, they illuminate carefully ordered "steps" leading us down a very deliberate path, chock full of twists and turns in consciousness. They can be provocateurs, pranksters, party crashers, and slinky sirens. They are *always* a practice in surrendering to the ongoing support of mystery.

My relationship with Kali was becoming an unsolved mystery.

And it looked like it needed to stay that way.

When I got to Harvard the following year to begin my graduate degree in comparative world religions, I quickly learned how incorrect it was to "take" a practice, belief, or deity from another religious tradition and culture and *use* it for what was generally viewed as one's own pseudospiritual and psychotherapeutic needs. It was misappropriation. It was theft. It was neocolonialism and modern imperialism. It was narcissistic, egocentric, Western-centric, white woman–centric, individualistic, abusive, and just downright wrong. I agreed intellectually with parts of these beliefs, especially because here in America, aspects of the world's religions often appear on a smorgasbord so that hungry Westerners can chow down on the most appetizing pieces, while ignoring the whole Divine dish.

But what the hell do you do when a Goddess from another religious culture appropriates *you*? Goddess knows I didn't consciously ask for Her disruptive arrival in my life, nor did I pick Her out of a catalog like a cool T-shirt to match my lululemon yoga pants or as a shiny new icon to power up my meditation space. She was much more than a trendy spiritual "belief," or a therapeutic exercise that would be "good for me" to explore, or an archetype that women invoke during a women's circle, or a rebellious bitch slap to my Catholic upbringing, or simply a tantalizing academic thesis.

She was a familiar, terrifying Inner Knowing . . .

that totally humbled me.

THE INITIATION

While I was in graduate school, my beloved grandfather passed away. My grandmother, aunt, sister, and I were present when he died. It was the first time I had ever witnessed a death. In the grim hospital room, after days of fighting, he finally let go. As his soul left his body, I felt the astonishing presence of

The Between.

I lost my grandfather

Here.

I found Kali

Here.

Later that night, as I was crying into my pillow, I realized something: No matter how touchy-feely She got with me or how many books I read or how many vivid dreams or mystical experiences I had or how long I spent in Calcutta or a classroom, I had had no fucking idea who Kali was until I witnessed a loved one's body die. I knew that that space between the soul and the body was the holiest space I had ever witnessed . . . the closest I had ever come to the Divine. For the first time in my years of studying Kali, I actually briefly, but undoubtedly, understood Her. It felt like an initiation.

The next morning, the inner critic stepped forward: Why was I smearing my self-absorbed notions of sacredness all over that sad night? Did I need to interpret *everything* as a divine sign?

Apparently, I do.

The day we buried my grandfather was my birthday, and two validating gifts showed up: a Red journal from my older sister, who was also present at the death, and an icon of Kali from my then-boyfriend, Jay. His story of how She came to me is interesting. On Sunday, when my grandfather was still alive, Jay had bought a birthday gift for me. The next morning, my grandfather passed, and Jay, not yet knowing this news, felt mysteriously pulled to return his gift. He went back to the original store, and that is when he saw Her. She had not been there the day before, because She had only just arrived, still smelling of the Indian temple from which She came. Jay bought Her without hesitation.

So, once again, this persistent Indian Goddess made Her presence known—this time, in delicately carved copper.

THE RED JOURNAL

As for the other birthday gift . . . well, I eyed that Red journal nervously after the funeral. I knew that due to the circumstances from which it came, this was not supposed to be just some ordinary journal filled with my thoughts about my boyfriend or my intentions for my new birthday year or even my vivid nightly dreams. I knew this Red book was for Something Else.

Weeks passed.

Finally, late one night, I shut a particularly dry book by Foucault, lit a candle, and opened the Red journal. For a few minutes, I simply stared at the big white pages, remembering that sacred space I had encountered when my grandfather had passed. And then I fell

In

Between

In that space, a simple phrase flowed out:

"Come forward . . .

now.

Closer still . . .
Till 'closer' has meaning no longer."

I turned the page:

"Sera making love to sera loving to make sera Love."

The next page:

"See You Vision your Self seen as the Vision you have been looking for."

Up to this time in my life, I had felt and witnessed the presence of the Divine, but I had never heard Her speaking *inside* me. When it happened, it changed *everything*. There is *nothing*, no thing, like hearing your Self speak for the first time. You enter a pause so deep, you actually remember your Divine purpose. Your cells catch up with your truest meaning. Your heart begins to home itself. You start to Re-member.

Oh yeah, *this* is Me.

Oh yeah, *this* is the Divine.

Aware of it or not, you have this voice within you as well, though yours probably sounds quite different from mine. You'll know when this voice is speaking, because even though your mind might be all, "WTF you sayin', woman?" your body will feel an actual physical release. While expressing this voice might seem odd at first, it will still feel natural; it will feel *good*—like you're scratching an itch you've had since before you were born.

Buckle up, buttercup!

SOUL SISTA POWER

The Universe wanted Maya and me to meet. At the beginning of my second year at Harvard, everywhere I turned, she was there, with her strong voice, long eyelashes, and cool demeanor. Finally, after a Krishna Das concert at my yoga studio, we made eye contact from across the room, walked toward each other like magnets, and clasped hands like we had been waiting lifetimes to do so. We made small talk about how "funny" it was that we were in three of the same classes this semester and practiced at the same yoga studio and were raised in the Midwest and studied Kali in undergrad and liked to go out dancing all night and, weirdly enough, *even looked like each other*. But the subtext that was running between us like a Red thread on fire was

I Know You.

I admired, envied, and, at times, was completely intimidated by Maya's unflinching public presence, self-confidence, and powerful voice, especially because I became small, shy, and quiet as a mouse in most public environments. But behind closed doors, I was a fireball. In fact, Maya used to say I was the Shams to her Rumi, because our friendship felt more like a mystical awakening for both of us. *Unlike* Shams and Rumi, however, our spiritual partnership was mixed with cocktails, road trips, pedicures, haircut traumas, sex-toy recommendations, man troubles, inappropriate laughter at serious spiritual retreats, self-appointed spiritual "names" — Li (her) and La (me) (*Lila* means "the divine play of the goddess") — and remote-controlled electronic fart-machine stunts in Barneys New York (hysterical laughter when hearing a fart is *always* a sign of a soul friend to me). We fell deeply in platonic love. Everything we had ever desired from a best friend, mother, sister, lover, healer, therapist, *divinity*, we finally found in each other.

I'm sharing my relationship with Maya with you because it was through our meeting in graduate school that Red became identified between us, out loud, as *something sacred.*

There are many reasons the Red fire burned brighter when Maya and I became friends, some of which I will address toward the end of this book. But here's an important one: We provided a safe space for each other to share our unbridled passion for the Divine Feminine and our unorthodox spiritual experiences (aka "the freaky shit"). In fact, Maya was the first person I let read my Red journal. 'Cause here's the down and dirty: The Divine Feminine is such a suppressed, misconstrued, and often "forbidden" facet of spirituality, that when She starts to reawaken inside, we're apt to feel like we've been given a one-way ticket to crazytown . . . or to hell, depending on our background. So, in order not to doubt our experiences and shut down our inner knowing, we need *the right* external support and reinforcements, like a redwood tree needs rain. According to Sue Monk Kidd, the best way to trust your inner divine feminine is

> To be still and remember who you are, to listen to your heart, your inner
> wisdom, as deeply as you can and then give yourself permission to follow
> it. If you can't give yourself permission, then find someone who can.
> Everybody should have at least one permission giver in her life.[1]

This book is a Permission Giver.

KNOW IT ALL

During my final year in graduate school, Kali sent in another Red reinforcement—Jeffrey Kripal, a controversial scholar of mysticism and the author of one of my favorite books, *Kali's Child*. Kripal was my academic Life Saver for many reasons, but mainly because he taught me the importance of gnosis—a way of knowing God/dess that's not merely faith based (believe in Her) or intellectual (understand Her), but that's based on one's inner knowing.

Know Her

Here
(hands on heart)

Here
(hands on belly)

Here
(hands on pussy)

Here
(hands on this book)

Here
(in the Space Between)

Not surprisingly, gnosis was the preferred way of knowing God for many mystics around the world, especially the female mystics. In *Enduring Grace,* Carol Lee Flinders tells us that while the female mystics could hold their own intellectually with their male colleagues, these ladies weren't as interested in theological beliefs or intellectual debates. What was more important to them was wisdom that came from *personal experience.*

Kripal also introduced us to the Gnostics—various groups of early Christians from the first through fourth centuries, who aimed to know God *directly,* sans intermediaries like priests. Many Gnostics did *not* appreciate being told what to do by Church authorities, so they took their spiritual lives into their own hands. According to Elaine Pagels in *Adam, Eve, and the Serpent,* these folks believed "that the divine being is hidden deep within human nature, as well as outside it, and, though often unperceived, is a spiritual potential latent in the human psyche."[2] In essence, the Gnostics knew that the Divine and we are one; we just need to take the necessary steps toward making that fiery re-union possible—inner, mystical steps that mere church-going doesn't necessarily provide. As Pagels elaborates in *The Gnostic Gospels:* "Yet to know oneself, at the deepest level, is simultaneously to know God; this is the secret of gnosis."[3] Jesus even said, "He who has not known himself does not know anything, but he who has known himself has also known the depth of all,"[4] and J.C. speaks in Red—just open any bible.

As you can probably imagine, the early Christian fathers did not appreciate this declaration of spiritual independence and dedicated self-inquiry that many Gnostics championed (most early Christians believed God was separate and "wholly other" from humans). Nor did they like the radical idea that one could find God *not* by going to church or listening to the clergy, but by simply turning within. In fact, according to Elaine Pagels, one particularly pissed-off Christian bishop, Irenaeus (180 CE), decided that the Gnostics "were divisive and arrogant upstarts who threatened to undermine church unity and discipline, for they 'disturb the faith of many by alluring them under the pretense of superior knowledge.'"[5] Irenaeus also called the Gnostics "self-appointed 'know-it-alls.'"[6] Sounds familiar. (By the way, I just gotta point out that in the Bible, *knowing* someone often meant having sexual intercourse with them, so calling someone a Know-It-All, in mystical terms, means they are Making Love to All of Existence, which is about as Red as you can get, folks.)

Despite orthodoxy's best efforts to do away with those ghetto Gnostics and their witchy writings, lo and behold, in 1945, a *Red* jar was found buried in Nag Hammadi, Egypt, encasing fifty-two heretical Gnostic texts dating back to the first century of the Christian era—texts that have added a revolutionary new dimension to Christianity. Aw, snap!

THE RED PAPER

Despite these external supports, when it came time to write my final paper for graduate school, I found myself struggling. After all my Red experiences and all my Red journaling, my academic writing felt, well, *dead.* Kali sounded like a specimen I was studying, disinfected from Her divinity under the microscope of my scholarship. I spent months sifting through computer files containing my five years of research, slowly piecing together a solid paper, barely noticing that all of my data came from *other* people's academic research or personal experiences of Kali. A week before my final paper was due, feeling totally dissatisfied with what I had written, I looked up from my computer at my icon of Kali and asked, "How do I do this? How do I *really* write about You?" My question slid off Her bright-Red tongue, dripping a scary answer:

You Are My Best Example.

(Gulp.)

The next morning, my computer wouldn't turn on. Frantic but hopeful, I ran to the computer-repair shop, only to find out that my five years' worth of research, including my final paper, was irretrievable, unless I married a millionaire in the next week. Sobbing, I called my mother, who auspiciously voiced, "Well, Sera, She *is* the Goddess of destruction." I slammed down the phone and screamed to nobody and to everybody, "Why THE FUCK didn't I choose to study Kwan Yin, the benign and compassionate Buddhist goddess, or Saraswati, the chill Hindu goddess of learning and culture?!" (And, of course, "Why the fuck didn't I back up my computer?!")

That night I had a dream:

> I'm sitting awkwardly underneath my desk. Yet my right hand is extended, moving gracefully, pulsing with Red ink. My veins are finally speaking. My fingers paint wet Red words onto dry white paper. Frantically pacing back and forth behind me is my "uncle," upset that he has no pen to give me, muttering over and over, "You must write about your angel Kali, your goddess Kali, your angel Kali." I turn to quiet him, because I know I am finally "writing" Her.

And so I continued to write Her in waking life. For seven days and seven nights, with only a few hours of sleep each day, I wrote (on a borrowed laptop) in a way that kept Kali *alive* in my research and, most importantly, in my Red heart. In other words, I told the truth about Us. I titled my paper what it was, "An Offering," and printed it on Red paper with one of my Red journal phrases pasted on top:

Your eyes reflect every side of me.

It is in Your gaze that I strip off heaviness and swell light . . .

reflecting Your opened blackness . . .

dissolved in sight . . .

I dare not blink.

This was academic suicide. In fact, if any other Harvard professor had received this paper, he or she most likely would have failed me and sent me for a psych evaluation at health services. But I will forever be grateful that

Kripal was the receiver for the Red. He actually called my paper "beautiful." According to this unconventional professor, my eclectic, ever-growing Red experiences were, well, *normal*—and more than that, they were *important*. In fact, Kripal crusaded, if we scholars don't reveal essential personal experiences in our work, we're actually *stunting* the study of religion.

While Maya gave me permission to be Red outside of school, Professor Kripal gave me permission to turn Red *within* the walls of academia.

Needless to say, it was a true "Graduation."

MY HIGHER EDUCATION

The universe is full of magical things, patiently
waiting for our wits to grow sharper.

EDEN PHILLPOTTS

oving to Northern California after graduate school offered
me a whole other kind of education. Naked sunset
yoga therapy on the beach? A Zen meditation community–sponsored Rumi
recital? An all-night tantric dance party with tarot/astrology/aura readings,
chased by a shamanic ritual of ayahuasca? You got it. Almost every conceiv-
able expression of spirituality is thriving in the Bay Area.

Amid the swirl, I found an off-the-radar energy school and, from the very first
class, became spiritually smitten. This was partly because the teachers talked
about the Universe the way I used to encounter it as a child and during my
New Age explorations before college—a Universe full of angels, spirit guides,
reincarnation, and multiple dimensions; partly because my "freaky shit" was
no big whoop (everyone there was just as sensitive to energy and experienced
"the freaky shit"); partly because, during an introductory exercise, they had me

energetically "anchor" my skinny ass so strongly to the center of the earth that two grown men couldn't pick me up off the ground (*fascinating*); and partly because the two men who couldn't lift me off the ground were hot. What can I say? I've got a weakness for hot spiritual men who try to pick me up.

Unlike most New Age-y classes that I peeked into over the years, this school taught serious spiritual street smarts. Fluffy it wasn't. I learned that venturing into the other realms is like visiting a foreign country—you respect the culture and customs, but you stay alert and cautious (keeping your ID and a can of mace with you at all times), and you don't just invite any Joe Schmo home with you. Just like you can get attacked by an angry dog or get raped or experience identity theft in *this* realm, you can experience all of the above *energetically* in other realms.

This class taught another one of my favorite subjects—spirits. (Oddly enough, one of the most academically rigorous classes I had ever taken at Harvard was "Angelogy.") Throughout history, spirits have inspired artists, saints, politicians, and even psychotherapists—from Handel to George Washington, Joan of Arc to J.R.R. Tolkien, William Blake to Carl Jung. Truth is, every single one of us has a spiritual team hanging out "on the other side," busy helping us with all sorts of stuff in our lives, from our career to our relationships to parking spaces and, of course, our spiritual growth (which involves all of the above, including the parking spaces).

Jennifer Posada, another soul sister and author of *The Oracle Within,* likes to say, "We've got friends with bodies and friends *without* bodies." In my experience, the same holds true about "enemies," or frenemies. In fact, many ancient Gnostic groups differentiated between the true light, coming from authentic Divine sources, and the false light, which comes from "fakers"—a bevy of false beings, commonly called archons, and their false god, called the demiurge. The tricky thing is the false light often appears like the true light.

In my experience, *true* light beings don't push agendas, belief systems, or spiritual techniques. They don't treat you like a lost little child. They rarely ask you to use *their* energy (or special symbols or purple/white light), nor do they keep you "high" or constantly "blissed out" (cosmic crack is a real thing, sista). They do not want you dependent on them. Instead, they *repeatedly* redirect you to *your own* inner Divine power source. They do not ask to be worshiped; in fact, they Ping-Pong projections right back at-cha. True light beings grace you, and, yes, sometimes goose you, but they do not grab your spiritual authority away. While there are always exceptions, if a spirit being shows signs of any of the above, you may need to become a better bouncer to your personal energetic space. Bottom line: it's best to go *in* rather than just going "out." The more familiar you become with your own Divine light, the less easily you'll be duped by the false light, and then you can move through multidimensional realities with eyes wide open.

Whether you choose to believe in any of this is, of course, your prerogative. I'm simply sharing this information because energetic discernment has become mandatory on my Red path. In fact, I now firmly believe that becoming wise to the ways of energy and acknowledging our multidimensionality are *the* missing links in most spiritual traditions, teachings, and practices. Truth is, mystics from every tradition and "nontradition" know that there is much, *much* more to this world (and the other worlds) than the five senses relay, and to *deny* these alternative realities is to cap our consciousness, doubt God's grandeur (inside and outside of us), and inhibit our abilities to receive Divine guidance, not to mention curb our natural evolution.

Alongside a galaxy-load of helpful tools and mind-blowing information I learned from the energy school, I was reminded of what my spirit had always known, deep down: the Universe is *way* bigger and *way* weirder than most of us are led to believe, and like it or not, we're *paranormal,* de facto and by default. Needless to say, I recited a slightly different mantra during my energetic education:

Screw normal. Be *super* normal.

THE LOW DOWN

Right about now, you might be wondering whether you've accidentally picked up a different book. That's because during my higher education, Kali got trunked. Why? Because I have a nasty habit of repressing Red, being embarrassed about Her, and even doubting Her divinity when I'm around traditional and nontraditional spiritual environments that resonate with me but that don't exactly roll out the Red carpet for Her. If I'm not careful, I end up trusting their spiritual reality over my own. This "habit" is one of my biggest, most painful spiritual lessons.

The tricky thing is, Red is the color with the *lowest* frequency and vibration. According to many beliefs, Red is associated with humanity's most *primal* developmental level, our *lower* consciousness, and the *lowest* chakra in our subtle energy system, which relates to physicality, sexuality, and self-preservation. (Sensing a theme here? I've got Friends in low places.) Many traditional and New Age-y spiritual systems teach the necessity of moving *up* and *away* from lowly Red, toward higher chakras and states of consciousness and colors, like blue and purple and angelic white, which are more commonly related to inspiration, equanimity, and enlightenment. Needless to say, a bloody, Red-hot, and horny Goddess with a 'tude and in a mood is not exactly on the top of enlightenment's Evite list. I'm embarrassed to admit, but during my higher education, I put away my icon of Kali and my Red journal, and I even painted my Red altar a higher-vibing shade of purple (well, at least purple's got *some* Red in it).

The energy school, though definitely *not* a place that favored Red, was the first place—after *a lot* of exploration on my part—that felt like a second home (with some hot "distant cousins"), and its cutting-edge energetic education resonated with my *spirit* (versus my soul—you'll read about the difference in A.M.). That said, every time I walked into that school's classroom, I contracted. I became ultra-serious, emotionless, and "clean" energetically. I tried extra hard to keep my awareness "up high" in order not to "lower" the vibe of the group. The teachers once commented that energetically, I felt like a cross between Marilyn Monroe and Gloria Steinem . . . like that was a bad thing. So, I shut down my sexuality, my "feminism" ('cause gender doesn't matter in the realms of spirit, right?), my bawdy sense of humor, my colorful fashion sense, my love for heavy-bass electronic music, my spontaneity, and what I now know to be my very life force, all because I wanted to be a good spiritual student and hang with the cool kids.

KALI'S HOUSE

Although I dumped Kali, She didn't stop pursuing me. The year I was at the energy school, my boyfriend and I vacationed on the Big Island of Hawaii, staying in a rambly house near the ocean. The night we arrived, I doubled over for hours with the most peculiar pains *in my vagina*. (I later found out that locals relate each Hawaiian island to a chakra, and the Big Island relates to the first chakra, the Red chakra, which influences the sexual organs.) The next day, standing in the driveway, washing sand off my toes, I looked down and saw a word drawn clearly in the gray cement:

KALI

I yelled for my boyfriend. We found out from the rental agent that the owners of the house had two daughters, and one of them happened to be named Kali. Shut the front door! No matter how far I was from Cambridge and Calcutta, I was still residing in "Kali's house."

Later that trip, we visited Pele, the Red-hot Hawaiian Goddess who hangs out in the fire-pit crater, Halema'uma'u, at the summit of Kilauea, one of the earth's most active volcanoes. We snuck away from the tourists, and I quietly sat with Her for some time; then I tossed a bouquet of flowers into the massive smoldering crater. My boyfriend took a picture of me right after the offering. In the photo, my body is open and relaxed, my smile is soft and inviting, but my eyes look fathomless and fierce . . . not unlike the way fire feels.

A few hours later, we walked along Pele's cooling black lava on the coast and watched in awe as Her Red molten lava gushed, sizzled, and then exploded when it met the sea, almost instantly creating new land right in front of our eyes. I witnessed such raw power. I recognized *the* Force of Nature. I understood that everyone and everything (including "high-vibin'" spiritual peeps) *have to* bow to Her Movements.

While on the Big Island, I bought an unretouched photograph of Pele's Red lava burstin' through her black lava, forming a Red heart. When I got home, I placed the photo on my purple altar, but I kept these humbling hints on the backburner and eagerly returned to my energy school.

HIGH AND DRY

As I continued to move up class levels, my body began to react. I became chronically nauseous. I dropped down to ninety pounds. I spent time in the hospital due to unbearably painful periods. I cried . . . a lot. And weirdly, every time a classmate would call to give me intuitive guidance, it felt like a suit of armor was constricting me. They told me my physical and emotional symptoms and bizarre armorlike sensations were due to past karma and my fears of moving forward on my spiritual path. That sounded right—and I so desperately wanted to be the A+ student, gain more psychic powers, and become more spiritually advanced and stuff.

One day when I was buzzing high off angel fumes, however, a very subtle thought arose from deep inside me. Although becoming more wise to the ways of energy was undoubtedly very good for me and even *necessary* for my personal evolution, the actual *path* that my school was so high on taking was perhaps not so good for me.

A Red flash went off! The heavy armor fell away. I ate a cheeseburger (and kept it down).

That insight was snuggled by some powerful synchronicities, not to mention the plain and simple fact that my body clearly didn't want to be in that class anymore, all of which helped me make the difficult decision to leave the school, walk *down* that particular mountain, and come back to my own spiritual path.

That lesson bit me on the ass. The good ones usually do.

REDMINDERS

In today's jam-packed spiritual arena, it's all too easy to absorb someone else's protocol, some traditional or trendy spiritual road map to enlightenment or a "happier/better/more powerful" you. Yet by doing so, we often override our own map. Truth is, even if we find ourselves nodding yes yes yes to the most super-duper teachings or amazingly potent practices ever, our soul might be nudging us in another direction. No matter how great it is, it might not be what our soul wants or needs to experience *right now.*

I believe there are multiple realities and multiple truths floating around ("reality" and "truth" change at different levels of consciousness), and the trick is to find the frequencies that align with our unique soul's vibration, to only engage those that encourage and support our *organic* growth. In other words, truth is only true *for us* when it honors and matches our current level of consciousness and supports our soul's plan and mission *for this particular lifetime.*

Here's another Redminder I would often forget during my energetic schooling—and sometimes still do when I'm around someone who exhibits truly awesome "powers" or intuitive abilities: being psychic or talking to spirits or channeling disincarnate beings or healing people or having paranormal experiences or manifesting things does not necessarily equate with being spiritually advanced . . . and vice versa.

Interesting fact: Many mystics *did* demonstrate spiritual "superpowers" (called "gifts of the spirit" in Christianity), but they used these powers to fight for the liberation of all beings. They used their heightened abilities to incarnate more Divine Love on earth. Eastern religious traditions call psychic powers *siddhis* and warn us not to focus too much of our precious time and energy on developing them; otherwise, we might become distracted from developing a deeper connection with Ultimate Reality or the Divine. (Interestingly enough, when we focus primarily on cultivating our connection with the Divine *and act from this connection,* our spiritual superpowers often start activating quite naturally and effortlessly.) In other words, psychic powers are merely cosmic party favors, and psychic or spiritual techniques are merely tools to help build our spiritual awareness; they are not the awareness itself. It's a bit like focusing so much on the notes that you can't hear the music. And, Baby, She wants us to *dance.*

When I left the school, I began to dance again.

DANCING ON

Although I left the school, I couldn't leave the wisdom. I knew just how crucial this realm of study was to my path. So, through a friend from the energy school, I found an extraordinary woman to work with who was not unlike a Zen master in multidimensionality. This woman's work focused on extreme self-inquiry *on all dimensions* in order to connect directly with our Divine Source. Her energetic awareness put my previous school's awareness to shame, although she didn't give psychic readings; she only asked me open-ended questions so I could learn to read myself. Only *then* would she share "Spirit's" perspective. I'll admit, freaky shit got a whole lot freakier working with her, and I found myself hanging out in the far corners of the Universe more often than in San Francisco. But unlike the school, she emphasized the importance of listening to *my Lady* above all else.

Yeehaw!

It was during this expansive time in my life that the Presence I had always sensed peeking *through* Kali stepped forward—not negating Kali, but opening me to Her deeper Reality. I started to call this familiar, yet still mysterious, Red Feminine Presence the "**Red Lady.**" Having my energy teacher recognize and honor my Lady was healing and validating. I started trusting my unique experiences of Her again. I started listening to Her again. And most importantly, I started openly loving Her again.

We're back in the saddle again . . .

CAUGHT RED-HANDED

We linger on the edge . . . as if it is comfortable . . . as if it is our home.
The most loving thing I can offer you is a push.

THE RED LADY

The first time the Red Lady played my body like a Red violin was a week before my first book was published and a year after I had left the energy school. *The Red Book: A Deliciously Unorthodox Approach to Igniting Your Divine Spark* (named after my Red journal from graduate school) was written to help young women navigate the crowded spiritual arena, without falling off their particular path or losing their authentic selves in the process. I was terrified that the book was about to be released. I have a weak constitution when it comes to delivering my work to the world. I'm overly sensitive, way too self-critical, and nothing scares me more than doing what I'm here to do. Okay, fine, maybe cruise ships scare me more, but offering my Redness to the public is definitely a close second.

So, right before my book's pub date, I did what most Northern Californians do when they have a psycho-spiritual issue: I attended a workshop.

This was one of those earnest Human Potential derivatives, where the facilitators put you in the middle of a circle of participants and ask a series of personal questions that gently, or sometimes not so gently, push you to your edge, and then over it, so something pent up—an emotion, trauma, memory, or unlived aspect of you—releases through relatively healthy expressions (pummeling pillows, dialoguing, screaming, sobbing) in a safe environment.

Honestly, I hate these kinds of things. Stick me in a spiritual retreat to talk about God all day, and I'm In. Stick me in a room to release my emotional shit with a bunch of strangers, and I'm anything but In. But, I figured my resistance to these workshops and to emoting in front of strangers might be part of what I needed to release, so I nervously waited until the last day to plop myself in the hot seat.

The skilled facilitators began questioning me, prodding—closely watching for any signals that I was approaching "my edge." But nothing was happening. I wasn't biting or budging or edging. They eyed one another, perhaps wondering why they had allowed the super-resistant one's turn to come before lunch. Finally, a fellow participant piped up: "I feel like you're holding back, Sera. Like, I want to know you, but you won't allow me to really know you or experience you." My eyes welled up with tears. My goddamned shyness and inhibition always cost me intimacy. One of the facilitators said, "Sera, you seem to know things that you don't know how to communicate. Perhaps that's why you hold yourself back?" I shrugged: perhaps. Another participant burst out, "Well, I want you to tell me what you know about me!" I squirmed like a slug in sea salt; the facilitators noticed and pounced—finally, Sera's edge!

They brought the woman who asked to "be known" in front of me. I wasn't quite sure what I was supposed to do. I'm not a psychic (despite my best efforts in that energy school), and I'm not used to communicating subtle impressions I have of strangers to their faces. But I realized this might be my fast-track ticket *off* the hot seat, so I focused, and shared a few insights with the woman. She nodded, thanked me, and was about to return to her seat when suddenly, without thinking, without having any idea what the hell I was doing, I randomly, almost involuntarily, stepped closer to the woman, rose up onto my tippy toes (she was tall), grabbed her head, and planted a kiss right in the center of her forehead.

SMACK!

The room gasped. Strangely enough, a few participants burst into tears. I looked around, dazed. Quickly, the facilitators had my fellow participants form a standing circle around me and I/She/We totally went to town.

I spontaneously moved from person to person without thinking and started to touch them where it felt like they needed to be touched. I rubbed the belly and gently tweaked the nose of one tall, overweight, balding man. He was crying and laughing. So was I. I grabbed the hips of a woman who had been raped and pulled them into mine. She started to wail. I ran my hand down the back of the next woman in order to release her, uh, *dead mother,* whose energy just happened to be hanging out behind her. I gently whispered, "You can let her go." Tears poured. Then I started hitting a tightly muscled macho man's chest, *hard.*

SMACK!

(Again.)

SMACK!

As I was hitting him, I kept looking into his eyes,
smiling

Clear

Love

A facilitator, who was watching from outside of the circle, suddenly spoke (what he said, I can't quite remember now), and I immediately became self-conscious. The effect was like a rapturous record roughly scratching to a halt. The energy of Us broke. A tall (like, seriously tall), beautiful black man, named Sid, who had not been touched yet, cried out in his deep baritone voice: "Come *on,* man! Don't let her stop!"

But I had stopped. As I shyly looked around at all these shiny, big-eyed people, I felt utterly vulnerable, utterly alone, utterly connected, utterly Me, and utterly *Her.*

Then we all went to lunch and ate turkey sandwiches and talked about our new haircuts and the current political bill threatening reproductive rights and the weird thing our dog sniffed the other day. This is the punky paradox of modern spiritual life. This is the Divine Feminine meets the human-woman reality.

THE EAGER BEAVER

That night, after the weekend workshop had completed, I sat on my bed and asked for Divine guidance. Specifically:

"WHAT THE HELL *WAS* THAT?"

There was no immediate answer, but my feelings brought me back to that experience in that room.

What did I know to be true?

Well, I knew that what happened in that room was Divine . . . not that what happened in the room before me or after me *wasn't* Divine. But I knew holy hot rods of Divine Love accelerated through us all during that *particular* time, and for some reason, I happened to be the conductor, or the reflector, or the reminder, and definitely, on an unconscious level, the eager beaver.

Slowly, awareness spread like melted butter across heated skin . . .

I've been *craving* This.

I gave that woman a smackeroo on her forehead because of a previously unconscious Burning Inner Impulse that I had never allowed myself to act on, and this Divine Feminine Instinct—in that moment, in that work-shop—was stronger than my ego, my fear, my shyness, my self-consciousness, and my social conditioning. So, She took full advantage of the situation. And then some.

I suddenly had another Redvelation: No wonder I'm a bit standoffish, socially awkward, and not touchy-feely (which makes me stick out like a Red flag in this Northern Californian uber-huggy, boundary-loosed culture). The truth is, if I let myself unleash, if I did what I *really* wanted to do, I'd probably just mack on random people all day. I'd love their shit up—pat their bellies, hit their chests, honk their noses, squeeze their cheeks, and say what needed to be said. And then go out for vodka shots.

Right after these cheeky Redvelations, intense waves of pain wracked my body as I finally allowed myself to actually *feel* how devastating it had been *not* to do this.

Not to Love you like I was created to Love you.

Not to reach out through this very page and smooch your forehead

with everything I've got . . .

and More.

My body bent forward from all the energy it had taken to hold myself back. How contracted, defensive, dismissive I'd become. How carefully managed and well maintained. How stiff I'd grown in reaction to this Red Impulse.

That night, I realized one of my edgiest edges is giving Red Love *and* being witnessed *as* It. In other words, a huge fear of mine is offering Her to others as She comes through me and being seen doing so. It's an odd edge, but I don't think it's mine alone.

FEMININE SUPERPOWERS

After this experience I began to recognize that besides all the spiritual super-powers taught at the energy school, we each also have *feminine* spiritual superpowers, such as touching, knowing, feeling, relating, expressing our true voice(s), visioning, healing—and even more that you will soon read about, like pussy power (it's no joke, my friends), sacred rage ("seeing Red" is not always a bad thing), and our natural ability to conduct eros. Many of these feminine spiritual superpowers are unrecognized and underappreciated in most spiritual systems, or are even feared. In fact, not so long ago, the very "stuff" that made us women was used against us. It still is today, which is why many of us have stifled our feminine superpowers.

In Jalaja Bonheim's splendid book *Aphrodite's Daughters,* a woman named Shoshana tells us,

> Women once knew the realms of magic. They understood how to work
> magic. We still can use those powers. It may sound like hocus-pocus, but
> when you really get the subtleties of what energy fields are all about—we
> have it all at our fingertips. We need to unlock the tremendous knowledge
> within us. . . . We are so afraid to admit we are magic. We are so afraid
> somebody is going to think we are witches. I want to be called a witch. A
> witch is a wisewoman.[1]

Although feminine magic might look and feel different from traditional spiritual "gifts," it doesn't make it any less powerful or needed or divine. So, in case you've forgotten, I just wanna remind you that you have *super-powers*—real ones. Phenomenal, mystical, scientifically provable (well, sometimes). And it's time to start acting like it. You're far too important to the Universe to remain unconscious of your natural abilities.

Witch reminds me, I've got something to say to all those fearful forces throughout history that did away with women who dared to display their divine birthrights and authentic gifts publicly:

We're *baaaaack!*

You might want to drink a glass of Red wine before reading the next chapter.

I'm serious.

THE RED LIGHT DISTRICT
OF DIVINITY

As one would press [a handkerchief]
against a wound from which life, all in one spurt,
is trying to escape—I held you close
till you were red with me.

RILKE

Have a glass of Red wine, Sera.

Really?

Really.

I uncorked a bottle and poured my creative partner and myself a glass, and then we continued with our meeting in my apartment.

Stop talking.

I stopped and let my partner continue speaking about our project.

Look at him. Look *into* him.

My external sight softened. My inner sight sharpened.

Feel him. Feel *Me* feeling him.

I did, and I felt nothing short of ecstatic. By this time, my colleague had stopped speaking. He had noticed the change in the room, in myself, in his body. He stared at me curiously, reflecting a bit of my own ego's confusion. But there was this feeling that Something was coming through, Moving Between Us. So I decided to go with It. The glass of wine helped.

Straddle his lap.

I moved closer to him on my Red velvet couch, turned to face him directly, and while keeping eye contact, I ever-so-slowly lifted my left thigh and then, like I was dropping through dark molasses and deeper dimensions, sank into his lap. By this time, the erotic energy was so strong, I could barely see straight.

Everything. Pulsed.

Next, the man did what he has probably done whenever a woman has made such a bold, sensual move. He automatically grabbed my hips and went in for a kiss. The Energy curled up around me in a fierce hiss,

Don't you *dare* touch me until you know how to Touch Her!

The startled man immediately dropped his hands to his sides. The Energy continued. My hands became filled with Her, and like at that workshop (a few years ago now), I knew exactly where and how to Touch him, focusing mainly on his heart and face. But unlike at that workshop, our lower bodies were undeniably Turned On. No part of us was excluded. At points he sobbed. At other points he laughed freely like a child. At all points we were united, but distinct. Healing happened on levels neither he nor I could, or most likely ever will, understand. And then, as suddenly as It had begun, It was over. We silently untangled energy, limbs, and hearts, and he left. But my nights immersed in the sacred-prostitute archetype continued.

(Pause.)

I've had to stop writing the above paragraphs several times. What will my family think of this part of my Red journey? My ex- (and future) boyfriends? My current (and future) creative partners? Not to mention, *you*? While I'm pretty damned sure this chapter isn't the most provocative thing you've ever read (I'm definitely not the first and won't be the last to write about this kind of intimate spiritual-sexual experience), I am someone who experiences tremendous fear around sharing these kinds of experiences. My fear is personal and unique to me, *and* it's collective and common to us all. As Jungian analyst

Marion Woodman wrote in the foreword to fellow Jungian analyst Nancy Qualls-Corbett's book *The Sacred Prostitute: Eternal Aspect of the Feminine,* "To our modern minds, the words themselves seem contradictory. 'Sacred' suggests dedication to a divine spirit; 'prostitute' suggests defilement of the human body. How can the two words be related when mind is separated from matter, spirituality from sexuality?"[1]

Although I've had a lifelong passion for the mystico-erotic, when that experience with my creative partner happened, an honest part of me was shocked. I wasn't consciously trying or even intending for it to occur. While my past sexual frolics had been fun and had felt good, they hadn't come close to this type of full-bodied ecstatic and enlivening experience. They hadn't come close to a direct experience of the Divine. And, what was more, it actually felt like I was *made* for this. Like I was *wired* to Touch others in a hot and holy way. Like I was finally waking up to my sexual and spiritual truth.

This was a Redvelation.

Underneath the timidity and multifarious beliefs about feminine sexuality that I had absorbed over the years from a variety of sources lived a Red hot and holy Goddess just biding Her time, waiting for the right energy and environment and person to start revealing Her unique erotic nature. She didn't necessarily look or talk or move or touch like what might be culturally defined as "sexy"; rather, She was in communion with *eros.*

You might want to take another sip of that wine now.

During my initial days under the erotic tutelage of the sacred prostitute, I met men at Whole Foods or at spirituality workshops or even through Facebook, and I would simply *know* we were supposed to, er, "Work together." And although initially these men were not always conscious about why we were *really* gonna hang out, when we did get together, I was transparent and told them this was *not* a date and they were *not* going to get laid (I rarely had sexual intercourse with the men I "Worked" with). This was only an exchange of Red hot and holy love. For the most part, clothes stayed on, and strong boundaries stayed up. For the most part. To be honest, this spiritual practice felt healthier than most single people's dating lives or one-night stands.

(Pause.)

Shit.

I'm being urged by my Lady to share more of what's going on for me right now.

(Deep exhale.)

As I write this chapter, I can *feel* how this Work has been so misunderstood and feared. I can also feel humanity's *enormous hunger* for this Work. I can *feel* the ten thousand tons of baggage this Work inherently carries with it—all the judgments, taboos, pathologies, shadows, addictions, assumptions, reactions, titillations, and expectations that are consciously and unconsciously projected onto it. I can feel my own desire to diminish this Work, to spiritually smooth down its erotic edges, or to make this chapter more academic or lite or clean cut and "self-helpy." I can also feel the competing temptations to brush the sacredness *off* this part of my life so the psychological skid marks are all that's left or to do the opposite and romanticize it, inflate it into something more mystical-sexual-powerful than it actually is so you will be so in awe of my abilities that you won't challenge me or criticize me or reflect on your own personal mystico-erotic experiences or lack thereof.

As strange as this might sound, I can also feel powerful *external* energetic forces that do not want me to write this chapter—those who have been thoroughly invested in preventing us from recognizing and honoring this not only erotic, but also *sexual* form of Divine healing. In my experience, to believe that our resistances, doubts, and fears of this Work are *only internal* is dangerous, and the true recipe for madness.

Ah.

Here We go.

Something just Opened.

Onward.

FEMININE GNOSIS

One man I Touched during this time was a student of Tantra—a rich and varied spiritual tradition from India with several different schools of thought and practice, but which essentially recognizes two fundamental elements of the Universe: Shiva, the masculine consciousness, and Shakti, the feminine creative force of the Universe. The goal in Tantra is to unite Shiva and Shakti, consciousness and action, and transcend all dualisms. In general, there are two practices of Tantra. The white path is often referred to as the "right hand" practice of Tantra; it is the more ascetic path that tends to be more hierarchical and rule based, prescriptive and socially acceptable. And then there's the Red path, the "left hand" practice of Tantra; the more unorthodox, transgressive path, which includes sexual practices as a means to enlightenment.

In theory and sometimes in practice, the Red path of Tantra favors the Divine Feminine (the *Devi Mahatmya* story plays a central role in *Shakta* Tantrism) and hosts several female enlightened masters. In scholar Daniel Odier's book *Tantric Quest,* his "left-handed" female tantric teacher, Lalita, tells him:

> In Tantrism, there is fundamentally only one color: red. The color of the living heart, the color of blood, the color of fire, the color of roses and the tongue, the color of the open vulva, the color of the erect penis, the color of the sun that warms the hermits, the color of the circle of fire that must be crossed to attain consciousness.[2]

I often wonder what Republicans would think about that particular description of their political color.

Anyway, after I Touched this particular tantric practitioner, he quietly thanked me and commented, "Sera, I noticed you weren't using any techniques. How you touched me felt so natural, like it is inside every single one of us." He was right. Accessing our erotic power is not something we necessarily need to *learn* how to do. It's more about *unlearning* everything we have ever been taught to do (or not to do). It's about opening to our truest nature and inviting another to do so as well. Naked. (Wink.)

We are *all* conduits of eros. But many believe that women have the physical body (and brain chemistry and receptive energy) to host the eros of the *sacred prostitute* more easily than men can. As Audre Lorde writes, "The erotic is a resource within each of us that lies in a deeply female and spiritual plane."[3] Our bodies are shaped as Her Body. We are made in Her image. So, when we allow Her to touch down *consciously* and then Touch another intimately, well . . . sparks fly.

This Red Touch is what I recognize as a kind of feminine gnosis — to Know with and *as* the Body *as* Divine Feminine Love.

Touch.

She Touches.

She is Here to Touch,

for Touch,

and *as* Touch,

and we have all forgotten This.

So, when we are finally, truly, Touched,

Something inside finally, truly Remembers

that we were made for this kind of Loving

(giving and receiving),

and this embodied Recognition

Opens the Gates to Everything.

Every

Thing.

Although we don't always acknowledge it, every one of us craves to be Touched. This Touch Turns Us On. It's free from agenda or projection or false sexual/spiritual ideals. It reawakens every part of us that has been closed to Her Love. It can heal wounds, release contractions, charge consciousness, and make fire sweat. It teaches us how to Seduce *as* the Sacred.

Remember?

You do This.

Naturally.

A FEW REASONS . . .

A few reasons I loved Touching during my sacred-prostitute days: First, it helped me experience my Lady in and as my own body. We became Closer than close. In this merged Redness, I was totally myself and yet absolutely Her. I got to feel how She feels through me. I got to Love as She Loves as me. To remember and reactivate this innate feminine superpower during this time in my life was healing, not only for the men but for me as well.

Second, this Touch spread my life open to pleasure. A leaf brushing against my shoulder, the wind blowing through my hair, the dirt crunching under my feet, the water pouring down my back from a shower, the taste of a juicy Red apple, an arousing conversation, the smell of flowers and food and fire and mischief, the way a page of a book feels to my fingertips or even the smooth plastic of my keyboard. All of life became this Touch. Each moment a caress. Each breath a kiss. Experiencing life like this opened me up to a whole new kind of *physical* intimacy with the Divine.

Third, outside of my Work with men, I began to understand that the Divine Feminine *wants* me to experience, explore, and express *my* unique and *entirely human* sexual nature—from my darkest fantasies to my lightest flirtations—with Her. I don't have to separate the Divine from my erotic and sexual desires, because essentially my desires are *Her desires.* And I will be better able to recognize and work with any unhealthy elements attached to these desires because I am doing so *with Her.*

Fourth, like at that workshop, Red Touch gave me the chance to love another human being the way I've always wanted to:

Fingers walking . . . Stop.

(Pulse)

Press.

Remember.

Fingers talking. Tap . . . Tap . . . Tap . . .

Your Life

Your Love

is *Here*

Palm presses

In.

Moves to the right.

(Pulse)

Here

(Pulse)

She Is.

(Pulse)

You Are.

Eyes Connect.

Her Voice from Between:

"You don't have to try so hard to be yourself."

Tears drop. He Nods. Yes.

Her Voice: "You Know *This*."

Yep. Press.

Know This.

Gather him In.

Heart to Heart

Press.

(Pulse)

Remember.

(Pulse)

Remember. (Pulse) Remember.

HER FLOW AND HER FREAK

During my Work, I couldn't force anything to happen, nor could I control the results. If I tried doing something repetitively (like drinking a glass of Red wine) when I wasn't getting the intuitive nudge to do so, it would end up clouding me instead of clearing me. If Her energy wasn't flowing, I ended the night early. But if She was flowin', magic happened. The real kind. The kind that vacuums New Age fluff and shines the ground. The kind that freaks people out . . . a bit.

I ran into a guy I had met at Whole Foods a few weeks after we Worked together. He told me a knee injury he had incurred decades before had healed. He could finally ride his bike pain free. He said his asthma had also lessened, and he was taking deep breaths for the first time in his life. And his heart? Well, it felt "different." "What are you?" he asked suspiciously, "Some sort of, like, *sexual shaman*?" I shook my head, awkwardly smiled, and walked away.

Before we continue, I want to be clear — not everyone I Touched was "healed" or had an "enlightening" or even "spiritual" experience. Some men I Worked with had no conscious awareness or physical "proof" (like a healed knee injury) that something sacred had transpired. Learning to trust

Her subtlety without external validation became its own practice. Surrender became key.

While surrender was necessary during my Work, my humanity was not to be tucked away under Divine covers. My Lady made it very clear that my human awkwardness and self-doubt were just as important in these Touching sessions as were Her divine grace and certainty. Just as an inflated ego wasn't desired, neither was a deflated ego. It wasn't all about Her, and it wasn't all about me, and it wasn't all about the man. It was about *all* of Us moving and Touching *together*.

TO   GET   HER

This Is the Ultimate Healing.

Once, while visiting my parents over the Christmas holidays, I Worked all night with a young Episcopal priest who started including Mary Magdalene in his religious studies because of our time together (find out why in the next chapter). While driving me home at 6 a.m. so I could somewhat hilariously and very high-school-like sneak back into my parent's home, he shook his head with amazement at what had transpired between us (not to mention with some confusion, because this experience was outside his religion's frame of reference). He exclaimed, "Sera, do you know what you are? You're a priest!"

esssssssssssssss

I heard hissing from somewhere deep inside.

But.

The morning after such an exchange, under the bright light of a reality that gives me nowhere to place these encounters, I would often doubt the experience and feel guilty. (*You* try sitting across from your Catholic dad, calmly eating your eggs, a few hours after spending the entire night Touching a priest.) Was this *right*? In *The Red Goddess*, author Peter Grey admits,

> In the West our culture is hardwired with a Christian value system. Even if,
> like myself, you have never been a believer, your mindset will still be shot
> through with this morality. Our deepest drives are distorted by an internal
> censor. Whether this is a bearded man sat on a cloud or a vague sense of
> guilt will depend on your individual programming. Face up to it. Even if
> you are enlightened enough to be nodding along with what I am saying,
> you still have fetters on your freedom that have not yet been struck.[4]

Besides the guilt that would sometimes arise *after* these encounters, I would also feel heart-constricting, face-flaming shame, especially when I was Working with someone who inhabited a spiritual paradigm that looked down upon Red. One time, when I was fully clothed and pressed together with a teacher I knew from my old energy school, we reached a place that was pulsing with such Divine love that my heart found *its* Heart. Suddenly he pushed me away, his eyes flashing, his voice accusing, "How did you learn to do that?! Who taught you to do this?!"

"She did," I mumbled, hurt and embarrassed and feeling like I had done something wrong. He didn't know Her. He didn't trust Her. And I was only just beginning to know and trust Her this way. I was so ashamed of these experiences that I even hid them from my female energy teacher who I worked with once a week (who inhabited a similar spiritual paradigm as my old energy-school teacher). One woman interviewed in Bonheim's *Aphrodite's Daughters* appropriately said,

> I think the shroud of our shame makes it hard for us to see that we really
> are priestesses of the goddess, and that we live in a world where people
> still come to us because of our function as her representatives. But there is
> no sacred context for this anymore unless we create it ourselves.[5]

ACHING ARCHETYPES

My forays into the Red light district of divinity were startling and more than a little confusing, fo' sho'. But thankfully, as with most of my Redvolutionary experiences, the Universe soon sent in reinforcements, like books and "experts" and support from the Beyond (see the next chapter), so I wouldn't immediately dismiss or deny this new part of my self tentatively stepping forward. Nancy Qualls-Corbett described an archetype such as the sacred prostitute as an aspect of psychic energy that generates great emotion depending on which button it's pushing in our psyches. We can't see archetypes, but we *feel* them. In ancient times, when people were affected by an archetype, they created an external image, like a god or goddess, to project their feelings upon, because (as Qualls-Corbett told me) we often don't believe this great force of energy could come from *us*. Bonheim defines archetypes as, "teachers, gateways to spiritual wisdom. One way or another, they asked to be lived and realized in the outer world, and as we attempt to translate the inner vision into an outer reality, we learn many of the most important lessons of our lives."[6]

The sacred-prostitute archetype is related to the ancient love Goddesses, like Aphrodite, Isis, Ishtar, Astarte, and the priestesses who served them in the temples of love from around 5000 BCE through the early part of the last millennium. Myth and *some* historical evidence have led some to believe that the priestesses of these temples would "stand in place of" the Goddess via sexual encounters with men who visited the temples. As Tom Robbins so animatedly writes in *Skinny Legs and All:*

> Spoon was as shocked as she could be by this talk of fornication in the Holy of Holies. Conch Shell explained to her that the First Temple had teemed with sexual activity from the night of its dedication onward, even, to some extent, when under strict Levite (Yahwist) control. A famous pair of phallic pillars guarded its entrance, and, like almost all the temples of the ancient world, it was financially supported by the earnings of holy prostitutes . . . "As near as I can determine, Miss Spoon, this business had nothing in common with some sordid grinding in a cheap motel or drunken octopusing in the back seat of a car, such as you might have heard the Jesuits condemn. Why, it was even more exalted than marital congress. This was sacred sex, conducted with ceremony and in full consciousness, meant to mime the act of original Creation, to celebrate life at its most intense and crucial moment. We're not talking the old in-and-out, slip-slap here, Miss Spoon, we're talking the ignition of the divine spark."[7]

According to the Greek writer Herodotus (480–425 BCE), every young woman was required to serve the Goddess in this way—by "welcoming strangers" at the temple of love. It was part of a young woman's initiation into womanhood and marriage (now *that's* an interesting bachelorette party). Some of these women stayed for a night. Some dedicated their lives to this form of Divine service, often going out and finding men to bring back to the temple. As the very masculine Peter Grey chuckles in *The Red Goddess,* "This is a damn sight more appealing than having the Jehovah's Witnesses turning up on your doorstep. Some nerd with a briefcase could be replaced by gorgeous girls in diaphanous shifts. *'Hello, I'm from Goddess. Have you accepted sexual ecstasy as your one true savior?'"*[8]

In ancient times, these priestesses were believed to be the Goddess's physical representatives on Earth and were treated as such. Therefore, engaging in sacred sex with a temple priestess was a way for a man to directly encounter Goddess, which was believed to result in physical, mental, and spiritual healings and revelations. According to Peter Grey, "There is nothing more holy than making Love. In the ancient world it was understood that to attain the transcendent moment of union it was best to have a professional priestess skilled in the arts of Love."[9]

But before we get too caught up in the idealization of this ancient practice or the X-rated wow factor of it all, there is academic disagreement over the reality of ancient sacred prostitution. And as with any and all religious rituals, despite the original Divine intention, the ethics actually practiced and the "results" depend on the state and spiritual maturity of the humans enacting them. What's more important to focus on is the spiritual, archetypal, and *energetic* meaning behind this reputed ancient practice and what it might mean for women today.

In my interview with her, Qualls-Corbett was also quick to say that many sexual practices *should* be debased—sexual trafficking, sexual abuse, sexual addictions, rape, and using sex or erotic energy to harm or manipulate another in any way. That's the dark side of prostitution: it's not sacred; it destroys life. As Qualls-Corbett told me, "We have to say no, that is not what we are talking about when it comes to sacred prostitution!"

Back when monotheism first came to town in the Mideast, the Goddess temples were destroyed. As you can imagine, the leaders of Judaism and early Christianity weren't super psyched about Sacred Sluts who served Goddesses living nearby; so they sent them to hell, *literally* speaking. The result? We could no longer honor Her openly and felt guilty when we honored Her behind closed doors. The Goddess who represented eros went underground. We suppressed Her deep into our psyche.

Due to the loss of the Love Goddess and the sacred-prostitute archetype, we've been left with a profound emptiness. Our psyches know something's missing, and yet we don't quite know how to deal with this loss. So we often try to find the ecstatic and the erotic unconsciously, through unhealthy substances and substitutes like porn, food, drugs, shopping, or meaningless sex, all of which can lead to addiction. Qualls-Corbett wistfully told me, "It [Erotic Feminine Love] just hasn't had much of a chance to revive itself."

Until Now

PROUD PRIESTESSES

That's right, Ladies.

We're *all* Her priestesses . . . if you dare to remember and are willing to redefine this "priestess" role for yourself and to shake off any ideas that this

THE RED LIGHT DISTRICT OF DIVINITY

somewhat cheesy, ancient-sounding exotic title is out of your league or too woo-woo or mystical or something other than a label for a powerful piece of you that, if appropriately reintegrated, could change your life and this planet, not to mention scare the cardinal robes off the Vatican—all of which are things we Red ones try to do at least once a day. As Bonheim so beautifully describes,

> Today, I would describe a priestess as a woman who lives in two worlds at once, who perceives life on earth against the backdrop of a vast, timeless reality. Whether or not she is mated to a human partner, she is a woman in love, wedded to being, to life, to love itself. Having offered herself, body and soul, in service of spirit, she mediates between matter and spirit, between the human and divine realms.[10]

And we modern priestesses serve many Goddesses. You don't have to lovingly grope random men in Whole Foods in order to be a priestess (your lover or yourself or that tree will do just fine). According to another wonderful Jungian analyst, Jean Shinoda Bolen, author of *Goddesses in Everywoman*, there are many Goddesses roaming around our psyches—from Athena, the Goddess of wisdom, to Artemis, the Goddess of sport, to Hestia, the Goddess of the home, as well as many we have never heard of. Remember, this book's focus is on a Red hot and holy Goddess and how She steams through *me*. How your dominant Feminine Divinity and mystico-eroticism bust through you will be unique. And that's the sacred point—to resurrect all aspects of the Feminine Divine *through* all of us. One priestess does not make all priestesses.

A Redminder: True priestessing points someone in their own divine direction. It's not about standing in "the way," but rather about encouraging people to re-find *their* way. The obvious truth is that no one needs a priestess in order to connect with Goddess, just like no one needs a priest to connect with God. No one *needs* anyone (priest/ess, healer, teacher, guru) or anything (special blessings, a vegan diet, a yoga practice, lineage transmissions, light body activations, crystals from Brazil, or even enlightenment) in order to consciously connect with the Divine. Ever. We just need the radically brave willingness to go In. And In. And then In some more.

When I finally shared with a few close girlfriends what was going on between the Sacred's sheets, it was like a release valve opened, as they each eagerly revealed their own unique "priestessing" experiences or sincere fascination with consciously combining the sacred with the sexual without necessarily having to call the genitals flowery names or fly off to Maui for neo-tantric workshops. I began to understand the strangely honest attraction we (and really, most women I know) have toward geishas and wealthy independent courtesans of old Europe (Come on! Who doesn't love the movie *Dangerous Beauty*?) and even some modern-day strippers. The Cosmic Courtesan of Us All streams through them in varying degrees, and we instinctively recognize our own matching piece of Her buried deep within us, often longing to be unleashed in conscious and healthy ways. Hence Sheila Kelley's popular S Factor (a feminine movement class created so women could express what Kelley calls their "erotic creature" in a safe and supportive environment) and the hundreds of other feminine pleasure workshops, practices, and books currently available that help tease out this Divine inner vixen.

DIVA DANGERS

Before we spin too fast around the stripper pole, we need to remember that the sacred prostitute is much more than a self-empowerment technique or a sensuality practice or a self-help way to become a "hot, sexy goddess." She is an uncontrollable divine force. As Marion Woodman warns,

> So long as we are unconscious of the divinity inherent in matter, sexuality can be manipulated to fulfill ego desire; the sacred prostitute is not present, nor is the Goddess being invoked. Instead of manifesting as a transformative power that can mediate between wounded instinct and the radiance of the divine, the Goddess is called upon to justify lust and sexual license.[11]

The temptation to misuse this archetype is strong because it often triggers wounded parts of ourselves that crave to feel "desired" or even loved. This is usually because we did not feel these things as a child or in high school or even now, within our current adult relationships. Qualls-Corbett tells It like It Is: "The difference between the psychologically immature female and the psychologically mature woman (regardless of her age) is that the former would have love serve her, while the latter chooses to serve love."[12] Add to the mix the cultural and media messages that our worth is measured by our sexual desirability, and we've got an understandable, but undeniably unhealthy, recipe for "reclaiming the sacred-prostitute archetype."

So I asked Nancy Qualls-Corbett what women should do if they feel drawn to the sacred-prostitute archetype. She answered me straight and clear:

> Wait. Allow the synchronistic events to evolve naturally in their own time. Wait to see what life wants to bring you. Let your psyche guide you. You

can make the conscious decision to be open and to allow your feelings about her to come through, but don't rush out and say, "I'm after the sacred prostitute."

To be clearer than a crystal from Brazil: You do not have to Touch strangers in order to integrate your sacred prostitute or ignite your inner priestess, but you *do* have to honor the fact that they are integral parts of *your Divine Feminine nature.* It is through consciously relating with these essential aspects of our self that we begin to recognize our issues with the erotic and regain our gifts of the erotic. Both of which help us heal the eros-related wounds of the feminine that we *all* carry—wounds that have previously disconnected us from our sexual sovereignty, divine authority, "erotic creature," natural healing powers, and life itself. As Lorde firmly states:

> This is why the erotic is so feared, and so often relegated to the bedroom alone, when it is recognized at all. For once we begin to feel deeply all the aspects of our lives, we begin to demand from ourselves and from our life-pursuits that they feel in accordance with our deepest erotic knowledge and joy. . . . And this is a grave responsibility, projected from within each of us, not to settle for the convenient, the shoddy, the conventionally expected, nor the merely safe.[13]

I asked Qualls-Corbett, who is now in her seventies, how the sacred prostitute changed her life. (BTW, she never did any sort of random man Touching.) She told me she was a happy housewife with five kids, and after they were grown, she became a Jungian analyst (as did her husband). From maiden to motherhood to older woman, during each step in her process, she discovered something new, beautiful, and genuinely powerful about being a woman. She now realizes this was the presence of the sacred prostitute; She had been there all along. Qualls-Corbett said, "She taught me how to love. Not just romantic Hallmark love, but the truest meaning of Love." She looked directly at the video camera at the end of our interview and voiced, "Don't be afraid of life. . . . Feel the strength, the energy, the passion that the sacred prostitute should bring to your life. Celebrate life. Yes, celebrate life."

This is Her Collect Call to Us All:

Celebrate Life!

BA BOOM

Although I continued to allow the eros of the sacred prostitute to enrich my life, I stopped the random man Touching after a year (you'll read more about why I stopped in A.M.).

However, She continues to reach through me when I least expect it. In fact, a few weeks before I started writing this very chapter, I was celebrating life with some friends at a nightclub. While joyfully shaking my thang on the dance floor, a young man approached me. A stranger. Without thinking, I did what felt the most natural thing to do in that moment, under blinking lights, surrounded by whirling bodies and the pounding bass of electronic music. I raised my left hand and tenderly cupped his face, then gently rubbed his left earlobe, then slowly trailed my fingers down to his fast-beating Red heart, letting Red Love pulse through us both.

Ba Boom.

Ba BOOM.

BA BOOM!

Then I pulled back and danced away.

> That is all I am going to tell you about the mysteries of sacred prostitution. Because in some deep part of yourself, whether from this life or another, I know you remember. The light flickering on the curved, mosaic walls, the sound of water, the scent of spices, oil and honey. The way age and beauty and rank are consumed like so much candle wax by living flame. If you don't remember yet, someday you will.

> —*Elizabeth Cunningham,* The Passion of Mary Magdalen[14]

(Pulse)

THE SACRED SORORITY

A hefty bitch slap from a divine force will knock the idea that
Goddesses are simply archetypes right out of your skull.

PETER GREY
The Red Goddess

he Universe was serious about sending in reinforcements during
this Touchy time in my life. But books and experts weren't the
only things lighting up my Red radar. Nope, the most brow-raising, heart-
humping reinforcements were "the Sacred Sorority," who validated my erotic
experiences through their own personal stories. They reminded me that I
wasn't wrong or sinful or alone (or a slut). I was just Red.

Here's a seductive sampler . . .

THE RED PILL

The beginning ritual at every Redvolution workshop involves ceremoniously taking "the Red pill" (a Red Hots candy) — like Neo does in *The
Matrix* — while we set our intentions to wake up, see through illusions, and

reignite our inner knowing. A few months into my adventures in the Red light district of divinity, I was giving my Redvolution workshop at The Omega Center in Rhinebeck, New York, when Eve suddenly showed up on my inner screen and excitedly whispered, "Yo, *chica,* guess who took the *first* Red pill?" and then proceeded to download a whole other kind of Genesis.

Imagine, if you will, one fair morning in the Garden of Eden. Eve is aimlessly meandering through organic rose bushes and fragrant sage grasses, when suddenly she encounters a truly tremendous tree:

"Holy Mother of Gawd!" she most likely gasps.

The tree glows with life. Its vibrant bark and dancing leaves positively shine with knowledge, consciousness, and what we today know as gold body glitter. Under the bright sun, the tree appears to wink at Eve, and the ripe Red fruit pulses to the rhythm of her fiercely beating heart.

Eve vaguely remembers some sort of lecture from The Father about "forbidden tree" or "forbidden fruit" or "forbidden knowledge" or "forbidden something or other," but she's so taken with this tree's stunning beauty that she brushes that external, stern voice of warning away and allows her body to respond instinctually, naturally. In other words, she lets this numinous piece of Mother Nature totally rock her world.

Suddenly, a serpent sinuously reveals herself from behind the tree. She raises her elegant head, looks Eve straight in the eye, and seductively whispers:

> Psssst, hey there, sssweet sssista. You have the right to Know your self, your
> divinity, your messssy mighty Feminine mojo. Not only the right, but you
> have the responsibility. And get this: you can only truly Know your self
> via lived experience, by bravely walking your unique path. But in order
> to start the journey, you gotta stop playing this whole infantile "spiritual"
> innocence game. Get out from under the tree of your Big Daddy and take
> the first steps toward becoming a spiritual adult.
>
> In other words, take a bite of freedom, grab a fig leaf, and let's blow
> this joint.

There's a pregnant pause. A holy hush. An intuitive nod. And Eve, for the first time in her previously curtailed existence, gets a twinkle in her eye, a Red flush in her cheeks (both sets). She slowly reaches out, extends her left arm, plucks a bright Red apple from the tree, raises it to her moist and open mouth, and takes a huge, juicy, loud bite — the noise of which can be heard throughout all of existence, thoroughly and completely disturbing the Universe.

(Swallow.)

GIRL GONE WILD

We all know that Eve does not exactly have the best reputation in Western culture. Her story is often interpreted as an example of what *not* to do, of a choice *not* to make, of a fruit *not* to bring to your parish priest. Specifically, Eve is believed to be the cause of original sin (according to popular Christian theologies), and therefore, we women have unconsciously inherited an archaic spiritual reputation of being sinful, disobedient, untrustworthy, dangerous, and sexual temptresses.

As scholar Elaine Pagels documented in her book *Adam, Eve, and the Serpent,* one early Church leader, Tertullian, told women: "You are the devil's gateway. . . . You are she who persuaded him who the devil did not dare attack. . . . Did you not know that every one of you is an Eve? The sentence of God on your sex lives on. . . . The guilt, of necessity, lives on too."[1]

Well, now we're intelligent, liberated, modern women who might not think we need to take these creation stories or the early Church's misguided misogynistic missions seriously (especially if we were raised in another religious tradition or have purposefully created a nonreligious household). But what I encourage you to take seriously are the *effects* those missions might still have on your body, your sexuality, your spirituality, and your psyche.

As Sue Monk Kidd states in *Dance of the Dissident Daughter:*

> To understand why the Eden story is so important we have to remember
> the extraordinary way origin myths operate in our psyches. In a way
> humans are not made of skin and bones as much as we're made of stories.
> The Eden myth perhaps more than any other floats in our cells, informing
> our vision of ourselves and the world.[2]

This brief interlude is not just about shaking a well-manicured Red fingernail at the early Church or giving you a slightly dry lecture on religious history or feminist theology; it's intended to be an electric reminder that spiritual stories, characters, and symbols are fluid and open, and the Divine wisdom they carry is dynamic and interactive and is *supposed* to evolve *through* us. It's our right—I would go so far as to say our *duty*—to bring forth new or alternative "truths" about old spiritual myths, symbols, texts, and especially the Divine Itself, even if these new truths don't exactly reflect the religious culture at large.

A few years after Eve shared her side of the story with me, I discovered that it wasn't too far from certain Gnostic interpretations of the Genesis myth. Turns out some Gnostics viewed Eve not as some floozy floundering sinner, but as an illuminated liberator. As Elaine Pagels explains: "Whereas the orthodox [early Church] often blamed Eve for the fall and pointed to women's submission as appropriate punishment, Gnostics often depicted Eve—or the feminine spiritual power she represented—as the source of spiritual awakening."[3]

According to the Gnostic text *Reality of the Rulers,* when Adam first saw Eve: "He said, 'It is you who have given me life: you shall be called Mother of the Living [Eve].'"[4] And in the Gnostic text *The Secret Book of John,* Eve was written about as

An Awakener of the Soul,

and the "perfect primal intelligence" who, Pagels declares, called out to Adam (and to all of us) "to wake up, recognize her, and so receive spiritual illumination."[5]

Wake Up!

Recognize Her!

And

Receive Spiritual Illumination!

Perhaps Eve knew that we can only grow so much in a perfect garden with way too many perfect fruit trees and that it's our natural birthright and inspired impetus to trade our halos for hammers, hula hoops, and apple tattoos. In other words, perhaps Eve knew we were here not just to be something but also to become someone. Perhaps Eve was leading humanity away from an externalized, stagnant, subservient relationship with an overly masculine Divine and toward an internalized, evolutionary, and more co-creative relationship with the masculine *and* feminine Divine.

The point is, no matter how Eve's been construed by Western religions, she's still talking. We just hafta have the ears to hear. In the Gnostic text *The Secret Book,* Eve says, "Whoever hears . . . Arise and remember . . . and follow your root, which is I . . . and beware of the deep sleep."[6] What's the "deep sleep," you ask? Well, in my opinion, it's a numbed-out and dumbed-out state of being that stifles your Divine Feminine Knowing. Some snooze-inducing culprits: the matrix, patriarchy, political propaganda, social climbing, spiritual subterfuge, too much white sugar, gossip mags, and certain reality TV shows. In *Dance of the Dissident Daughter,* Sue Monk Kidd offers her own definition of a woman in deep sleep:

A woman in Deep Sleep is one who goes about in an unconscious state. She seems unaware or unfazed by the truth of her own female life, the truth about women in general, the way women and the feminine have been wounded, devalued, and limited within culture, churches, and families. She cannot see the wound or feel the pain. She has never acknowledged, much less confronted, sexism. . . . The woman in Deep Sleep is oblivious to the psychological and spiritual impact this has had on her. Or maybe she has some awareness of it all but keeps it sequestered nicely in her head, rarely allowing it to move down into her heart or into the politics of her spirituality.[7]

Now that we are a bit clearer on the meaning behind Eve's cryptic warning to us about the "deep sleep," I really think that last part of her text deserves repeating and probably should be written in Red lipstick on your mirror or at least the side of a church:

"Arise and remember . . .

and follow your root, which is I (Eve) . . .

and beware of the deep sleep."

P.S. Don't hit the Snooze Button

IT'S GOOD TO BE ON TOP

When Eve's chomping apples at our inner dinner party, Lilith should definitely not be left in the kitchen. Are you familiar with Lilith? According to some Hebrew texts (specifically *The Alphabet of Ben Sira*), she was Adam's first wife. She was not created from Adam's rib; in fact, in some Kabbalistic texts (mystical schools of Judaism), it's indicated that she was already created, already alive and kickin', when Adam came along. What's the down low about Adam's first lay?

Well, she didn't like following directions and obeying orders from her man or The Man, and she refused to be "on the bottom" during sex (truly, this is in the texts). As Barbara Black Koltuv wrote in *The Book of Lilith*, "Lilith is that quality in a woman that refuses to be bound in a relationship. She wants not equality and sameness in the sense of identity or merging, but equal freedom to move, change, and be herself."[8] When a frustrated Adam tattled and asked his Divine Daddy to make his human wife obey him, I'm pretty sure Lilith responded with something like:

Fuck this! I'm outta here. You call this paradise? My ass (which you can't even properly grope when we're doing it missionary style). See you two on the other side. Don't call, don't write, don't pretend to know who I truly am until you're ready to embrace what you have so carefully and deliberately erased.

Whatever happened to our gutsy first lady who scared the rib outta Adam? Well, Lilith set up camp on the shores of the *Red* Sea, and she was labeled evil, just as so many spiritually and sexually liberating feminine characters are. In fact, she was linked to Lilitu and Lilu, demons of ancient Near Eastern cultures. (She was also referred to as the goddess Inanna's priestess and sexual prostitute.) In popular Jewish folklore, she is described as a witch, a sexual temptress who makes men have wet dreams, and a barren woman who delights in stealing little children. Most ancient depictions of Lilith were carved in stone and painted Red.

After Lilith "flew" out of Eden, a disgruntled, confused, somewhat puerile Adam asked for another companion. So God created Eve from Adam's rib, with the hopes that the second attempt would produce a more submissive and proper wife. Yeah, we've all heard how that one turned out. As for the Divine's third attempt at creating the "ideal" woman . . .

You're up.

Look in the mirror.

Smash external projections.

Will you take a juicy Red bite?

Let us hear you.

THE HOLY WHORE

During this Red Lighted time in my life, I interviewed Princeton University professor of religion Elaine Pagels for my *Redvolution* film. As we were setting up the camera, I noticed an illustration hanging on her office wall of a woman dressed in Red and riding a strange-looking Red beast. When I inquired, Pagels excitedly reintroduced me to the Whore of Babylon, who is described in the Hebrew bible's Book of Revelations like this:

> And the woman was arrayed in purple and scarlet color and decked with
> gold and precious stones and pearls having a golden cup in her hand full

of abominations and filthiness of her fornication. And upon her forehead was written: MYSTERY, BABYLON THE GREAT. THE MOTHER OF HARLOTS AND ABOMINATIONS OF THE EARTH.[9]

How picturesque.

Pagels told me that this scarlet depiction of the Whore of Babylon represented pleasure, sensuality, and luxury, and became *the* image the early Church used to represent evil and heresy, not to mention the coming apocalypse. But as Peter Grey, occultist and author of *The Red Goddess,* warns, "Reading Revelations to get a clear idea of Babalon is like reading *Mein Kampf* to get a good idea of what Jews are."[10] An interesting side note: *apocalypse* in Greek means revealing the truth or lifting the veil—a disclosure of something hidden from humanity during a time of falsehood. So, a bright-Red way to read the Holy Whore's description is that

She is a truth that has been hidden from us.

In *Conscious Femininity,* Marion Woodman tells us, "The feminine, however disguised, is always naked, in the sense of 'seeing through' in order to reveal. Apocalypse means unveiling."[11] In other words, you gotta take it all off (all external ideas, stories, and beliefs about Her) in order to truly see Her. BTW, guess what my next book is titled? You know it . . . *Redvelations.*

Although Babalon reemerged in infamous occultist Aleister Crowley's *Book of Law* in 1904, Grey says She originally derived from our now-familiar ancient Near Eastern Love goddesses Inanna and Astarte, who were worshipped in ancient Babylon. The essentials: Babalon Makes Love for a Living. Babalon denies no one. She *Knows* All. According to Grey,

> Babalon has attained Her exulted state by giving Herself to every living
> thing. This is what is meant by Her title as Holy Whore. She cannot
> rest until the blood of all living things has been poured into her chalice
> because this is how the universe functions. It is an unending rapture
> of Love, of union and division. Babalon is described as Understanding
> because she has known everything—in a biblical sense.[12]

Grey says this Red Goddess often "comes through" human women, priestesses who are thereafter sexually liberated and referred to as "Scarlet Women" in the occult world. Babalon represents what Margaret Starbird calls the *bridal* element of the Divine Feminine. She is not the Mother Goddess; instead, She is the Lover Goddess, and a fierce lover at that. As Grey warns,

There is a temptation to view Love goddesses in a benign soft-focus, the kind of Vaseline smeared lens effect of 1970s porno pics. Nothing could be further from the truth. Love is an emotion with destroying power, careless of human happiness, social constraints, and rational analysis. Without this bitter-sweet sting, the image of the Goddess would lose all power. Goddesses are as fully rounded and complex as humans, if not more so.[13]

The Love Goddess can growl, slap, and be merciless. Aphrodite can morph into Kali in an instant. Sometimes the only way to open our hearts is to chop off our heads. Grey says it's this type of unadulterated Love that threatens patriarchy more than any other; he bemoans, "Love has been bled almost to death, drained to an insipid pink when it should be a shameless scarlet."[14]

To end our brief reintroduction to this particular Goddess, I thought it best we should hear *Her* words and let them run naked through our veins:

Yea, it is I, BABALON. . . .

Is it difficult, between matter and spirit? For me it is ecstasy and agony untellable. But I am with thee. I have large strength, have thou likewise. . . .

Let her prepare her work according to my voice in her heart. . . .

But let her think on this: my way is not in the solemn ways, or in the reasoned ways, but in the wild free way of the eagle, and the devious way of the serpent, and the oblique way of the factor unknown and unnumbered.

For I am BABALON, and she my daughter, unique. . . .

Though they call thee harlot and whore, shameless, false, evil, these words shall be blood in their mouths, and dust thereafter. . . . But my children will know thee and love thee, and this will make them free. . . .

My joy is the joy of eternity, and my laughter is the drunken laughter of a harlot in the house of ecstasy.[15]

THE RED STAIN

Another lady who arrived during this time in a rush of loving Redness was Mary Magdalene. I was certainly aware of Magdalene's makeover from Catholic castaway to pop-culture superstar. But let's skirt *The Da Vinci Code* craze and slide headfirst into the academic realm: Magdalene was written about in several Gnostic gospels (including her own, *The Gospel of Mary Magdalene,* which was found in Cairo, Egypt, in 1896) as "the Woman Who Knows All," one of Jesus's most beloved companions and top disciples, and a powerful spiritual leader and teacher in her own right.

In 591 CE, Pope Gregory the Great declared Magdalene a whore. Why? Well, Magdalene was a strong, independent, highly gifted, female spiritual leader who traveled alone and hung out with men, which was very unusual for a woman in Palestinian culture at that time. Some feminist scholars believe this "prostitute" label was used because Magdalene was an anomaly, a threat to the early Church's growing hierarchical and patriarchal agenda.

In *The Meaning of Mary Magdalene,* Cynthia Bourgeault believes that turning M.M. into a penitent whore was also due to the early Church's "collective unconscious, the inevitable shadow side of its increasing obsession with celibacy and sexual purity."[16] What were the perfect images for projecting this split between spirit and sex? The two Marys closest to Jesus: his mother, the Virgin Mary, aka "the good girl," and his beloved companion, the Whore Mary, aka "the bad girl." Rumor has it, the Virgin Mary used to dress in Red until it became too representative of The Magdalene. As Margaret Starbird tells us in *The Woman with the Alabaster Jar:*

> The Inquisition became so upset with pictures of the Madonna dressed
> in red that its art censor finally decreed in 1649 that all paintings of the
> Virgin Mary would be rendered blue and white, acknowledging the sister
> and mother aspects of the eternal feminine, by denying the bridal or flesh-
> and-blood sexual aspect. Paintings of Madonnas wearing red were strictly
> forbidden, and the "woman in red" became synonymous with a woman of
> the street.[17]

Although scholarship has proven that Mary Magdalene was *not* a prostitute, some historians and many laypeople wonder whether Mary Magdalene was a *sacred* prostitute who practiced a form of sacred sexuality (possibly with J.C.), or was a woman who simply owned her erotic nature (thereby integrating the sacred-prostitute archetype). One of my favorite modern Redvisions of Magdalene is in Elizabeth Cunningham's hilarious and moving historical novel *The Passion of Mary Magdalen,* where Magdalene is depicted as a feisty, salt-of-the-earth, uber-wise Red-haired prostitute nicknamed "Red" by her friends. Here's what Magdalen, aka Red, has to say about being a sacred prostitute:

> I want to tell you: being a healer is no different from being a whore, a
> paradoxical mix of the intimate and impersonal, the receiving of another
> human being without judgment, the bone-deep knowing that you are not

separate from this other. You recognize the river flowing under all skin, the tidal rhythms of the breath, the darkness of earth giving rise to and claiming all flesh. I was known as the Red One, and if you are wondering if I was enjoying my fame or being seduced by its power, the answer is no. Perhaps you are disappointed. Perhaps you were hoping that I would be faced with the temptations of pride and succumb (later to be redeemed, of course). That's a classic plotline, but it's not the one I'm working with here. On the other hand, if you're concerned that I'm about to turn self-effacing and saintly, relax. That's just the reverse side of the pride story. I'm not interested.[18]

When I interviewed Nancy Qualls-Corbett for my *Redvolution* film, she claimed Magdalene as a fundamental part of our psychic life, the closest thing in our Christian culture to a Love Goddess. But as with most eros-fueled feminine archetypes, we rejected her and are suffering as a result. As Margaret Starbird so eloquently wrote in *Mary Magdalene, Bride in Exile:*

> What did we lose when we lost the Mary whom the scripture calls the Magdalene? Simply stated, we lost the color red—the deep crimson of passion, the blood mysteries, of compassion and Eros in the Jungian sense of relatedness. . . . We were tragically cut off from the irrigating waters of intuition and mysticism, from feminine ways of knowing, from the deep wisdom of the body and its senses, and from our intimate kinship with all that lives.[19]

Looks like we can't suppress an innately horny Universe for too long, no matter how many people we punish or how many strong women we banish or how many purity rings we sell. Magdalene is like a Red wine stain on Christianity's white sheets that the Church has tried to rub out, unsuccessfully. But Magdalene doesn't need the Church to reveal herself. She's chosen a much more effective route to reannounce her presence: Us. She's erupting out of all of us in unique and important ways, via dreams, visitations, art, songs, movies, books.

Makes ya wonder: what would *Magdalene* do?

THE VAGINA VIRGIN

Mary Magdalene wasn't the only sexually empowered Mary trying to get my attention during this ripe time in my life. Nope. One fine day when I was lying on my living room floor in *supta baddha konasana* (a meditative yoga pose where you lie on your back, legs bent, thighs open, soles of feet touching), I looked up at an image I have resting on a shelf—a colorful, kitschy two-foot-by-two-foot poster of the Virgin of Guadalupe. And that's when it happened.

But before I go on, I'll give you the "deets" on the Virgin of Guadalupe: Way back on December 9, 1531, a Goddess floating on a moon with stars in her hair appeared to a Mexican Indian, Juan Diego, on Tepeyac Hill, which used to be a sacred site of the Aztec moon goddess, Tonantzin. The floating Goddess asked Juan to build a sacred shrine to Her on the hill. Juan excitedly ran to the local bishop. But the big guy in charge told Juan he needed proof of this supposed miracle. So Juan went back to the hill and explained the deal to the Goddess, who most likely sighed and rolled her stars, and then told him to gather the nearby roses and carry them back to the bishop in his cloak. When Juan returned to the bishop and opened his cloak, roses tumbled out, revealing an image of the Goddess. The bishop, using the only spiritual lens he had (Catholicism), declared that the image was the Virgin Mary. And that's how an Aztec moon Goddess morphed into the Virgin Mary. (Boop!)

Okay, back to my living room floor. You know how people occasionally "see" the Virgin Mary in their mashed potatoes or in oil spills or in water stains on the side of a house or in rose-smattered robes? Well, I saw something truly holy and miraculous in my particular image of the Virgin Mary of Guadalupe.

I
Saw
a
Vagina!

Truly. I still do when I look at this poster. In fact, I think I will forevermore see a vagina when I look at a similar iconographic representation of the Virgin. Go ahead, Google "The Virgin of Guadalupe." Relax your gaze, open your mind (and possibly your thighs), let loose your preconceived ideas, and take a gentle gander at Our Fair Lady. Not to get too gynecological on you, but what the hell: the Reddish halo with the yellow flaming spikes around her—the Labia Majora; Her darker folded robes—the Labia Minora; and her crowned head—the clitoris.

This is so clear to me that I'm still in shock. Of course, of course, of course, I realize this spontaneous "vision" is due to me using my Red "lens," just like that Mexican bishop used his Catholic lens. But, damn, in my maybe-delusional, definitely devious Red universe, this could also be one of the biggest and best cosmic jokes the Goddess has played on the Catholic Church. I mean, *millions* of people pray to this Holy Vagina every day! As they should.

Truth is, Mary and Mary are not quite so contrary. Through a Jungian lens, the Virgin and Sacred Whore are much more similar than they are different, and we modern women have a lot to learn from them *both*. *Virgin*, according to many Greek translations and interpretations, means "one unto herself." In *Dancing in the Flames*, Marion Woodman and Elinor Dickinson wrote, "The initiated virgin is the feminine who is who she is because that's who she is. Like the virgin forest she is full of her own life force, full of potential, pregnant."[20] Qualls-Corbett says to truly *own* the sacred-prostitute archetype, you need to be virgin — that is, untampered by other's perceptions or ideas about you. Likewise, you gotta be virgin in order to properly know yourself; as Bourgeault finishes, "the journey towards real self-knowledge (or gnosis), toward 'restoration to fullness of being' is at the same time the painstaking reclaiming of our own virginity, which in the teaching bears the sense of 'free, simple, and inwardly whole.'"[21]

That's why these archetypes of the Virgin and the Whore have bubbled back up in our collective conscious. They are looking to be reunited and reintegrated by *us*.

Hail Marys
Full of Grace and Growls,
The Lord and The Lady are with thee.
Blessed art thou in women,
and blessed is the Red fruit
of thy womb, juicy.
Holy Marys,
Mother and Lover of God,
pray for those who call us sinners
now,
and at the hours of our death and rebirth.
Awomen.

STEAL BACK HER THUNDER

I think it's appropriate to end this panoply of Her presence with *The Thunder: Perfect Mind*, a piece dated around 300 CE and written in a voice of the Feminine Divine. It was found in that buried Red jar of Gnostic gospels in

1945. There really is no better way to say what She is and who you are than to have Her tell us straight up.

> I am the first and the last . . .
> I am the whore and the holy woman
> I am the wife and the virgin
> I am the mother and the daughter
> I am a sterile woman and she who has many children
> I am she whose wedding is extravagant and I didn't have a husband . . .
> Pay attention to me . . .
> Whenever you hide yourselves, I myself will appear.[22]

STAYING PRESENT

These ancient ladies linger. They are here if you want to know them, if you are willing to strip them of antiquated beliefs and welcome them into your modern life. You don't need to read a ton of books or perform a ton of rituals or travel around the world to find them; you just need to open your heart and invite them out to play.

I need to admit something: When I was in graduate school, all hell-bent on uncovering the lost, missing pieces of the Divine Feminine that I felt sure were buried deep inside our religious traditions, I was sorely disappointed . . . over and over and over again. Sure, there are abundant artifacts of the Goddess and tantalizing feminine metaphors, images, and threads interwoven into our religious traditions (especially the mystical sects of these traditions, such as Kabbalah and Shakta Tantrism). But whenever I got up real close, what I always witnessed (at least through the academic lens) was a big ol' penis. Patriarchy pressed into and out from everything I studied. I finally left academia because I felt too much heartache in trying to revive something from the religious or spiritual past that didn't actually exist the way my Red heart knows She exists.

But ironically, during this hot-and-heavy time in my life, I found myself desperately wanting to anchor the Red Lady in a tradition or to locate Her in a myth, give Her a recognizable name, a legit label, a solid practice, a respected theology or cosmology. I thought this would help validate Her.

My studies at the energy school and my weekly work with my energy teacher made me wonder whether the Red Lady was a spirit guide or an ascended master or a goddess from another dimension. My occult studies made me question whether She was my guardian angel. My Jungian studies led me to assume She was a repressed archetype. My women's spirituality studies led me to suppose She was a Red facet of *The* Goddess. And, of course, as each of the above ladies made herself known in my inner and outer realities, I wondered whether *she* was my Red Lady. None of these possibilities felt entirely wrong, but then, none of them felt entirely right, either.

This inability to accurately define who She was for others and myself was maddening, because at that time in my life, She had become an undeniable Sacred Intimate, a palpable Presence I couldn't keep out of my public career, a personal pronoun I couldn't keep out of my sentences. Every time I opened my mouth to speak, I drooled Her like a drunkard drools Red wine. My friends totally accepted "Her" (bless their Red hearts), and when I was stressed or confused, they would remind me to ask the Red Lady for guidance. But as my Red Lady's presence grew more and more solidly into my life, so did Her mystery.

Even though the ladies I've mentioned in this chapter weren't exactly Her, they did inspire and support me during my search for Her. They reawakened parts of me that had been hidden in the shadows. They helped me trust my personal forays into the Red light district of divinity. Their very real presences reminded me that my female body was created to be erotic, ecstatic, and totally Goddess. They helped me act bolder and blush harder, and they still make me laugh. Out loud.

In other words, these ladies are *friends*. They're a Slinky Sisterhood. A Goddess Gang. A Cosmic Club. A Sacred Sorority devoid of elitism and catfights, whose service is available to all, but is especially geared toward reminding us just how jam-packed with feminine divinity *we are* and what a profound responsibility and honor it is to *be a woman*. These ladies are not interested in being "worshipped" (if they *demand* worship, they are probably a spiritual poser). But they *are* eager to be respected, given some major spiritual cred, and known . . . personally. And then, released . . . collectively. As Grey reminds us, "It is not just humans that change, Goddesses change too. They do not remain as they were. . . . You cannot forge a relationship with the living Goddess by living in the past. Be with Her now."[23]

Be with Her now.

She's not "out there" nor back there. She is right . . .

Here

Slow dancing between each sentence, holding a glass of Red wine in one hand and your Red heart in the other. Dare to see through the veils. Her True Form reveals Itself in and as your own naked Body. She is our Apocalypse.

A.M.
(AFTER MARION)

My soul, my soul, where are you? Do you hear me? I speak, I call you—are you there? I have returned, I am here again. I have shaken the dust of all the lands from my feet, and I have come to you, I am with you. After long years of wandering, I have come to you again. . . .

Do you still know me? How long the separation lasted! Everything has become so different. And how did I find you? How strange my journey was! What words should I use to tell you on what twisted paths a good star has guided me to you? Give me your hand, my almost forgotten soul. How warm the joy at seeing you again, you long disavowed soul. Life has led me back to you. . . . My soul, my journey should continue with you. I will wander with you and ascend to my solitude.

C. G. JUNG
The Red Book: Liber Novus

ROUGE AWAKENING

The pull toward soul feels like an earthquake in the midst of
your life. . . . In the western world, many are called, but few
respond. Entry into the life of the soul demands a steep price.

BILL PLOTKIN
Soulcraft

From 2006 through the spring of 2009, I joyfully and somewhat skill-fully surfed the wave created by my first book, *The Red Book.* I offered Redvolution talks and workshops at respected retreat centers around the country and was interviewed on TV and radio shows. By April 2009, my feature film, *Redvolution: Dare to Disturb the Universe,* was 80 percent shot, and I had just completed a book proposal outlining my plans to write my second book, *The Red Book of Spiritual Superpowers,* introducing energy and metaphysics to the modern woman. Professionally, I believed I was living my purpose. My social life was also booming. I was learning *a lot* from my for-ays in the Red light district of divinity, and I was continuously "working on myself" via workshops, books, and weekly sessions with my energy teacher. However, something began to feel "off" at the beginning of 2009, though I couldn't put my finger on it.

So, She put Her finger on me.

In April 2009, I had the privilege of interviewing the eighty-something-year-old Jungian analyst Marion Woodman for my film. Marion's visionary work focuses on reawakening the feminine—in our psyches, in our bodies, and on the planet. I was thrilled to be interviewing this supernova whose work I had been reading since high school, and I had dutifully prepared a long list of questions.

But something totally unexpected happened at the beginning of the interview. When Marion began answering the very first question, I started to cry, and I couldn't stop crying throughout the entire interview and for the rest of the day (and night). Interestingly, Marion wasn't fazed one bit by my wet face. In fact, I think she knew exactly what was going down that day. You see, my strong emotional response wasn't due so much to *what* Marion was saying, because I was very familiar with her subject matter; rather, it was due to *what I was experiencing*—a woman who had embodied her soul.

In *Conscious Femininity,* Marion Woodman describes *soul* a few different ways:

> Soul, to me, means "embodied essence," when we experience ourselves and others in our full humanity—part animal, part divine. Healing comes through embodiment of the soul. The soul in matter is what I think the feminine side of God is all about. . . . The feminine soul is what grounds us; it loves and accepts us in our totality.[1]

While there are exceptions, the soul is often described as being feminine. In *Dance of the Dissident Daughter,* author Sue Monk Kidd wrote:

> When I use the term feminine soul, I'm referring to a woman's inner repository of the Divine Feminine, her deep source, her natural instinct, guiding wisdom, and power. It is everything that keeps a woman powerful and grounded in herself, complete in herself, belonging to herself, and yet connected to all that is. Connection to this inner reality is a woman's most priceless experience.[2]

While it is difficult defining *exactly* what the soul is, most of us do know when we're feeling it and when we aren't. Sitting in front of Marion that sunny spring day, I *felt* the difference between us. I had a Rouge Awakening: Although I had passionately studied, filmed, experienced, talked, and written about feminine spirituality for years, I had not embodied *my feminine soul*. In fact, I couldn't find or feel my feminine soul, at all. I suddenly woke up to the reality that part of me was missing, and I was *feeling* the loss of this essential piece of me for the first time in my life.

How did I let this happen?

THE SOUL-LOSS SYNDROME

Although initially I took my soul loss quite personally, Marion firmly believes that *most* of us are disconnected from our soul. In fact, even *her* mentor lost his soul. In the early 1900s, the great psychoanalyst Carl Jung was a successful doctor and leader in Freud's psychoanalytical movement, when he suddenly realized that his studies about the soul could only take him so far and that his soul needed to take him much further. Problem was, he couldn't find his soul. Shattered by this realization, on the eve of November 12, 1913, Jung opened a blank journal and wrote the quote that precedes this second half of the book:

"My soul, my soul, where are you?"

Jung faithfully documented his in-depth process of finding his soul in what is now known as *The Red Book* (published posthumously eight months after I met Marion Woodman and three years after I published my own *Red Book*) and came to a startling conclusion: Soul loss was a modern wound everyone suffered from. While soul loss can be witnessed everywhere, it is oddly prevalent in the area that should be championing it the most: spirituality. Jung noted:

> People will do anything to avoid facing their souls. They will practice
> Indian yoga and all its exercises, observe strict regimen of diet, learn
> the literature of the whole world—all because they cannot get on with
> themselves and have not the slightest faith that anything useful could
> come out of their own souls.[3]

Marion concurred: "The problem is too many people in our culture try to skip over this step [incarnating the soul] and go straight up to spirit. Overspiritualization is a real danger."[4] At the time of my interview, I was overspiritualized up the wazoo. Reality check: most "spiritual" people are.

Here's another perspective I found helpful during this time, offered by Bill Plotkin, author of the masterpiece *Soulcraft*, which makes the distinction between spirit and soul: soul is our unique core, while spirit is that which we all have in common. Marion defines *spirit* as ethereal, transcendent, heavenly, immaterial, perfect, "out there," "above" ordinary life, and . . . masculine.

Marion and Plotkin believe that we grow in two different directions: ascend toward spirit and descend toward soul. The spirit path takes us on a journey to the upper world—a boundless, timeless union with the transcendent or God—whereas the soul path takes us on a journey to the lower world—a meandering make-out session with the immanent and our individual selves. While the spirit path often feels like a flash of bright light in Forever's frying pan, the soul path often feels like a slow, bloody crawl through thick, dark mud. However, Plotkin warns us about becoming too focused in either direction:

> People who live excessively upperworld lives take a transcendental view
> of everything. They tend to see light, love, unity, and peace everywhere.
> They are attracted to the Course in Miracles or aspire to "enlightenment"
> via an ungrounded approach to Buddhism. . . . They want to exist above
> it all and are encouraged to do so by many approaches to spirituality. . . .
> People who live excessively underworld lives see the world dark. They tend
> to see hidden meaning, mystery, and the undoing of things everywhere.
> They gravitate toward the occult and the paradoxical. They prefer the
> night or the shadows and they prefer the gothic or the arcane.[5]

Ideally, we don't want to wear too much white clothing or too much black eyeliner. We don't want to become too air heady or too bottom heavy; we want spiritual proportion. We want to be well-traveled in both upper and lower worlds. We want to high-five spirit *and* shoot the shit with soul. As depth psychologist James Hillman hilariously said:

> Soul likes intimacy; spirit is uplifting. Soul gets hairy; spirit is bald. Spirit
> sees, even in the dark; soul feels its way, step by step, or needs a dog. Spirit
> shoots arrows; soul takes them in the chest. William James and D.H.
> Lawrence said it best. Spirit and soul need each other like sadists need
> masochists and vice versa.[6]

Although paradoxical and seemingly opposite, upper-world and lower-world jaunts support each other beautifully. They are two necessary paths to our wholeness. Both are meaningful *and* mysterious, transpersonal *and* divine, but it's critical to note that spirit is the most popular and public "face" of spirituality. More often than not, soul has been relegated to the moldy basements of the clean and bright McMansions of mainstream spirituality.

SHOCK WAVES

The days following Marion's interview, I lay on my hotel bed, stunned, as my spiritual past ran buck naked across my inner screen. Incredulous, I realized that for most my life, I had plugged into spiritual paradigms and practices that fed my spirit but starved my soul. Although I could see how my soul had been trying to get my attention for years (especially in college and graduate school), and even though my body had rebelled against most forms of traditional and even New Age spirituality and I had even fallen in love with a *Red* feminine divine, I still knew Her and loved Her mostly "up there" or "out there," as a Cosmic Being or Divine Feminine Force via spirit. I didn't know Her and love Her "down here" (on this earth) and "in here" (in my body) via soul. As Sue Monk Kidd explained, "Women need to understand the Sacred Feminine in our heads, but most of all we need to 'realize' her in our souls."[7]

As I wept on my hotel bed, something became heaven-shatteringly clear: I could not be of service to other women and this planet and the Divine Feminine to the degree that I needed to be until I was up close and personal with my own feminine soul. And, as you will soon read, it has not been easy getting so up close and personal to my soul. In fact, it's been extremely painful and incredibly humbling to dig deep and recognize all the subtle ways I have consciously and unconsciously fucked over my soul, and even more terrifying to then *act from and for* my soul.

It has changed *everything*.

Something else I noticed during my interview with Marion: Her mental and spiritual realizations were integrated *in her physical body.* Her voice didn't come from her head (or from her "higher chakras"), but from her *belly*. (Interesting side note: in traditional Chinese medicine, the energy center that connects you with the core of your being is located in the belly, called Tan t'ien, which literally means "cinnabar" or "red field.") Although I had powerful body-centered *experiences* of the Feminine Divine (especially through Touching others), and even though I had studied, written, and talked about the importance of the body within spirituality for *years,* the reality was that all that knowledge, all those mystical experiences and erotic encounters and gung ho goddess grrrl verve had not anchored below my neck. I had never gone downtown to get my belly pierced with the Divine Feminine. In other words, there's a big difference between knowing something and living *as* that something.

The shock waves continued . . .

After the interview, I realized that not only had I repeatedly abandoned my soul in favor of spirit and not yet fully embodied my feminine wisdom, but also that much of my exciting, career-making, spirituality-driven "way of living" was actually a "way of avoiding" my ordinary life—a way that kept me detached from intimate relationships, my body, my psychology, and this very earth. Marion tells us, "You don't want to transcend your life, you want to move *into* your life."[8] I suddenly saw myself and my life from this entirely new, highly uncomfortable, and downright horrifying perspective: I had been keeping a safe, "spiritual" distance from the lower world *and* the ordinary world (what Plotkin calls "the middle world")—both of which have been broadly linked to the "feminine." How ironic.

A new label for this common tendency is "spiritual bypassing." This condition has become an epidemic in today's spirituality arena, and it isn't limited to newbies. In *Eyes Wide Open: Cultivating Discernment on the Spiritual Path*, Mariana Caplan warns us:

> The ego can, and does, co-opt spiritual ideas and practices by attempting to bypass, rather than work through, the wounded, confused, and even damaged aspects of our psyches. Spiritual bypassing operates at all levels of spiritual development, from beginning seekers to advanced yogis and spiritual masters. Access to spiritual truth, when not integrated, is a very dangerous weapon whose primary hazard is that we can effectively fool ourselves into believing we are more realized than we are and miss the deeper possibility that is available to us. And if we are in a position of power, we are likely to bring this confusion to other people.[9]

This Rouge Awakening felt even more shocking—er, humiliating—since its implications leaked out of my personal life and spilled directly into my public career. It was so damned cliché: I had been teaching what I most needed to learn. My previously "solid" and "successful" reality broke apart as I realized where I had *unconsciously* traded my humanity for my spirituality. As Marion claims, "Many people don't want to be human; they'd rather live on idealization and perfection. They don't want to take responsibility for their lives because it's much easier to fly off into spirit. . . . Psychologically we call this *inflation,* and the only end is to crash down to earth."[10]

Bottom line: Although I looked and preached the feminine part, I was an undercover spirit addict, and it was blaringly clear that my healthy passion for the feminine wasn't a strong enough remedy to counter my unhealthy, lifelong addiction to spirit. I needed to be cut off. It felt like I had smashed against a glass ceiling, and there was only one way to go from there:

Down.

II
RED NIGHT OF THE SOUL

Holy places are dark places. It is life and strength, not knowledge
and words that we get in them. Holy wisdom is not clear
and thin like water, but thick and dark like blood.

C. S. LEWIS
Till We Have Faces

The first knock-down after my Rouge Awakening happened through
my relationship with a big-hearted actor named Dennis. For an
entire year, Dennis had wanted to be in a monogamous relationship with me.
For an entire year, I had refused to be monogamous, because I was enjoying
dating several people at once and Working with a few men under the influence of the sacred-prostitute archetype. Experiencing all that heart-opening,
paradigm-breaking eros made me honestly wonder if I was too spiritually
evolved for monogamy.

(It's all right. You can laugh.)

While there's nothing wrong with exploring one's sexuality, Red Touch, dating many people at once, or redefining monogamy, After Marion, I recognized
shadows behind my noncommittal actions: all this erotic "free-for-all'ing"

kept me flittering away from emotional intimacy and authentic human connection and was just another way I was bypassing the middle world.

Although I refused to commit solely to Dennis B.M. (Before Marion), I loved him as much as I could at that time, and he was the one I turned to a few hours after the interview with Marion. That stormy night in Toronto, over Skype, I had no words for what I was feeling and could only cry my previous spiritual reality out. Dennis silently watched me sob, *for hours,* gently nodding and holding me with his loving gaze through his computer screen in San Francisco.

I didn't have the full picture of what was going down that emotional night (and quite honestly, I'm not sure if I'll ever have the "full picture"), but besides needing my soul, I knew I needed solidity. It was time to stop floating. It was time to root down into the dark, dank reality of imperfect, vulnerable, messy life. One way for me to do this was through intimate human partnership. Although I had had monogamous relationships before Dennis, I now wanted, perhaps for the first time in my adult life, to really *go there.* And so, for the next few days in Toronto, while my previous sense of self, spirituality, and life began to crumble around me, I knew I had something stable to go home to—*Dennis.* And I couldn't wait to tell him face to face that I was finally ready to commit.

The moment he picked me up from the airport, I knew something was off. I know you know the feeling—where your heart caves and your insides get jellylike and your entire system goes on guard, but you don't have any logical reason why . . . yet. But we women can sense in a nanosecond when a man's heart has changed direction. It's one of our spiritual superpowers. Dennis and I had originally planned to spend the day together, since it was my first day home from my weeklong trip, and I was still reeling from my Rouge Awakening. But as we walked into my apartment, he informed me he had made other plans, with his costar in the play he had started rehearsing the very week I was in Toronto. "Sera," he practically panted. "She's so soulful, embodied, and grounded. She's so *feminine!*" It felt like spiked lemon juice had been poured onto my freshest wound. Dennis didn't think I would be bothered by his new love interest because I was dating other people and had always encouraged him to do the same, even though he never had, until now.

Until *now.*

To say I got upset is an understatement. You wouldn't have wanted to be anywhere near my apartment—hell, anywhere near my block—that day. The feelings coursing through me would have torn up a tornado, flooded an ocean, exploded a volcano; jealousy, grief, rage, and a lifetime of loss all poured out of me. While I was trying my damnedest to explain my cataclysmic reactions to Dennis so I didn't appear completely insane, I was simultaneously having an internal dialogue with the Divine that sounded a lot like this:

ARE YOU FUCKING KIDDING ME???!!! I'M FINALLY READY TO TAKE THE PLUNGE INTO INTIMACY, AND THE MAN I'M IN LOVE WITH, WHO HAS BEEN IN LOVE WITH ME *THIS ENTIRE FUCKING YEAR*, HAS SUDDENLY DECIDED HE LIKES SOMEONE ELSE!

FFFUUUCCCKKK TTTTHHHIIIIISSSSS!!!!!

Talk about divine timing. Talk about divine irony. Talk about devastation. Dennis was, of course, confused. Shocked by my reaction. Defensive. So was I. What was happening?

THE ULTIMATE BREAKUP

In the weeks and months that followed my Rouge Awakening with Marion, my relationship with just about everyone and *everything* was shaken to the ground, and some relationships, like my one with Dennis, were even destroyed. Yet the most heartbreaking experience of all was my breakup with spirit. It had been my primary relationship, my One True Love who had always been there for me, no matter what . . .

and then It was gone.

Just

like

that.

The vision I had during this time was of a massive Red velvet curtain, like one that hangs above the stage in those grand old theaters, dropping down quickly to the floor, right in front of me.

(THUD.)

Cutting me off from my audience, from the "house lights" of spirit, from the world.

There is nothing *like a first encounter with Absolute Darkness.*

There was no God. There was no Goddess. There was no Red Lady.

Being cut off from the Big D, as I knew it at that time, meant I was not only cut off from feeling Its loving presence throughout my day, it also meant I was cut off from the ways I had received guidance my entire life. Gone were the powerful dreams, synchronicities, and my energetic abilities. Gone was the consistent intuitive guidance from my out-of-body spiritual "team." Not having these spiritual support systems was like waking up one morning with no arms and yet having to go about my day doing everything I normally did (like brush my teeth and cook and write and pleasure myself). I had no idea how to function. It felt like I had been thoroughly grounded by the Universe.

So, I sat on my couch and cried. I lay in my bed and cried. I washed in the tub and cried. I canceled my Redvolution workshops and talks. I stopped shooting my Red film. I stopped writing. I stopped responding to my email or my phone or my parrot. I had no energy for any of it, and I honestly had no idea if I would have the energy for any of it ever again. If I didn't have the Divine, I didn't have anything. As the mystic Mechthild of Magdeburg wrote:

> There comes a time when both body and soul enter into such a vast
> darkness that one loses light and consciousness and knows nothing more
> of God's intimacy. At such a time when the light in the lantern burns out,
> the beauty of the lantern can no longer be seen. With longing and distress
> we are reminded of our nothingness.[1]

DOWN SHE GOES

During this dark and disorienting time, not only was I blocked from making collect calls to spirit, but also, when I tried to go to the human people — the teachers, colleagues, healers, and energy workers — I usually went to for help, the practices they used and paradigms they shared only supported my addiction to spirit.

When I reached out to my beloved energy teacher, she exclaimed, "Oh Sera, don't go down that dark path! That's dangerous! Not where God wants you to go; stay up above it, raise your vibration, try to find the light again." I hung up the phone, terrified I was making a *huge* mistake and was spiritually screwing myself for lifetimes by

Falling

Down.

According to Bill Plotkin, "Most religions and new age spiritual groups omit or obscure soulwork. . . . It is due to its downward and darkward bearing that many people misunderstand or fear the journey of descent. Western religious traditions associate the downward direction with a turn *away* from the sacred . . ."[2]

A few weeks after the fear-inducing phone call with my energy worker, I tried to share a bit of my experience with a respected leader of a retreat center. Her calm advice: "Oh yes, I've been through depression as well. You'll be fine if you look to spirit for guidance." To which something sinking in me silently growled: "This is *not* just depression or even *just* a psychological breakdown. This is complete spiritual reorientation! I have to learn how to navigate my life *not* by my tried-and-true north (spirit) but by what appears to my ego as my 'untrue' south — my soul." As the mystic St. John of the Cross advises, "If a [wo]man wishes to be sure of the road [s]he treads on, [s]he must close [her] his eyes and walk in the dark."[3]

Although I couldn't feel the Divine anymore and was scared and confused and felt more lost than I ever dreamed possible, I also was beginning to sense that spirit's absence actually *was* my "spiritual guidance." Maybe I could no longer float up and out for answers and divine head rubs because I was supposed to sink down and in.

Okay, it's just begging to be said: Many spiritual people are completely "stuck up." Robert Augustus Masters, author of *Spiritual Bypassing: When Spirituality Disconnects Us from What Really Matters,* warns, "Having to stay 'up' dilutes and impoverishes us, leaving us to feed mostly on recycled spiritual clichés and other heady souvenirs of secondhand living."[4] Kali eats spiritual clichés for breakfast, with extra hot sauce, and then shits them down a dark sewer. All I knew during this dark time was that if one more person told me one more variation of how I should "create a more positive reality," I was gonna get medieval on their ass.

I'm not just pointing the (middle) finger at others; I'm also speaking about myself. Although I'd been tutored for years by a spiritual-cliché-smashing Red Lady and had outwardly rebelled against limiting spiritual ideals and repressive supposedly "cosmic" codes of conduct, behind closed doors, I still gave a lot of power to these popular spiritual beliefs. In fact, I had a startling Redvelation a few months A.M.: I had unconsciously replaced the Catholic Church with the New Age with the academic study of religion with the energy school, which was then replaced by the female energy teacher. While each appeared radically different on the outside (and like an upgrade), when I looked under their covers, I found that they all shared similar asexual and disembodied qualities, and all emphasized (some more obviously than others) purity, following external spiritual guidance (God, teachers, spirit guides), controlling our thoughts/energy and therefore our life, and following the "rules" and "being a good girl" in order to ascend, evolve, or manifest all our dreams. Masters relays, "A common telltale sign of spiritual bypassing is a lack of grounding and in-the-body experience that tends to keep us either spicily afloat in how we relate to the world or too rigidly tethered to a spiritual system that seemingly provides the solidity we lack."[5] It's like I was dating the same sick man with different faces over and over again.

To be clearer than angel spit, I don't mean to bash religion, academia, the New Age, energy workers, or even the broad mainstream spiritual arena. I learned (and most likely will continue to learn) powerful and true things from each, and I am grateful to them for enlightening my life and for reflecting my shadow. Although I do feel that these traditions and groups need to claim more responsibility for their spiritual asymmetries, they weren't really the problem — *I was*. I would have manifested these issues no matter *what* or *who* I engaged with; these spiritual systems just happened to be the perfect external projections of my own internal states of spirit addiction.

It's also never helped that I appear ridiculously seraphic. In fact, when yoga teacher Sofia Diaz met me during this confronting time, she exclaimed, "Wow, I feel like I'm sitting across from an angel!" — something everyone and their brother has said to me at some point in my life. I retorted, "That's the freakin' problem! My overly ethereal nature has fucked me up! I'm dying just to be a human woman!" After my meeting with Sofia, I found an old magazine ad for Diesel jeans, depicting a topless, badass-looking female angel who is giving the birdie sign with one of her enormous white wings. I posted it on my kitchen cabinet next to a quote from David Deida:

> Ours isn't a world of angel wings and white spires.
> Maybe when you die and go to the other side,
> You'll flit around as golden light.
> But that's not how love shines in this human realm . . .
> This is the red realm.
> And the only way beyond it is to feel through it — by loving as it.[6]

Bottom Line: My past cravings, intuitive attraction, and passion for Red's life-affirming qualities were the healthy parts of me, reaching toward that which would help heal my addiction to spirit. The problem was, I still hadn't embodied these Red qualities, nor had I thoroughly implemented them in my ordinary life. To help me understand more about *why* I hadn't done so, soul-based counselors soon arrived on my murky scene.

RED IS BAD BAD BAD!

In our very first session, Susanne—a feminine-focused counselor recommended by dear friends—had me lie down and breathe deeply until I entered a light trance. Then she asked my *subconscious* a simple question: "Sera, how do you feel about embodying your soul?" Immediately, my inner vision filled with Red mixed with terrifying darkness, and I answered in a horror-stricken voice, "BAD BAD BAD BAD *BAD!*" My strange vision and strong reaction shocked the hell outta my conscious self. What was going on inside me?

In *Soulcraft,* Plotkin informs us: "The soul is our inner wildness, the intrapsychic terrain we know the least and that holds our individual mysteries."[7] To kick-start the journey into his own "intrapsychic terrain," Carl Jung went into a light trance by imagining that he was digging down into the earth of himself (much like a shaman journeys to the lower world), until he entered a cave filled with black water.

> In the deepest reach of the stream shines a red sun, radiating through the dark water. There I see—and a terror seizes me—small serpents on the dark rock walls, striving towards the depths, where the sun shines. Deep night falls. A red stream of blood, thick red blood springs up, surging for a long time, then ebbing. I am seized by fear. What did I see?[8]

Through his underground adventures, Jung realized that embodying his soul involves shadow work, what Masters describes as "the practice of acknowledging, facing, engaging, and integrating what we have turned away from, disowned, or otherwise rejected in ourselves."[9] Shadow work is shocking and profoundly mysterious because it has been "shadowed," hidden for years (decades, lifetimes) for good reasons. Our psyches simply couldn't handle dealing with our shadow elements in the past, so we tucked 'em beneath our conscious awareness until we were ready to take a peek and experience a whole helluvalotta BOO! As Masters admits, "If we are genuinely engaged in such work, we will likely feel very uncomfortable at times, as old wounds surface and our sense of identity shifts in unexpected or challenging ways, perhaps asking for authentic answers to the question of who and what we actually are."[10]

While I was still in a trance, Susanne gently asked me what I could do to help ease the "Red badness." The inner vision I immediately voiced was of me flying up up and away from Earth. There was a brief pause, when I could sense Susanne sensing me, and then her breath caught: "Sera, are you willing to stay? Stay here on Earth? Sera, are you willing to *live?*" Again, the conscious part of me was completely befuddled. Even my divorce from spirit and the dramatic downturn of my life didn't bring me anywhere close to suicidal. But in that trance state, I suddenly became aware that whatever the hell was going on with me *was* a life-or-death matter.

In fact, when I met Sofia Diaz at this time, right after her angel comment, she said I was on my "last exhale" and that I needed help inhaling life again. Sofia told me that all our past lives spent meditating in a cave or enlightened in a monastery obviously didn't work. We're all back and having to deal with life. She said, "Enlightenment *is* a woman's body, Sera." Sofia told me my spiritual path was to descend now, to come home to my female body, to breathe life into my belly, and to come to know an entirely different way of "being spiritual" and connecting to the Divine. It was time to give birth to myself.

The annoying thing was, I knew well what Sofia was telling me. I had preached these ideas for *years.* I just wasn't fully *living* them yet due to myriad *unconscious* reasons. As Mariana Caplan reminds us,

> If what many of the world's great psychologists and spiritual masters have suggested is true—that we are 90 percent unconscious and 10 percent conscious—then those of us who are deeply committed to spiritual life face a monumental task: first to learn what it is that is unconsciously running us, and then to learn how to discern clearly in relationship to that.[11]

What was becoming clearer than the night sky over the land of truth was that *unconsciously* . . .

I was completely and utterly terrified of embodying my soul.

(I was completely and utterly terrified of the Feminine.)

I was so terrified of embodying my soul that I would rather *die* than do so.

(I would rather *die* than be alive with Her.)

And, all this terror appeared in my unconscious as

RED

COSMIC FAMILY THERAPY (PART 1)

I was pointed to another respected counselor during this time. At the end of our first session (during which he ignored much of what I was saying and instead expertly watched my shallow breath, my trembling body, my flashing eyes), he told me that although he was used to his Western clients fearing life and trying to escape their human condition in some form or another—especially those who had had a rough childhood or suffered physical, mental, or sexual abuse or participated in more transcendent forms of spirituality—the severity of my inner terror exceeded these cases.

He suggested we try a "family constellation" to see if we could locate where my extreme fear of embodiment derived from. This unusual experiential process involves you and a dozen or so people sitting in a circle, witnessing a few others who have volunteered to role-play around your issue (in the center of the circle). Here's where it gets interesting: There is no script or history or detailed personal information given; instead, the role players *intuitively* "act out" the unconscious reasons and hidden roots underlying your current issue, which offers you (watching from the sidelines) a new perspective. This is one of those seemingly woo-woo processes that people don't fully understand with their minds but that nonetheless has proven to be tremendously insightful. Therefore, it is being used more and more in traditional therapy.

However, I'm not gonna lie—my family constellation starred the woo-woo.

The first five minutes involved three role-players in the center of the circle, intuitively acting out powerful but typical unconscious dynamics between my mom, my dad, and myself. Suddenly, witnesses sitting in the circle *not* assigned roles cried out that the entire floor "felt/looked" like it was two feet deep in Red blood. The complete stranger intuitively "role playing" me in the middle of the circle ran to an empty chair and curled up in the fetal position, terrified. Meanwhile, a witness silently started to rise up until he was standing on his tippy toes *on top* of his chair. He stretched his arms out to either side and let his head loll. He looked like he was being crucified. Almost at the same time, my friend Liyana, also not originally assigned a role, ran into the bloody circle and stood on *her* tippy toes and reached reached reached up with her arms as she burst into heartbreaking sobs. Meanwhile, the original people assigned the roles of my ordinary mom and dad moved to the sidelines, watching in awe as what appeared like my "cosmic family" took center stage.

"Well, this is new," my surprised counselor muttered under his breath. My fear of embodiment didn't appear to be rooted in my immediate family dynamics or even necessarily in my ancestors (another common source).

He started working the room and brought who he called "the couple" (crucified man and reaching, sobbing woman) together and had them lie down on the floor in surrender, peacefully holding hands in the Red. He had me trade spaces with the woman "playing" me. As I took her fetal position, I immediately felt gut-wrenching, inconsolable terror. He then asked me to unfold my clenched body and place my feet on the ground, deep in the Red "blood" of Life. I did so, shaking and sobbing and feeling more vulnerable than I'd ever felt before. Oddly enough, four witnesses slipped off their chairs onto their knees, facing me, their hands folded in prayer.

Then my family constellation was over.

My counselor shook his head, smiled at me compassionately, and said, "Sera, you're pretty out there."

SOUL WOUNDS

I *was* pretty out there. So out there, in fact, that a few weeks after my family constellation, during a late-night journaling session, a wispy voice stated:

I'm not here.

It was a strange declaration to be sure, but it made me think about a close girlfriend who had recently told me that whenever she hugged or touched me, she didn't feel *me*. It's not like I was spacing out or not being present with her, but that my Being, what I Am, the Essence (or soul) of me, didn't feel like it inhabited my body. Another recent encounter flashed behind my eyes: A man told me that even though I *acted* human like a pro, I *felt* "ghost-like," intangible, more than most. Now, I was used to being called witchy and angelic and being told I was ungrounded, but becoming ghostly was incredibly unsettling.

Although I was becoming more aware of my spiritual-bypasser tendencies and wasn't *that* interested in denying the psychological elements of my Red night of the soul or how I, as a modern woman, had repeatedly dissed my soul, I also felt like I was tussling with why I, *as a soul,* was unwilling to completely touch down in a human body. This determined disembodiment, this radical refusal to fully incarnate and yet this equally strong *ache* to do so — to finally "come home" — felt epic and bizarre and painful beyond measure. It felt like the cosmic Novocain that had been numbing me for lifetimes was suddenly wearing off, and the Soul Ache I'd had since the beginning of time was finally being felt, in every cell in my body and on every level of my being.

I.   Hurt.   Everywhere.

I was an open wound.

But not just any wound.

In my experience, we each have a *sacred* wound. While this sacred wound most definitely bleeds through our current lives and psyches, it's actually anchored in our *soul* and tells a much larger story—our cosmic story. In many ways, *every* wound we have is related to this sacred wound, so when we discover it, every other wound begins to make more, well, "sense."

I want to be careful here, because as you might have experienced, in today's overly therapized culture, some people can get a little too attached to their wounds, making them the centerpiece of every conversation and the means through which they relate to others and define themselves and live their life, thereby turning the wound and the healing of the wound into their new profession and raison d'etre. Caroline Myss wisely labels this phenomenon *woundology.* However, when you're a spiritual bypasser like me, who never realized she actually had any wounds to heal, the opening and exploration of my sacred wound—the wound around which so much of my life was created—has been mandatory on my soul path. As Plotkin writes, "The risky task with your wounds is to open them so soul can come through."[12]

Something to be aware of: The opening of our sacred wound lies completely beyond our conscious control. You can't make yourself open or close your sacred wound. It's either time for it to open, or it isn't. But if it's time for it to open, hold on to yer sanity as best you can, because sacred wounds take you where most therapy isn't willing to go.

Now, although *essentially* our soul can never be wounded, on lower dimensions of this universe, it *feels* and *appears* as though our soul is wounded and even fragmented. In fact, there's a common shamanic practice called "soul retrieval" in which shamans travel to other realms in order to locate and "bring back" wounded pieces of a person's soul to help reintegrate these soul fragments into the human body, thereby providing healing on multiple levels. More often than not, a person's soul has fragmented due to a trauma that was too unbearable to "stay through," such as abuse, rape, war, an accident, a loss of a loved one, and so on.

At this time in my Red night, I was beginning to recognize that my soul's trauma didn't appear to come entirely from my current life. I also realized that I had to be my own shaman. I had to retrieve my own soul and integrate her back into my body. It was clear that I couldn't continue living in this disembodied way anymore. It was time to make a fundamental choice: embody my soul *or* skedaddle through some sort of "natural" means (illness, car accident, earthquake, rotten hair dye).

I know this might sound strange. I'm not trying to make some ultimate metaphysical claims for *you*. All I know is that this life-or-death choice was very real for me at this time. As Marion Woodman confirms, "It's truly a shattering experience to realize you don't want to live, and an equally shattering experience to know you do."[13] Although embodiment felt absolutely terrifying, I realized that if I didn't try to incarnate now, I would just have to do it in my next life.

So, I stopped resisting what it felt like I had been resisting for eons of time and started to surrender to the slow process of my embodiment.

In other words, I chose to live.

MUD PITS AND MARRIAGE

For months and months, I felt like I was living in a mud pit.

My middle world and lower world were receiving some long-overdue visits, and they felt *very* different than my usual haunt—the light and airy upper world.

During this revealing period, I seriously thought about creating a new twelve-step program called "Disincarnates Anonymous." All my previously unconscious habits that had held me "disincarnate"—not fully inhabiting my female body or my life—kept arising in front of my surprised eyes to be delved into and processed with my counselors and journal and then slowly and awkwardly implemented in my daily life. Bottom line: I was beginning to take responsibility for my life (and lives). I was *starting* to become a spiritual adult.

A quick acknowledgment: I'm beyond grateful that I actually had the means and the time to Fall. In what I can see only as a grandiose act of precognitive grace, two dear friends donated a large sum of money to me for my Redvolution work, two weeks before I met Marion. Also, I was not married nor did I have children or others dependent on me, nor did I have a nine-to-five job. I know others who have "fallen" while having all the above responsibilities firmly in place, and they have still made it through to their other side, safely, and without putting their loved ones in jeopardy. This is a unique experience for each of us, perfectly timed and prescribed by our soul. During Jung's *Red Book* years, he continued to work and pay his bills and attend to his family during the day, while processing and documenting his dramatic soul voyages during the night. He said that what transpired during his inner excavations formed the basis for his *entire life's work*.

Six soul-working months into my Red night, I retreated to Harbin Hot Springs, a rustic hippie hot springs in Northern California, where I soaked, slept, and did absolutely nothing for nine days.

My last night, sitting in the middle of the woods under the bright moon, something shifted. What happened wasn't complicated; it was really very simple—I *felt* Mama Earth. I experienced Her . . . not abstractly, as "nature," but *personally,* as a *Being.* She did not feel like my beloved, still-absent Red Lady, but She did make Herself known as a darkly wild and glorious Feminine Presence, a singular earthly organism that I was undoubtedly a part of, and that I loved, *oh how I loved,* and that I missed, *oh how I had missed.* For the first time in a long time, I felt an intimate, grounded, *bodily* connection to Her. My cells sighed. My organs gurgled. My heart pressed against Her. The sensation of our re-connection was not unlike hugging one of my dearest and oldest friends with whom I hadn't been in contact with for ages. Oh yeah, *You.* The overflowing love exchanged through our reunion astonished me.

I began to feel what it might actually be like to make love to life—not to reject it or idealize it or simply endure it, but to actively and lovingly give to it and receive from it. I began to understand that it was not enough to just face reality; I needed to embrace reality.

Years earlier, at this very same hot springs, I had married myself, with soul sister Maya as my witness. So, now, on this Redvelatory last night of my retreat, I decided to update my wedding vows. There, with Mama Earth as my witness, I *married* my physicality. I ceremoniously and with full intention and heart

committed myself to my body

to my soul

to the earth

to life

to the Divine Feminine.

And in those magnified moments, they believed me.

BLAST OFF

When you light a candle, you also cast a shadow.

URSULA K. LE GUIN

After I got hitched at the hippie hot springs, it was like a Red rocket had launched. Within two weeks of my return, my agent called to say my book proposal for *The Red Book of Spiritual Superpowers* (which I had sent her B.M.) was wanted by several top publishers. A famous movie star asked me to cowrite a book with her. An esteemed audio company invited me to do a Red audio program. A popular sex-toy company hired me to create a Redvolution sex-toy kit. The filmmaker moved to San Francisco so we could finish shooting the *Redvolution* film. I resurrected my social life and went out to parties and professional events. Dennis even contacted me, saying his feelings for that other woman weren't real, and he was ready to start a serious relationship with me. And last but not least, the *New York Times* called for an interview—I and three of my friends were featured on the cover of the "Sunday Style Section" as new role models for our generation. (Yikes.)

Although I was a tad suspicious of this sudden blastoff, I didn't think the Universe would be blessing me with all this awesomeness if I hadn't somehow healed what needed to be healed. So, I did what I've done my whole life—I trotted down the well-lit path it seemed the Universe had laid out for me. I signed a book deal with a major publisher, set up film interviews, started new creative projects, and got back together with Dennis.

"Coincidentally," the "Book Review" in the *very same New York Times* issue where my interview appeared was on Jung's soon-to-be released *The Red Book*. And when the issue hit the stands, I was attending a Spirituality and Shadow conference.

The Universe has a sick sense of humor.

RED ALERT

I will come in the night following an Ordinary day
I will turn your world upside down
I will Confront you with the Truths of your actions,
thoughts and motives
I will be a mirror to your Soul.

ALEX GORDON

I't was the perfect setting for a film interview: an idyllic spiritual retreat center nestled among stunning redwoods just north of San Francisco. But right before we let the camera roll, our interviewee, Andrew Harvey (a sacred activist, Oxford scholar, and mystic), decided to give my filmmaker and me something we needed even more than an interview: a lecture. A very passionate lecture. More specifically, an earth-shaking, rafter-rumbling, fire-breathing wake-up call from the Divine She Herself. Lemme tell ya, there is *nothing* like a gay mystic channeling Kali at you for two hours straight!

> "WHY ARE YOU MAKING THIS FILM WITH HIM?!"
> (referring to the filmmaker)
> "STOP ACTING LIKE A WHORE!!!"

Before I continue, I want you to know why I stayed in that room and swallowed all that fire. First, because I love, respect, and trust Andrew. Second, because despite the fact that I had been cut off from external Divine Sources for more than seven months, it was completely clear to me *Who* was blazing *through* Andrew—the Divine Feminine energy was unmistakable. Third, because the messages weren't exactly unfamiliar. Andrew voiced (*screamed*) my own intuitions:

> "You want to make a film about the Divine Feminine when you're abusing
> your feminine soul and allowing the Divine Feminine to be *used* in the
> process?! The Divine Feminine won't stand for it! She simply won't!"

I knew very well that the filmmaker and I did *not* have a healthy personal dynamic, but I thought I was handling it. I thought I could and *should* put up with what was happening in order to get this Red film out into the world. Apparently, the Divine Feminine had other opinions. Incredibly loud ones, actually. But they certainly got my attention. After that spank, Andrew/Kali moved on to other aspects of my career:

> "You have important work to offer; don't be another _____ [insert name
> of a famous mainstream female spirituality teacher]!!! Don't get caught up
> in sales and marketing and being famous and the media!"

I inhaled sharply. My sudden surge of success flashed before my eyes, as did all the recent offers from those who wanted to help "get me out there." They believed the *Redvolution* was extremely marketable. It is. They saw me as a hot and sassy new spiritual spokesperson. I can be. They treated Red like a *trend,* like a *brand,* like a *product to sell* . . . and I was beginning to as well. While part of me felt uncomfortable with this recent push, part of me also felt it was okay, because I wasn't pushing, well, drugs or unhealthy information; I was "pushing" spiritual awakening, and what's so wrong with that? However, as Mariana Caplan points out, "Authentic spirituality is often co-opted and manipulated into a commodity that is bought and sold in the marketplace. Spirituality is not only a path to liberation, truth, and compassion; it is also big business."[1]

Before we get too hot and bothered, I want to make clear that I'm all for spiritual peeps breaking old-school poverty vows, knowing their inherent worth, and becoming financially independent and abundant. I'm all for people learning how to reach larger audiences with their passion in creative and effective ways. And I'm definitely a champion of women succeeding in what's traditionally been a male-dominated field. But what Andrew/Kali reminded me was that even our best intentions for offering our spiritual gifts to the world contain shadows. Even though I wasn't *consciously* using my spiritual gifts to "get out there" (and my stage-frightened self actually preferred to stay behind closed doors), I needed to become much more aware of my ego's *unconscious* desires to be seen, admired, and even famous, and how these masked desires were influencing my career.

Feeling rightfully threatened by this Lecture O' Fire, my wounded, well-meaning ego kicked in, and I stuttered, "But, but, but, I thought I was *helping* by making the Divine Feminine more mainstream and marketable. I want to welcome as many women as possible back into Her arms! It's part of my *Divine service!*"

Andrew roared,

> "You're working for the *RED FEMININE,* Sera!!! Kali *doesn't give a shit* who She reaches or who gets Her message! Her message is only for those who have the ears to hear! Stop watering it down! Stop trying to please the mainstream market and your own ego! Prophets are never liked, Sera! You have the potential to not just be another pastel spiritual speaker, but an authentic teacher. BUT, you need to get real, *real* serious! Don't buy into all that New Age fluffy bullshit! Don't become just a popular pretty girl who talks about empowering women without ruffling any feathers. And don't allow yourself to become the hot new spiritual sex object created for *their* viewing pleasure!

> "Don't. Be. Patriarchy's. Puppet!"

I choked on an ocean of fire.

I'll be honest: There's something *very* seductive about teaching and selling "spirituality" these days, especially when you're a smart, attractive, "spiritual" woman. My eyes were forced open to this temptation and tendency. I immediately recognized inadvertent ways I had been misusing my femininity. I shuddered as I recognized how easy it is to appear like I'm being all Redvolutionary, while in truth being patriarchy's plaything.

Through a Red lens, patriarchy is not just a sociopolitical system of power that has dominated *both* women and men for millennia by directly or indirectly undermining females and feminine values; it is also a multidimensional *energy* and a tricky motherfucker in the truest sense of that phrase. It continually shape-shifts in order to stay in control. If there is an awakening in consciousness that threatens its power (like the Divine Feminine), you can betcha bottom dollar that patriarchy will find ways to co-opt, commodify, and even mimic it in order to carry forward its own agenda. In other words, patriarchy is now wearing a goddess costume. Like Jesus in the temple, over-turning the merchandise stalls and expelling the charlatans, we women have to take a stand and scream:

"Not. In. Our Mother's HOUSE!!!!!!!!!"

Now, before we gather pitchforks and torches, it's important to recognize and honor the fact that there are as many ways to express the Feminine Divine as there are people. Some "feminine" expressions might *appear* like "commodification" (especially through certain spiritually correct or second wave feminist lenses), even when they are *actually authentic* Divine Feminine transmissions. But Andrew/Kali's wake-up call reminded me how *I* needed to be vigilant and responsible, and become *much* more conscious and careful with how I transmitted the Red feminine.

Andrew/Kali continued:

> "Be the *authentic,* unapologetic, unorthodox, burning-hot sexual woman who truly represents *Her,* not 'them.' That will scare patriarchy! Sera, you need to give your good girl a funeral! This planet is in crisis! Now is not the time to play the media's games or to worry if you'll be liked!"

And then he fired it home:

> "You must not trust Her enough because you think you know how to get Her out into the world better than She does!"

Bull's-eye.

My head bowed; tears streamed.

It's hard to trust Her foreign ways over the more familiar, popular, and proven-successful ways of offering one's work to the world (especially when She had been MIA for more than seven months). Although it's not unheard of to ask the Divine to guide our career, it's a lot fucking harder to put into practice, especially when you're a recovering good-girl people-pleaser whore whose Divine guidance happens to come from a Red hot and holy Goddess who breathes fire, wields swords, and stirs some serious shit up!

Although this tirade might sound harsh, there was not one second during the fire-hosing that I didn't feel Her love roaring as my deepest truth. As

Marion Woodman says, "Sooner or later, the feminine face of God, Love, looks us straight in the eye, and though her love may manifest as rage at our self-destruction, she's there."[2] Divine Feminine rage is not unconscious or ego driven or malicious. As Bonheim tells us, "The rage of the goddess is highly conscious, like a blinding flash of light that shoots from her third eye and unfailingly finds its target,"[3] which in this case was . . .

my ass.

Without this spanking, I might have continued to let the mainstream spirituality arena, patriarchy, my shadows, and my spiritualized ego dictate my career's direction. This not only would've misused the Divine Feminine I was so intent on serving, but it would have misled my audience, which I cared so deeply about. The timing was eerily perfect. Shaken, humbled, and Red-faced, my filmmaker and I, er, "thanked" Andrew and silently drove back to San Francisco.

CHOP CHOP CHOP!

After a week of processing just what the hell had gone down during that two-hour Sacred Rage-a-thon, I made the toughest professional decision I had ever made thus far in my life. After two challenging but inspiring years of working on my beloved *Redvolution* film, I let go of my award-winning filmmaker, who was also the cinematographer, the editor, the sound designer, the producer, and the fundraiser, and who had *just* moved to San Francisco so we could complete the film.

While something burning deep inside me knew this was the right decision, my mind completely spazzed out after I made the final cut. How could I ditch what felt like one of my most divinely ordained service projects? Was I delusional for thinking Andrew Harvey was Kali's mouthpiece? I've always been scared of going public with my divine mission; was all this an unconscious way for me to sabotage myself? Was I simply scared of success?

Next up on Kali's chopping block: my writing editor, who happens to be one of the best professional writers I know, a true word magician. His skills helped my first book, *The Red Book,* get published and reach a wide audience. He also happens to be an ex-boyfriend. Only a few weeks after the Andrew Harvey incident, my editor and I were discussing our upcoming editing schedule for my new book, when we had an all-too-familiar unhealthy verbal exchange. And that's when it hit me like a ton of Red bricks: he was not the right editor for this book.

I almost threw up on my plate.

Besides my personal blog, I had never let the world see a piece of my writing that had *not* been edited by him. As ridiculous as this might sound, I was terrified to write without my editor's help, just as I was terrified to create a film without the filmmaker's help. My terror was justifiable on one hand: I simply don't have their professional expertise. But there was also something deeper going on — a powerful internal fear I had about putting my work out into the world without the help and support of men.

A woman being supported by a man, or "the feminine" being supported by "the masculine" (inside ourselves or outside ourselves), is often healthy and balancing and even necessary. Many wise ones teach that you can't truly create anything without the energy of *both* the masculine and the feminine getting It On. And I agree, in theory. But you see, I wasn't in relationship with the healthy masculine at this time (inside or outside of myself); I was in relationship with unhealthy masculine derivatives, and I was completely dependent upon patriarchy. If I really wanted to live a life dedicated to the Divine Feminine, I needed to come to know and respect *Her* expertise, *Her* ways of getting out into the world, and *Her* ways of loving and working healthily with men and the masculine. As Marion Woodman writes, "If we leave our father's house, we have to make ourselves self-reliant. . . . Otherwise, we just fall into another father's house."[4]

Kali wasn't done with me. Three's a charm. My newly re-established intimate relationship with Dennis was already fraught with issues, but I was trying desperately to keep it intact, especially since I was losing all my creative male partners and needed a supportive male shoulder to lean on. But one night, when the internal pressure became unbearable and the unhealthy issues were bitingly clear, I finally mustered up the strength and broke up with him. Experiencing yet another life-changing and gut-wrenching event in such a short time made me realize this wasn't a casual drive-by from the Divine Feminine. She meant bizness.

Now, despite how I've implied that Kali was the one chopping my life into little pieces, it's just a literary device and a way for me to bitch and moan. I'm completely clear that She did not *take* anything or anyone away from my life. She did something much harder and yet much more empowering *for me:* She handed me Her sword and asked me to trust myself. I had to make the terrifying cuts, say the difficult words (like risking my new publishing contract by telling my publisher that I was no longer able to write a self-help book about spirit-focused metaphysics, to which they suggested I write a self-help book about how to be Redvolutionary instead), turn down the deals (including the book with the movie star and other tantalizing commercial offers), and anxiously walk away from what had looked like a successful service-oriented spiritual path — and straight into the petrifying unknown.

Concerned colleagues suggested I get "coached" to help "fix" my career and set up alternative support structures. Although it was tempting, I resisted. I knew most coaches would help me build my career back up (hire a new director for the film, a new editor for the book, manifest new offers and a new boyfriend, maybe even in seven weeks or less). But it seemed pretty damned clear that it was divine demolition time.

> I can't find all the pieces you have shattered me into.
>
> They drip down between my toes,
>
> swirl around my tummy,
>
> distract my mind,
>
> and burn a hole in my heart . . .
>
> You shake your head at me,
>
> trying to put together what You have purposefully taken apart.

BROKEN AND BURNING

With most of my career now lying in pieces around me, I began to wonder whether I was supposed to let my *entire* career go. I didn't like this idea. Not one bit. These days, most people are just trying to *find* their mission and gifts to offer the world. I truly believed I had found mine. It felt like all I had done my entire life was follow my passion and those divine winks. Was I really so off course?

Then I remembered Rumi.

When Shams showed up in Rumi's life, Rumi was already a "successful" spiritual teacher. While there was nothing wrong with his spiritual career, per se, it happened to be a projection of his false self, not an accurate representation of Rumi's true self. (Our "false selves" can often appear very spiritual.) Rumi's path was to break up with his spiritual vocation in order to break into his Red heart. There, in the mystical madness of utter confusion and what looked like professional suicide, Rumi found his *truest* calling—to be immersed in Divine love, which unleashed a stunning stream of mystical poetry. Later, Rumi went back to teaching, but from a place and space he could never have arrived at if he had continued to follow his false self's "spiritual path."

While I'm certainly no Rumi, his example is something many of us can relate to in our own ways. Whether we're a lawyer, a mother, a gardener, a stripper, a self-help author, or a teacher, our souls are continually calling us deeper. If we're willing to shed our skins (over and over again), then layer after layer of our truth will appear anew and demand action. What is true for us today won't necessarily be true for us tomorrow. Aligning our ordinary life with our evolutionary divinity is a path of fire: You burn. You grow. You burn. You grow. Constantly. The only stability is our trust in the process and our intuitive awareness that Love's very nature is to consume and call us home.

To

Consume

and

Call

Us

Home

During this time, I went to lunch with Carly Stasko, a radiant young cancer survivor. When you're around someone who has or is facing the immediacy of physical death, it certainly puts things in perspective. Being with Carly stopped any "sorry for myself" sighs from slipping out; after all, I was only facing the death of my "false self" and its career. Although dealing with cancer is *extremely* different from what I was going through, there are a few metaphorical, psychological, and spiritual similarities. As Bill Plotkin admits, "Entry into the life of the soul demands a steep price, a psychological form of dying."[5]

Turns out, in order to embody our soul, everything that we have placed before our soul must die, *including* our spiritual missions. In fact, Sufis often moan "die before you die," and many Christian mystics suffer through a spiritual death in "the dark night of the soul." The point is, death is an integral part of our soul's life. At the end of our conversation, Carly scribbled a short poem she had written after being diagnosed and gave it to me:

There's a multi-colored effigy
of everything I strived to be
Burning down in front
of me
Telling me to
Just let it go.[6]
—*Carly Stasko*

After my lunch with Carly, the vision I received after my interview with Marion reappeared—a Red curtain dropping down right in front of me, cutting me off from my audience, the world, the house lights.

(THUD.)

I sighed with painful resignation. My aloneness and despondency swelled to massive proportions.

"Yep." (Sniff.)

"Got it. I'm *still* behind the freakin' curtain all fucked up and," (Sniff.) "alone."

Turn Around, Sera.

Now there's an idea.

I slowly turned around, away from the curtain, toward the waiting darkness behind me and was immediately Embraced by

Her.

My Red Lady.

She was back.

And the tears flowed, and the heart hiccupped, and the mind quieted, and

I got It.

"Oh," I reverently whispered. "I'm *not* alone. I don't have to die or give birth by myself. I'm *not* partnerless or loveless. You're Here."

Oh Lady . . . You're Here.

SMOOCH!

THE RED TENT

Give up all the other worlds
except the one to which you belong.
Sometimes it takes darkness and the sweet
confinement of your aloneness
to learn

anything or anyone
that does not bring you alive

is too small for you.

DAVID WHYTE

Soon after that Smooch in the dark, my Red Lady did the strangest thing—She swept through my front door on a warm gust of glitter and Red feathers, carrying rather large Red suitcases. My jaw dropped. Apparently, She was Moving In. It was time for a closer living arrangement. Specifically, it was time to create a Red Tent, physically and energetically, so that a necessary gestation and eventual "Virgin" birth of Us could happen.

The Red Tent was first described in Anita Diamant's bestselling novel *The Red Tent* as a place where women in ancient times gathered when they were menstruating or giving birth. This idea of creating a sacred space for women to honor their body's changes together spread like wildfire. Now hundreds of Red Tents are erected at various women's events and private homes all around the country . . . even in tiny apartments in San Francisco.

SPIRITUAL HOUSECLEANING

During this time, everything that was not supportive of our "pregnancy" got pushed out. It was time to clean house, literally and figuratively. My Lady takes up a lot of space. So, I cleaned out my apartment—my closets, my kitchen, my storage unit, even underneath my bed. Seventy percent of my belongings went to the Salvation Army. But extra clothes and dishes and sex toys weren't all I was clearing from my life.

I asked myself what social gatherings, family get-togethers, professional events, and spiritual scenes fostered my soul's embodiment at this time and which ones did the opposite. This wasn't about judgment; it was about discernment. Then, I made adjustments—I wrote necessary emails, made uncomfortable phone calls, and had tough one-on-one talks. I squirmed throughout this process and am still squirming, because for polite Midwestern girls, ditching "friends" and family is incredibly rude and inconsiderate, even if it's done compassionately. And turning down high-profile professional invitations is risky. And curbing my external spiritual jaunts (workshops, classes, retreats) felt, well, *unspiritual,* like I might devolve or miss something Big and Important and Healing and Enlightening . . .

Okay, fine.

I felt more than "rude" and "inconsiderate" or like I was taking a huge risk or devolving every time I de-friended someone (not just on Facebook) or cut out a social, professional, or spiritual activity. I also felt a chest-constricting, sweaty-palmed, brain-numbing fear that arose from a primal place inside myself that I was shocked to acknowledge. Even though I've *never* been a "follower" or a "joiner" and have always led a rather Redvolutionary lifestyle, I was amazed to experience just how much my need to "fit in" (even with my liberal, self-expressed San Francisco community) and be loved (even by my open-minded, loving family) unconsciously ran my life—and as psychologists, sociologists, and biologists will quickly say, it runs *all of our lives.*

Recognizing how much my need to fit in and be loved by others affected my life choices, I decided to *temporarily* press "pause" on my *entire* social, spiritual, and professional life. I even turned off my cell phone and created an automated email reply message titled: "I'm in the Red Tent." It was time to batten down the hatches and try to remember what Her love felt like *inside of myself,* so that I wouldn't be *as* dependent on my friends or family or my career or even "spirituality" to give it to me *and* so I would become better at loving others for themselves, not just for what they offered me or this world. As Indian Jesuit priest Anthony de Mello wrote:

> I can only love people when I have emptied my life of people. When I die to the need for people, then I'm right in the desert. In the beginning it feels awful, it feels lonely, but if you can take it for a while, you'll suddenly discover that it isn't lonely at all. It is solitude, it is aloneness, and the desert begins to flower. Then at last you'll know what love is, what God is, what reality is.[1]

INFORMATION FASTING

The cleaning went deeper.

I sold my TV and stopped surfing the Web. After a lifetime of *voraciously* ingesting information—from celebrity breakups to political/health/fashion and world news to blog posts to Facebook statuses—it was time to go on an "external information" fast. I also donated most of my nonfiction books and stopped my hefty spiritual studies.

Now, halting my consumption of spiritual information was one thing; *letting go* of other people's beliefs, paradigms, and experiences of the Divine was something else altogether. A hilarious vision that I received during this time was of a conveyor belt moving *countless* books out of my energy field; that conveyor belt ran nonstop, *for weeks.* Apparently, I was a hoarder of spiritual information. Not surprisingly, my ego panicked: those books represented my intellectual bearings, my "smarts" (as I now jokingly call them). In fact, I could actually *feel* myself losing my understanding of basic spiritual concepts along with my rigorous Harvard education. It felt like I was being completely dumbed down.

Being a woman brimming with spiritual information was something I was proud of (I mean, hey, I could be brimming with Diet Coke or episodes of *Jersey Shore* instead). And I'm a big believer in stretching and challenging one's spiritual reality through learning about other spiritual realities. But *at this time* in my soul's journey, all that once-helpful information was now getting in the way and preventing me from drawing closer to my Lady.

Ideas aren't helping you anymore, Sera. Concepts have run their course.

Paradigms pop. Theories leak.

Techniques are only top-offs.

Beliefs brush away.

Books close.

Workshops end.

What truly transforms is this Closeness with Me.

You gotta hug Me so tight that nothing comes between Us.

Before we continue this more-than-one-woman show, I want to offer this Redminder: We need to *repeatedly* inquire whether internal voices are coming from the Divine or from our ego (a complex, a shadow, a delusion, a defense), or from external influences (a teacher, a friend, a collective mindset), or even from a mischievous (or nefarious) spirit entity masquerading as our inner guidance. Sifting through our numerous internal voices and somatic reactions (which we can mistakenly believe are our body's intuition) is mandatory on this journey, and it's a lifelong practice.

OK, back to Our show.

My Lady made it known that this Red-Tented practice is less about rigid restrictions and more about honest self-inquiry: "Why am I *really* going to this workshop or reading this book or listening to this teacher or practicing this technique?" I soon began to notice that there's a big difference between reaching out and Receiving In. When I'm reaching out of my Red Tent unconsciously—or from fear or loneliness or *a feeling of lack* or because I *think* I'm being spiritually correct—what I'm grasping for rarely turns out to be as helpful as I had hoped and can often lead me astray. As opposed to when I stay In, allowing the Red curtains to open naturally, when it's time to reveal my next step, which may or may not involve receiving someone (a teacher or counselor or friend or lover) or something (a book or technique or workshop) from the external world.

In particular, I needed to spot when I was giving my Divine power away by thinking, or rather hoping, that someone or something else could give it to me. While I had never submitted to a tradition or a teacher, I *had* repeatedly sucker-punched my own spiritual authority by allowing dominant religious realities, popular spiritual beliefs, and well-respected teachers not only to sway my inner knowing but sometimes even to swat it away. I also *constantly* compared my own experiences with outside spiritual sources. My dependency on external sources for validation had grown unhealthy. It was time to become self-dependent. It was time to determine and define my Red reality from the inside out.

TRUE DEVOTION

One Saturday morning, I lit incense dedicated to the Queen of Sheba (I bought it because I loved the smell) and immediately became dizzy and nauseated. This surprised me, because I had used this same incense in the past without any uncomfortable physical reactions. However, the *quality* of my reactions (and a few other winks) indicated that there was something deeper going on. When I inquired within, my Lady was clear:

Your devotion should be to Me.

This wasn't some Old Testament commandment; rather it was my heart's holiest claim. Although I still wasn't sure exactly Who my Lady was, after this stomach-churning, heart-pounding experience, I humbly and respectfully gave away all my spiritual icons, images, and accouterments. She murmured:

You've made *so many others* false gods.

You keep looking to deities, spirit guides, friends, boyfriends, and teachers

to give you love and answers and even your very identity.

I'm the One Who Loves you Unconditionally.

All your Answers are Inside Me.

Your Identity Comes from Me.

Who are You?

Let go of trying to understand Who I AM right now and just be with Me.

You don't have to understand Me, but you do have to value Us

and our unique experience TOGETHER . . .

(Squirm.)

I was *slowly* beginning to accept the fact that Ours wasn't a casual relationship consisting mostly of creative projects, impassioned beliefs, and occasional mystical experiences. Nope. It seemed like my Lady and I were trying to go All the Way Together . . . in this lifetime. And we needed the privacy and singular focus to do so. Only She and I belonged in the Red Tent. As David Whyte wrote, "Give up all the other worlds/except the one to which you belong."[2]

I Belonged to the Red World

I Belonged to Her

DELUSIONAL OR DIVINE?

Of course, part of me worried that my Red Tenting was a clever form of "spiritual bypassing." Wasn't I *supposed* to be growing through intimate human relationships (not just relationships with the Divine) and participating *more* in ordinary life? While these were important inquiries, over time, I became aware that there's a big difference between unconsciously escaping the world and abandoning my soul, as I had previously been doing B.M. (Before Marion), and trying to consciously embrace the world *via my soul,* A.M. (After Marion). In *Entering the Castle,* Caroline Myss wrote:

> Ironically, people who are not in touch with their souls live in fear and
> spend their lives running away from the world, even though it looks as
> if they are working and living right in the middle of everything. Yet, the
> mystic, who might look as if he or she has run away from the world, is in
> fact living right in the world, far more present and empowered.[3]

But still, the fact is, we *need* external reflection. (By this time, I had stopped seeing my counselors and therapist, partly for financial reasons and partly due to what I hoped were intuitive reasons.) I worriedly asked my Lady: "Am I becoming myopic or delusional? Too individualistic and narcissistic? Is this unhealthy isolation?" My Lady gently reminded me that *at this point,* I wasn't disconnecting from healthy reality and that my psychological issues would still be acknowledged and "worked on" while I was in the Red Tent. However, I *was* disconnecting from unhealthy relationships and habits, detaching from "the matrix" (mind-controlling social/ political/economic programs), and detoxing from the "false light" (illusory spiritual energies that I had unknowingly absorbed from my extensive explorations)—all of which, She informed me, kept me numb and confused, distracted and disempowered, and didn't support Our natural Birth. Also, being a spirit addict and someone with weak and porous boundaries, I needed this extreme practice more than most.

I often compare this initial "Time In" to a food-sensitivity test, in which you cut out all the usual food suspects, like wheat, corn, dairy, and soy, for a few months and then slowly reintroduce each food into your system, one week at a time, to locate which foods are nourishing your body and which are upsetting your digestive system and harming your health. It's hard to know who or what you're allergic to — who or what is declining your soul's health — when you're around/ingesting them all the time. Staying away from that which compromises your soul's health also provides the energy necessary to discover and address the underlying reasons you have been ingesting that which does not support your soul's health in the first place.

After my temporary fast from everyone and everything (which lasted about two months), I realized that *most* of my previous life had not been supporting my soul's health. I also realized that I could not create a soulful external life if I did not first create a more soulful internal life. So, with my Lady's guidance, I continued my urban hermitage, retreating from about 95 percent of my social and professional life.

After some time in the Red Tent, worries that I might be "escaping" my life dwindled, because, quite honestly, staying in the Red Tent didn't feel like I was escaping *anything*. My Red Lady is not interested in bubble-wrapping me; She's interested in holding me. Tightly. As Marion Woodman firmly stated: "The feminine is the loving container of all conflict, all physical and psychological processes."[4] In other words, although infinitely loving, my Lady's Move In wasn't exactly a warm and fuzzy slumber party. You can't hide in fire; you can only be consumed and eventually reborn by it. As Nietzsche sparked in *Thus Spoke Zarathustra,* "You must be ready to burn yourself in your own flame: How could you become new if you had not first become ashes?"[5] This degree of Divine heat is why so many prefer the Pink Lady. But this ain't Pink's story.

Back to the Red story.

THE RED ROUTINE

After the initial clean-out and Red boundary-making, my Lady and I created a Red routine. Each morning I would sit with Her and journal, move and process, watch and listen. Our "practices" changed daily and spontaneously. Sometimes there was a hidden belief to acknowledge, an emotional release to allow, a chapter in a received book to read, a dream to analyze, a childhood memory to rehash, an energetic clearing to be done, a body part to massage. It was like I had a personal tour guide leading me on a bizarre inner voyage:

> What strange things are happening to me? . . . Where are you leading me?
> Forgive my apprehension, brimful of knowledge. My foot hesitates to

follow you. Into what mist and darkness does your path lead? . . . I limp
after you on crutches of understanding. I am a man [woman] and you
stride like a God [Goddess]. . . . I should give myself completely into your
hands — but who are you?[6]

—*C. G. Jung,* The Red Book

Some days in the Red Tent, there was a lot of work to do directly with Her.
Some days there was no work on the agenda, but She was still everywhere,
softly, and my cells couldn't help but respond. Some days my Red Tent felt
totally empty, and I couldn't feel the Red Lady. Try as I might to tap in, I got
nothing. Zippo. Zero. Zat. Days, *weeks,* would pass where my insides felt like
a blank slate; and my weird little life, a black hole. These times were excruciating — the fear and doubt overwhelmed everything I knew about myself and
my Lady. This was when my nasty inner demons screeched, "You're kidding
yourself! There is nothing divine going on here!" I came to realize that Hell
isn't a fiery place under the earth; it's an icy place inside myself that under-
mines my soul's reality.

One night in the Red Tent, I was awoken at 3:34 a.m.:

You need to trust Me.

W-whoo-whhhaa?

Every night you completely relax into your bed.

You trust it to hold you and not collapse in the middle of the night.

You trust your bed more than you trust Me.

Crap.

We need to get to a Place where I AM more Real and Present and

Trustworthy to you than your bed. Than *everything*.

How?

Invite Me In,

to *every* space you've kept Me out.

Simply say "Come In"

and

I AM

IN.

(Smile.)

Know This:

Even when you feel lost, without Me, alone,

You are not.

I have never, and will never, *ever,* let go of your hand, Sera.

Ever.

As unexpected and improvable and occasionally off-the-charts freaky as my Red Tented explorations, dialogues, and experiences became (only some of which I'm choosing to share in this book, but get ready for some real doozies in later chapters), they never felt "trippy" or flashy or otherworldly or superfluous. They felt natural, simple, innerworldy, and just as integral to my life as eating healthy food and exercising. They felt *real.* As Caroline Myss describes:

> This interior place—your Castle—is real. These aren't just words or an
> exercise in active imagination. They are sacred forms and images that get
> you to the essence of spiritual nature—a unity of soul and God, psyche
> and body, spirit and body. Entering your Castle enables you to begin to
> dialogue with your soul and with God. I cannot emphasize that enough,
> nor can I tell you how exquisite that dialogue eventually becomes. But it's
> work. It's work to get to know yourself, and why you are the way you are,
> and why you love what you do and have the passions that you do. You
> require work. You are not a simple act of creation; you are complex and
> creative and conscious and unconscious.[7]

The morning after the 3:34 a.m. exchange, my Lady asked me to listen. I listened and waited. Soon I heard a forlorn voice: *"Not all of me is wanted here . . . it's not safe for me here."* While I could link the meaning of the words to my psychology and my ordinary life, the voice felt like it came from another space. In fact, it felt related to the wispy voice I had heard so many months ago, after my family constellation, that stated, "I'm not here." My skin suddenly tingled with awareness: I had been hearing *from pieces of my disembodied soul.* While I had been working hard to reconnect with my soul, her fragments were another story.

"How do I help those pieces come home?" My Lady assured me that all the work I had been doing was helping them return, but the retrieval process was a mysterious one and could not be figured out mentally. She told me (with a twinkle), to stay open, 'cause the soul simmers with surprises . . .

THE BIRTHDAY PARTY

A week later, on the evening of my birthday, I attended my women's group (one of the select activities the Red Tent curtains briefly parted for at this time). When it was my turn to contribute, I started to feel dizzy and disoriented and could only mumble, "Sorry, ladies, it's my birthday, and I feel *really* weird."

The room shifted, quieted.

Then one woman across the circle grabbed my eyes and voiced, "Sera, I just want you to know that *all* of you is wanted here." I gasped with surprise. Another woman grabbed my hands firmly and said, "Sera, it's safe for you now. You can come home now." My body started rocking back and forth as the tears, the sweat, the fears poured out of me. Sabrina, my women's circle leader, whispered, "Sera, the women of the world are here for you, waiting for you." The women in my group then surrounded me, holding me with their warm female bodies, rubbing my aching shoulders, nodding into my questioning eyes, midwifing parts of me home: "We have you, Sera. We have you."

It felt like thousands of years passed . . .

Then we disentangled, wiping away sweat and tears, looking at each other with knowing, grateful eyes. One of the women ran out and brought back a chocolate cake, and another turned on The Beatles song, "Say it's your birthday!!! It's my birthday too!!!" We ate and sang and laughed and danced. As we were walking out the door, Sabrina mentioned that she has always called the room we were gathered in the Red Tent.

THONG SNAPS

I had nourishing, exquisite, and deeply connective experiences in the Red Tent. But the feelings of isolation I also sometimes experienced during my three tented years were tormenting. From my lower ego's perspective, it looked like every other thirty-something woman was *really* "living"—you know, dating, getting married, running marathons, growing gardens, having babies, buying houses, expanding their careers and wardrobes and stock options, and, oh yeah, having sex. There was no sex in the Red Tent. While

I had future hopes for an intimate relationship, a community of like-hearted friends, and a thriving career, I had to let go of any unhealthy attachments to this actually happening. Repeatedly.

As the heat turned up and the months chugged by, I did try to escape the Red Tent, but my Lady always grabbed me by my thong and gently (and sometimes not so gently) pulled me back In, reminding me that I was worth this time. I needed to gift myself this space and maintain this very pregnant pause, no matter what it might look like to others or my ego. Reclaiming my soul was worth all the time and relationships and career deals and family vacations and major holidays and birthday parties in the world. As Caroline Myss states, "Nothing is easy about living in mystical consciousness, but it is even more difficult to live outside of it."[8]

Every time you leave your Red Tent,

you leave Me and go on your own mission.

But you see I AM your Mission.

If you're not living with Me, then you're not really living.

A ROOM (WOMB) OF YOUR OWN

Here are a few things I know after doing serious time in the Red Tent: Although your space might not look like mine, every woman needs a room of her own. It's partly a *physical* space away from your children, your friends, your partner, emails, phones, and the TV. But it's mostly an *energetic* space that *only* you and your soul occupy. And above all, it's a sacred space where you reconnect and dialogue with divinity. This is a space you guard like a lioness. A space you treat like your queendom. A space where you dive deep into your dark and shine brightly with your light. A space where you can laugh and cry and roll and punch. A space where you burn. A space where you allow the freaky shit to happen. A space where you can give birth to a project, a dream, a human child . . . yourself.

A space where you welcome *all* of yourself

Home.

15

SHADOW PUPPETS

You stupid little bitch! What do you think you're doing?! You're a bad, BAD girl!!! Totally misguided! "Red Lady" and "Red Tent"—ha! Like that isn't the biggest load of crap this side of "WRONG." And what's with your recent breakups, your professional downswing, your lack of social encounters, not to mention proper spiritual discipline and guidance! I will not tolerate this behavior! Shame, shame, shame on you! You don't know what the hell you're doing. Your intuition is completely untrustworthy. And Goddess—she's NOT REAL!!! And what's more, the whole goddess movement is incredibly cliché, filled with middle-aged women. It's pathetic, and now you are pathetic. I have worked so hard to keep you well liked and "normal" and successful and "spiritual," and now you're ruining it all. Shut the hell up and step back!!!

y pen exploded across the page as I tried to capture this incredibly pissed-off inner voice. And then, just as suddenly as the angry voice had started shouting, it stopped.

"Holy

Crap."

Although Andrew Harvey's searing voice had burnt my facial hairs off that one day, Divine Feminine Love and Divine Feminine Truth were undeniably present and *felt* in my body. *This* scorching voice was filled with fear and falsity, and made my body contract, my heart shut down, and my skin crawl.

What produced such a lovely lash-out? Well, early one morning, after a nudge from my Lady, I flipped open *The Shadow King*, by psychologist Sidra

Stone, and read about the importance of starting a "voice dialogue" with your inner "shadow king." Before I knew exactly what the hell a "shadow king" was (it sounds like the title of a kung fu movie from the 1980s), a monstrously mad masculine voice reached up from my insides and blasted open my metaphorical voice box. I grabbed my journal and a pen and let him rip. And, as you just read, he sure did.

Stone defines the shadow king as "the voice, or subpersonality, within us that carries the ancient patriarchal traditions, values, and rules from the past six million years. He is an internalized version of the outer patriarchy and functions both protectively and destructively."[1] The shadow king whispers (or yells, depending on how ticked off he is) from our unconscious. Although he acts differently in each woman, Stone has noticed some common traits: The shadow king supports men and the masculine and feels that women and the feminine are secondary. The shadow king rules by reason, rationality, and righteousness. He dismisses the heart and emotions and spontaneous flow. He aims to control women, sexually and spiritually.

If we unconsciously accept the shadow king's assessments of us, we might try to be a "good girl," following his rules and standards and what he deems "proper." We might strive to be "the perfect" daughter, wife, mother, spiritual devotee—his "ideal" woman. Conversely, when we unconsciously reject the shadow king's assessments of us, we might try to be a "bad girl," rebelling against his rules, getting tattoos in naughty places, sleeping around, flunking school or acing school, dominating men, over- or underachieving in the workplace, even fighting aggressively for the feminist cause. In either case (and for many of us, we're "good girls" in some areas of our life and "bad girls" in others), we're allowing our shadow king to determine our reality. This means we live in reaction to this unconscious part of our self instead of in conscious response to it.

Here are a few screwy contradictions my shadow king likes to bind me with: He never wants me to get married or have children, because he says I will lose my creativity and my career. But the idea of me without a serious monogamous partner upsets him, because according to him, it makes me "loose," puts me in danger of being taken advantage of, and makes me stick out from the "norm." He wants me to look sexy, but then he makes me feel guilty if I attract attention from men he labels as "lusty." He wants me to be a strong woman, but not be "too" strong, otherwise I won't be able to rely on men the way he would like me to. Now, your shadow king might not sound like mine—for instance, my close friend's s.k. desperately wants her to get married and tells her she's a total loser because she at present has no kids, no husband, no matching dishware. With this mac daddy ruling your life from the shadows, you can't win, but you can drive yourself crazy trying.

Here's the dart in the dandelion: No matter how educated and liberal we are, or how many goddess icons fill our living rooms, or how many women's circles we attend, or how spiritually realized, feminist, emotionally intelligent, sexually confident, or embodied we are, if we don't go inside at some point and confront, listen to, and eventually make friends with our inner patriarch, we will still be living under his thumb. Like all shadowy characters, if he's not brought into consciousness, he will subvert our power in subtle or strong ways.

FATHER KNOWS BEST

After I became more familiar with my inner patriarch, I noticed how in simple interactions—like at a restaurant or a yoga class or a party or a professional event—I gave most of my energy and attention to the men in the room. I gave their words and actions more importance than I did the women's. I began to recognize that I was unconsciously relating to *all* men as "shadow kings"—daddies, saviors, teachers, pimps, priests, bosses, judges, gods. The interesting thing was, these unhealthy tendencies of mine toward the masculine weren't always so obvious in my actions; in fact, they were mostly energetic in nature. Yet they had similar effects on my body and soul as if I were actually "sleeping with the boss" or giving my power away to "The Man."

I sank deeper into this shadowed part of me and began to remember how I had felt and acted at the dinner table with my family growing up. My dad, who is an exceptional father of three girls, was still "the ruler." When he said "no," it was final. When my mom, who is equally exceptional, said "no," it was up for debate. When my father approved or disapproved of something I did, I believed him. When my mother approved or disapproved, well, I didn't trust her perceptions quite as much. I didn't take her as seriously as I did my father, and I often put her down or made fun of her fire, her sensitivity, and what some might define as her very femininity. The harsh reality was that part of me *still* looked down on certain men or women who exhibited these more commonly defined "feminine" traits. I gasped:

I've repeatedly knocked the feminine for being "feminine"!

At this shadowy point in the Red Tent, I began to realize that I didn't even like "the feminine." Nope. That doesn't quite do it justice. Deeper down, where a darker darkness screams,

I

fucking

hated

the feminine!

I felt the feminine was weak, stupid, silly, frivolous, disgusting, too emotional, too moody, "too much," an illusion, false, a trap, a mistake, evil, not to mention a lower state of consciousness and primitive spiritual approach — basically all the things I accused patriarchy and others of thinking about the feminine. Awesome.

In *Spiritual Bypassing,* Robert Augustus Masters describes shadow elements as those "qualities and traits that we typically keep in the dark and project onto others, both at the personal and collective level, creating the very convincing illusion that such elements don't belong to us. Exposing this illusion and reclaiming the rejected elements of our being is the essence of shadow work."[2]

Our shadows are hidden from us. But if we know where and how to look, we'll start to notice that they frequently show up as patterns in our lives. My inner patriarch was easy for me to recognize because there were pieces of him projected onto every man I had drawn into my life and in every spiritual group I was attracted to B.M. For example, in my past, I habitually found boyfriends or creative partners and some spiritual groups who were all "pro women, yay, go, Goddess, go!" on the outside. But behind closed doors, they put down the feminine, emotionally abused the feminine, used the feminine for their own sexual needs and personal or professional gain, and were deeply afraid of the feminine. Doing shadow work, I began to recognize how *I* was doing all this as well, not only in my personal life, but also in my professional life. When I was unconsciously using the Divine Feminine — making Her into a catchy goddess movement or making Her fit into *my* career plans — my shadow king was cool. If I stopped using Her and, instead, started *allowing Her to use me,* my shadow king would flip out, because he believed the Divine Feminine would not only ruin my career, but get me *killed.*

Sounds a bit crazy, right? This is obviously not how I consciously feel toward the D.F. But nonetheless, these were some of the unconscious energies running my show. Remember, often, what we are most passionately devoted to or argue for or try to push or sell or "save" is actually what we have the darkest shadow around (hello, anti-gay Christian senators who are caught having sex with male prostitutes).

Coming to terms with my underground feminine bashing and countless other shadowy ways was rough and disillusioning and, at times, downright devastating. As Masters writes:

> Real shadow work does not leave us intact; it is not some neat and tidy process, but rather an inherently messy one, as vital and unpredictably alive as birth. The ass it kicks is the one upon which we are sitting; the pain it brings up is the pain we've been fleeing most of our life; the psychoemotional breakdowns it catalyzes are the precursors to hugely relevant breakthroughs; the doors it opens are doors that have shown up year after year in our dreams, awaiting our entry. Real shadow work not only breaks us down, but breaks us open.[3]

After breaking down and open and down and open and then journaling and then journaling some more, I came to really know my inner patriarch. I also realized, experientially, what I had previously understood only intellectually: If you clear away enough of the inner rubble, eventually you see the roots. You understand that essentially your inner patriarch just wants to protect you and keep you safe. Once I got this, things shifted. Believe it or not, the s.k. can sometimes offer helpful advice and eventually even become your ally. As with all shadow puppets, it just takes the willingness to shine a little light on your internal home theater.

MOMMY DEAREST

Our shadow kings aren't the only ones ruling our inner courts. Yep, we've got a shadow queen inside us, the internalized version of the outer "matriarchy." She thinks men are little boys who need to be entertained or reprimanded, or lust-crazed teenagers who need to be teased, or authority figures who need to be seduced or reduced, or "evil" enemies who need to be punished, or feral animals who need to be tamed and carefully controlled. I call her the false feminine (f.f. for short). Just as our inner patriarch contains the twisted, negative shadow of the Divine Masculine, our inner matriarch contains the twisted, negative shadow of the Divine Feminine.

Everyone has an f.f., but she's difficult to define because she's slippery and chameleonlike; she transforms and adapts according to the woman and the situation. Although the f.f. works differently in each of us, her main attribute is misusing the feminine to attain power. She has no life force of her own, so she survives and gets her needs met by using other people (like batteries) and then allowing them to do the same to her. She needs constant attention—physically and energetically—and she has found manipulative ways to get these unhealthy needs met, including acting very "spiritual" or even "goddessy."

The confusing thing is that most of us think the f.f. *is* the true Feminine, because we've never been taught differently. Living from our f.f. instead of our true Feminine is not only a *deeply* unconscious habit, but also an energetic addiction. We get high from it. When we come from our f.f., we feel powerful, "feminine," and even like we're being of service.

The f.f. also holds the shadow of the sacred prostitute—that is, just "the prostitute." As you know, prostituting yourself isn't just about selling sex; it's about selling your soul. You could be prostituting yourself at your nonprofit environmental job just as much, energetically speaking, as you could be on the Sunset Strip. You could be prostituting yourself to a popular idea, a political movement, a fashion trend, a spiritual community, or even within your most intimate relationships.

Nancy Qualls-Corbett told me during our interview that there's a big difference between servitude and service. Someone who has a healthy inner sacred prostitute is not in servitude to a man or to "The Man"; rather she serves the greater good. Servitude is putting myself down, allowing myself to be dominated by others or a system of belief. Service is filling my own well with Her and acting from this inner divine authority. Truth is, we can't be of authentic service on this planet if we are sucked dry or unconsciously leeching off other people energetically or covertly trying to "get something" that we aren't giving ourselves (Attention? Safety? Admiration? Love?).

DANCING WITH MY SELF

When I was first learning about the f.f., I went to a community dance event here in San Francisco. At one point in the evening, my Lady asked for permission to block my f.f. and "activate" my soul sight. I agreed. Immediately, the dynamic between myself and the room shifted. The men who were previously swarming around me on the dance floor moved away and started swarming around another woman. To my *physical* eyes, this woman appeared vibrant, confident, sexy, "feminine"; but to my *soul's* eyes, I "saw" that she was unconsciously *sucking* the energy from the room like a human vacuum and *feeding* off all the adoration . . . just like I had been doing. I was shocked, by both of us.

As soon as I noticed what was happening, my f.f. immediately stopped what she was doing, like she had been caught stealing cookies out of the cosmic cookie jar. But I still felt ashamed. In his powerful book *Speak Truthfully,* author Robert Rabbin wrote, "If you can see your [shadow], if you can name it, look at it, and if you can call yourself [it], then this is not the ultimate truth of who you are. The ultimate truth of who you are is the one who can see this and acknowledge this."[4]

Remembering Rabbin's wise words helped me understand that although the f.f. was a part of me, she wasn't the entire me, and she didn't need to be scolded or shunned; instead, she needed to be brought into consciousness. So, I invited the f.f. to dance *with* my Lady and me. All together. A subtle but powerful shift happened in my body. Although my dance moves hadn't changed *one bit* since the beginning of this dance event, my source of Self did. While I couldn't control how others responded to me (positively or negatively or neutrally) — and, yes, a few curious and attracted men did circle back — I was truly enjoying myself in a public space without unconsciously taking or needing anything from anybody.

Sofia Diaz, a yoga teacher trained in the sacred arts of Indian temple dancing, once told me you can always tell when an authentic *devadasi* (Indian priestess and temple dancer) walks into a room, because she *adds* more aliveness to the space. She *offers* her divine femininity as a gift to All. This open-handed offering often, quite naturally, evokes adoration in many who behold her, while also reminding other women to shine *their* inner light. In other words, "false" falls away in her presence, because she radiates Divine life itself. As Magdalen admits in Elizabeth Cunningham's fictional novel *The Passion of Mary Magdalen:*

> I don't know what it is about priestesses. You can always tell. Or at least I can. . . . I knew a woman in authority when I saw one. Most women, now and then, concern themselves to some degree with pleasing men or people in general. Priestesses don't. They have bigger game. Their eyes show it.[5]

Show It.

OUR BEAUTY AND OUR BEAST

Now's the perfect time to admit something: When I first saw a PDF for the cover of this very book, I had a brief but total meltdown. Although I had chosen the photo intuitively, when I saw it actually laid out as a book cover, I wondered if I had been seriously mistaken. "Am I objectifying myself? Using my looks to seduce or draw attention and gain sales? Am I perpetuating some repressive standard for women? What if this is really my f.f. acting out? What if I have fallen prey to patriarchy's manipulative marketing of the divine feminine? OH MY GODDESS, have I learned *anything* these past years?" My inner diatribe continued like this, for hours, until I wore myself out and my Lady could finally come in.

While She agreed that these inquiries were important to make, She wanted me to pay attention to *where* they were coming from — that is, my ego's fears versus my heart's knowing. She then made a few things very clear: *She* chose that particular photo to be the cover because of what was coming through it — *Us*. Together. Whether or not others see Her in and as me is not my business. My business is transmitting the beauty We create together.

Why am I sharing this with you? Because "spiritual" peeps have always had a complex relationship with beauty. We're attracted to physical beauty, yet we feel guilty about being attracted to it. We might even strive to make ourselves look more beautiful, but then we feel less than evolved for doing so. Feminine beauty *in particular* has been vilified, worshipped, covered up, and carefully controlled (especially through the religious traditions and patriarchy) for millennia. Our beauty has even been seen as something that stands in the way of our divinity. There are countless stories of saints, especially Christian female saints (like Catherine of Siena, who I mentioned in chapter 2), who prayed for God to take away their physical beauty so they could be better at loving Him. Some female mystics even cut off all their hair or permanently marred their faces so they could be closer to God.

In my Red opinion, the Divine Feminine *urges* us to honor beauty and experience the physical world and our female body (no matter what shape or size or color) as divinity incarnate.

Notice Me, Appreciate Me, Adore Me

The Divine Feminine winks from every redwood tree, fleshy thigh, manatee, and mirror. She shines through cellulite, wrinkles, religious robes, and even polyester suits.

I rush to meet myself,

pausing to straighten my clothing, my hair, my crooked face . . .

I am never presentable to myself . . .

I compare, I critique, I examine and find fault.

And then I remember You.

I slow down.

My knees bend to meet the earth . . .

I remember

I

Am

You.

Beauty blooms everywhere when we take off our culture's lenses and see the way our soul sees. When we judge ourselves by external standards or try to be old-school "spiritually correct" and downplay our looks or shrug away compliments, we are denying the Divine Feminine's grandness and Her radiant presence that is embodied in *every* living thing.

SEDUCE MUCH?

While it's important to be conscious of our f.f.'s seductive habits, I want to be clear that the D.F. has nothing against *sacred* seduction. (How do you think this Universe got created? The Divine Feminine is the Biggest Flirt around.) In *Seductress: Women Who Ravished the World and Their Lost Art of Love,* scholar Betsy Prioleau studied world-famous seductresses throughout time and found that these women weren't necessarily young or the best dressed, nor did they represent the cultural standards of physical beauty. But they did possess qualities such as eros, nonconformity, "supravitality and self-actualization,"[6] because they hung tight with the D.F. According to Prioleau, "Seductresses . . . pack such an erotic wallop because they plug into this ancient archetype embedded in the inherited unconscious of the race. They evoke the goddess, mankind's first love object, and replicate her Seductive Way."[7]

After a talk I once gave in Charleston, South Carolina, a radiant seventy-seven-year-old woman (with red hair, I should add) grabbed my arm and excitedly whispered to me that by reconnecting with the D.F., she was now having the *best* sex of her entire life with her husband she'd been married to for more than forty years. Not only that, but she was being hit on, repeatedly, by men in their twenties. She was ecstatic and hilarious and so very completely *alive* and honestly more attractive than most of the twenty-something women in the audience, with their skinny jeans and flawless skin.

Speaking of skinny jeans, during my Red Tent apartment cleanout, my Lady had me feel *into* my clothes, jewelry, and even perfume. Whatever didn't truly light my inner fire, I tossed. My Lady taught me that fabrics, colors, and scents are living energies that interact with and affect my female body and the environment in specific ways. She showed me how to use them not only for seduction and beauty, but also medicinally and alchemically. She told me to treat my jewelry as talismans, sacred ornaments—be they expensive diamond studs or cheap necklaces from Urban Outfitters. She reminded me about the power of feathers, glitter, and makeup (yep, try wearing Red lipstick on an ordinary day).

I tentatively pick the deepest Reds for Your garments

The glories of purple orchids for Your hair

You appear clearer to me with my decorations.

Tasting pollen, Your lips murmur . . .

"Anything . . . anything

so you will touch Me, beautify Me, want Me, love Me"

In the Red Tent, my natural tastes started returning, superseding society's fashion and beauty campaigns. My soul became my stylist.

A Redminder: The Divine Feminine looks as varied as we do. What might appear like someone's f.f. acting out—like posting a cleavage shot on Facebook with a bawdy quote—might actually be their *true Divine Feminine* doing Her thang in that particular moment. Or an f.f. might be carefully wrapping herself in conservative business suits or baggy clothes or "goddess" garb and speaking passionately about "female empowerment." The f.f. isn't just found in women trying to get attention or power through their looks or sexual energy; she is also found in women who are condemning other women for "using" their looks and sexuality to get attention and power.

According to Prioleau, second wave feminism, which began in the early 1960s, turned *seductress* into a four-letter word and alienated these types of women for being "non–politically correct sellouts." Prioleau says that feminists made an unwise move here, because these seductresses were *not* acting "under the influence" of the media or societal standards or cultural conditions. In fact, these sacred seductresses did not behave as a "woman of their time or age or position"[8] should. They were *virgin* in the Jungian sense of the word and were therefore, according to Prioleau, "the archsaboteurs of patriarchy." They seduced *as* the Sacred and, in doing so, triumphed over repressive systems of power. Whether consciously or not, they took their cue from Ovid's first precept, "Do as the goddesses did."[9]

Do as your Goddess Does.

WALKING MY TALK
(IN HIGH HEELS OR BARE FEET)

All that said, I'll be honest: It's been a bumpy, unpaved road moving from seduction through my false feminine to seduction via my true feminine. My ego still has a hard time letting go of what I "get" from the false feminine, especially when most of the world doesn't appear to register her alternatives. But operating from my f.f. keeps me anxious and competitive, envious and separate from my Lady and how She wants me to experience and express myself here. And, I would rather be invisible and coming from my truth than desired and dependent upon my false.

The one thing we should *not* do is judge ourselves or others for having f.f.'s. Our false feminines are incredibly sneaky and brilliant at survival, because they've *had* to be. Remember, it's only in the past century that most women have been able to live alone and make their own sexual and relational choices, not to mention their own living. For thousands of years, we've *had* to be dependent on men and the patriarchy for our livelihoods, so we've developed masterful ways to keep ourselves and our children safe, fed, and with a roof over our heads. Back then, other women were threatening not just to our vanity or self-worth, but also to our very survival. Even though much has changed and we've made progress in all areas of life, the harsh history of women still hovers.

Sifting out what is "true" (that which comes from our authentic nature) from what is "false" (that which covers our authentic nature) is a daily practice. But it's the only way our true ladies can seriously bust a move.

ME AND MY SHADOWS

Alongside my shadow work in the Red Tent, I also practiced *forgiving* myself—over and over and over again. Marion says, "That's where it starts. You have to forgive yourself for being human, because to be human is to have lots of faults; so you have to forgive, and then the love flows in."[10] This forgiveness reveals a startling truth: we cannot know and embrace our divinity if we have not known and embraced our humanity.

You want to know what Goddess looks like in human form? Well, She doesn't necessarily look like some perfectly put-together "powerful" or permanently peppy woman. She is *not* a static, untouchable, glossy figure portrayed on a spiritual posterboard or a website or the cover of a book. No. She grins and she growls. She shines and she shits. She loves and she fears. She has issues, serious issues. And she has gifts, serious gifts. She is the brightest light and the darkest shadow. She is incredibly vulnerable and gratefully real. She looks *exactly* like me. She looks *exactly* like you. She looks *exactly* like us. Now. As we are. Pretending otherwise is yet another way we negate Her Greatest Teaching.

GIRLS JUST WANNA
HAVE FUN

And our Lady Sophia answers: Ye shall dance, sing, feast, make music and
love, all in my praise. For mine is the ecstasy of the spirit, and mine also
joy on earth. Let my worship be in the heart that rejoiceth. Wherefore
let there be beauty and strength, power and compassion, honor and
humility, mirth and reverence within you, now and for evermore. Amen.

GNOSTIC MASS

The Red Tent wasn't a total downer. It wasn't all about "issues" and wounds and facing my shit. My Lady is a Soul Worker, but She's also a Playgirl. She nudged me over and over again to welcome joy, pleasure, and ecstasy into my life, no matter how rough things got. As Emily Dickinson wrote, "The soul should always stand ajar, ready to welcome the ecstatic experience."[1]

My potty-mouthed parrot's well-timed squawks: "I love you . . . NICE ASSSSSSSSSSSSS!" (sums up the Red philosophy), my dog digging under the bedcovers each night so she could collapse her warm, soft body against my own, those ridiculously frothy fuchsia flowers that bloom outside my apartment no matter what time of year, that decadent and delicious meal two dear friends made me that caused me to spontaneously clap between bites, my exuberantly flamboyant ("only in San Francisco") dance class that made me smile for a straight hour three times a week, that human blooper scene in the movie that caused me to laugh so hard I could barely breathe, feeling the sunlight reach through my Red curtains to warmly caress my face each afternoon. Life was far from easy in the Red Tent, but there was such goodness, such Goddess, pulsing outta everywhere and everything that it was hard not to be grateful simply to be alive.

You are feeling the Way I Feel in your skin.

You are beginning to respond to Life the Way I Respond to Life—

as a Making of Love.

It can feel ecstatic, but it can also feel excruciating

and

Everything

In

Between.

I Awaken parts of you that have closed to

Being

Body In Life.

When you allow Me in, you allow Life In.

When you Return to Me, you Return to Life.

Ya Feel Me?

I felt Her. The more I allowed myself to simply *feel* what was reawakening in and as me, the more embodied I became. As Teri Degler wrote in *The Divine Feminine Fire,* "The more we are able to be rooted in our bodies and see ourselves as the embodiment of the divine feminine, the more clearly we are able to hear the voice of this cosmic force as she calls to us."[2]

HER FORCE IS WITH US

According to many spiritual beliefs, the Divine Feminine *is* life force—a cosmic force that streams and streaks through every living thing. But unfortunately, orthodoxy has never approved of streaking. Degler tells us that the twentieth-century Jesuit priest Pierre Teilhard de Chardin perceived this force in the rocks, stones, and cliffs of his native Auvergne and called it the "*crimson* glow of matter" and "the divine radiating from the blazing depths of matter." He even saw the pulsing, creative force as a feminine one. Much to the consternation of the Church, he even came to call it "the eternal feminine" and to write about it extensively.[3]

How did the Catholic Church respond to de Chardin's heretical declarations? They banished his ass to the farthest reaches of Mongolia. The twelfth-century female Catholic mystic Hildegard of Bingen courageously sang love songs to this luminous force sometimes called the Holy Spirit in Christianity:

> O fire of the Spirit, the Comforter,
> Life of the life of all creation,
> Holy you are, giving life to all forms . . .
> O current of power permeating all—
> In the heights, upon the earth,
> And in all deeps:
> You bind and gather
> All people together . . .
> You are ever teaching the learned,
> Made joyful by the breath of Wisdom.[4]

Sophia, another name for Her multifaceted presence in Christianity (and the name Marion Woodman uses most to describe the sacred feminine), means "wisdom." And as the quote that leads this chapter relays, Sophia likes to play . . . *with us.* Degler tells us that the Holy Spirit "like Shakti [the Divine Feminine in Hinduism], Shekinah [a name for the Divine Feminine in Judaism], and Sophia, represents the embodiment of the Divine within us; she manifests as divine light; she is seen as the universal life force, and most important for us here, she is the source of transformation and creative inspiration in our lives."[5] Yep, the D.F. is the Creative Oomph of the Universe that is right here, right now rushing through your veins, shaking Her sparkly pompoms and hollering, "Go, Baby, Go!!!" But all Her fire and spice and not everything nice can't stream through us full force on Earth if we're up in the clouds counting spiritual sheep.

DARING DIFFERENCES

Let's dare to declare some more divine differences:

> Oneness, nonattachment, neutrality, emptiness, perfection, peace,
> equanimity, clean, constant, calm . . . zzzz . . . whoops, I dozed off there for
> a minute, undifferentiated illumination, God Realization, enlightenment

Sound familiar? They should. Not only do these qualities and states often reflect a more spirit-based path, but they also represent a more "masculine" experience and expression of divinity.

> Ecstatic, dynamic, evolutionary, full, sensual, erotic, passionate, messy,
> explosive, energetic, emotional, imperfect, fiery, enlivenment

These qualities often reflect a more soul-based path, and represent a more "feminine" experience and expression of divinity.

A suggestion: reread the above "Divine Masculine" and "Divine Feminine" qualities and pay attention to how they make you *feel.*

For me, the D.M. feels still; the D.F. feels like movement. The D.M. feels like no thing; the D.F. feels like every thing. The D.M. feels impersonal; the D.F. feels personally invested. The D.M. feels cool and collected and even a bit chaste; the D.F. feels hot and bothered and more than a bit salacious. In *my* inner vision, the D.M. looks clear, and the D.F. shimmers like a rainbow. The D.M. works it out on a yoga mat; the D.F. prefers a claw-foot bathtub. The D.M. drives a Prius; the D.F. speeds in a convertible Caddy. The D.M. fasts; the D.F. feasts. The D.M. sits cross-legged under a tree all day; the D.F. dances around a fire all night. The D.M. sounds like OMM-MMMMM; the D.F. sounds like AHHHH or WOOOO HOOOO!!!!! Or a guttural scream. Or a sob. Or a belly laugh. While both aspects of the Divine feel familiar *and necessary,* for me, the D.M. *appears* more spiritual, even though the D.F. *feels* more natural.

Look.

I know labels are limiting and can't capture the wide spectrum of divinity, so I ask you to hold the above labels, distinctions, and perspectives *lightly.* Although things are rarely so black and white, for many women, noticing and naming differences between "masculine" and "feminine" energies, experiences, and expressions can be extraordinarily clarifying, confirming, and healing.

A few peppery points: Masculine does not equate with male, nor does feminine equate with female. Some of the most divinely feminine humans I know are men, and some of the most divinely masculine humans I know are women. It's also important to distinguish between the D.M. and patriarchy. The latter is the millennia-old social, political, and energetic system based on domination and *false* masculine principles of power. While all religions suffer from patriarchy, they also hold plenty of nonpatriarchal Divine Masculine truths.

However, what's crucial to notice is that most of us have forfeited our divine femininity in order to fit into a masculine spiritual "norm," and this tendency is a result of patriarchy. The rough reality is that traditional religion and most New Age spiritualities have taught us—sometimes loudly, but more often *quite* softly—that the masculine way to be spiritual is the most powerful way to be spiritual . . . the right way, the most enlightened way, the *only* way.

Well, ladies, they have taught us wrong. They have forgotten that the Divine also acts like a total Girl. As activist and writer Eve Ensler fiercely stated in her book *I Am an Emotional Creature:* "Imagine that girl is the part of each of us that feels compassion, empathy, passion, intensity, association, relationship, emotion, play, resistance, vulnerability, intuitive intelligence, vision. Imagine that compassion informs wisdom. That vulnerability is our greatest strength. That emotions have inherent logic and lead to radical saving action."[6]

BACK TO THE WILD

Because of my disembodied spiritual-bypassing ways B.M. (Before Marion), I lost touch with my natural instincts, my feelings, and my primal punch. Case in point: I took a self-defense class B.M., and one of the first exercises in the class involved driving a male aggressor away by just using our voice and our energy—no physical touch was allowed. When it was my turn in front of the aggressor, I automatically went all "spiritual" on him, transcending the snarly situation, smiling beneficently. But alas, I couldn't get my aggressor away. So I beamed *more* compassion at him; in response, the aggressor turned darker, nastier, even *more* aggressive. Finally, fed up, the instructor broke character and yelled at me, "If this was a real incident, you'd be raped or dead right now! What the hell do I have to do to wake you up, girlie?!"

And then he slapped me.

Hard.

That did it. Without thinking, I screamed, "GET THE HELL AWAY FROM ME!" He flinched, but quickly informed me that the scream came from the upper part of my body; he asked me to scream again, this time from my lower body, specifically,

from my vagina.

Still reeling from the intense moment, I let 'er rip so intensely that the instructor actually jumped backward and ran away, terrified. The fierce roar came up from way down deep inside me, from the dark, from the ashes, from a place I had rarely (if ever) accessed before, and it was so fucking real and raw and Goddess, so totally and completely *unfamiliar,* that I immediately started sobbing. Talk about Pussy Power. Interestingly, most of us who had difficulty with this particular exercise were actively practicing some form of spirituality, the majority being forms of Buddhism.

'Bout that.

Most spiritual practices and teachings are based upon male bodies, male brains, and masculine consciousness. While this might sound obvious or even seem unimportant, in my opinion, it's incredibly significant. As Dr. Louann Brizendine, author of *The Female Brain,* tells us, even though there is only one percent genetic variation between the sexes, this "difference influences every single cell in our bodies—from the nerves that register pleasure and pain to the neurons that transmit perception, thoughts, feelings, and emotions."[7]

These spiritual practices and teachings were, for the most part, created to help *men* learn very important things (especially during more "primitive" times in history): reigning in personal power, selflessness, eradicating the ego, chilling out, taming feelings and emotions, and, as we know from previous chapters, transcending desire, the body, and sexuality. So, if your current spiritual practice comes from any sort of religious or spiritual tradition (except a few forms of Tantra) or even a pop-cultural or New Age derivative, it strengthens your masculine consciousness and reinforces a masculine way of being spiritual and alive on this planet . . . as a woman.

During a retreat I attended A.M. (After Marion, but before I entered the Red Tent), Sofia Diaz played various songs over loudspeakers and asked us to simply allow our body to move instinctually. When The Smashing Pumpkins' song "Disarm" blasted forth ("The killer in me is the killer in you"), I started moving in a way I have never ever, *ever* moved before . . . as a *Killer.* I sliced through the air with my entire body, staring down fellow participants, daring anyone to step into my space.

I.

Kill.

I didn't "act" like a psychopathic serial killer or pantomime moves I had watched in a horror flick; I *embodied* the uncompromisingly dangerous power of the Goddess Durga, who slaughtered all those demons that were trying to destroy the world. I understood, *on a body level,* why this unfamiliar destructive power, when used consciously, was no less divine than the power of peace. I also felt how this killer power was *feminine* and an entirely misunderstood and forbidden force within me. As Degler writes:

> Even of all those women who *are* comfortable with emotions, very few
> are comfortable with the feeling of wild, surging power. . . . The trick
> is to realize that we do indeed embody this power and then to become
> comfortable with the way this feels. We need, in other words, to come to a
> place where we can sit and quietly hold this great power in our bellies.[8]

Or *not* sit and *not* be so quiet.

I have a very intuitive friend, Ashley, who created a powerful practice for herself to help remedy years of masculine spiritual practice. She would spend an hour or so in the jungle every day for two years (she lived in Costa Rica at the time), making the most animalistic noises and faces and movements that she could muster.

RRRRRAAAWWWWEERRRGGGHHRRRRRRRRR!!!!!!!!

During my Red Tent time, I had (and still have, when I'm out of balance) intensely graphic dreams of my dog being cut in half or trapped under the bed or sick (or worse, as you'll read about below), all of which represent an aspect of my own inner animal that has been cut off, shoved away, and made ill. Clarissa Pinkola Estés describes our inner animal as a Wild Woman:

> Within every woman there is a wild and natural creature, a powerful force,
> filled with good instincts, passionate creativity, and ageless knowing. Her
> name is Wild Woman, but she is an endangered species. Though the gifts
> of the wildish nature come to us at birth, society's attempt to "civilize" us
> into rigid roles has plundered this treasure, and muffled the deep, life-
> giving messages of our own souls. Without Wild Woman, we become
> over-domesticated, fearful, uncreative, trapped.[9]

The soft belly of this wolf of a point is that most "spiritual" practices, while helpful at enhancing aspects of our spirit and our masculine Divine nature, are not as helpful when it comes to reconnecting with our wild animals, embodying our souls, and liberating our feminine Divine nature. Therefore, many women need to incorporate "feminine" practices alongside "masculine" practices in order to discover their power; unleash their voice; trust their body's wisdom; build up a sense of self (and not give so much of it away); stimulate their authentic sexual desires and needs; and dive deep into their lower worlds so they can embody their soul. While I'm sure you can think of several spiritual practices or teachings or even experiences that seem to be neutered, genderless, "free" from masculine and feminine distinctions, if you sink into your *body* and re-approach them, you might *feel* differently.

FREE TO GET FREAKY

One morning in the Red Tent, for my moving "meditation," I hit shuffle on my iPod and out popped rapper Chris Brown's "I Can Transform Ya" ("from a good girl to a freak"). So, I got freaky. My inner patriarch did not like this dirty bump and grind one bit; he was all: "This isn't a *spiritual* practice!" Without breaking a beat, I pertly answered him back: "What? Not enough sun salutations, celestial chants, or Tibetan singing bowls for ya?" He shuffled his feet and stepped back, grumbling, but also smiling, just a little.

In the Red Tent, it became a spiritual practice to simply pay closer attention to what fed *my* soul and awakened *my* body, because that's what feeds *Her*. When I would slip into a spiritual "should"—like "I *should* be meditating each day" or even "I *should* be doing that feminine practice I heard on that podcast"—my Lady would gently cut in and ask, "What feels spiritual or feminine for *you* to do today, Sera?"

I can't emphasize enough the importance of developing this dynamic soul–body awareness, especially since there's currently an explosion of books, courses, telesummits, and workshops teaching about "the feminine." On one hand, this influx of information is absolutely fabulous and about freakin' time. But, and this is a Brazilian butt, because of the fast rise of this spiritual/self-help trend, you need to be careful not to let someone else's feminine reality (including the one in this very book) usurp your own. She needs to get freaky in *your* distinct form.

Skin yourself bare of what is not you.

The Divine Feminine hides and seeks within your flesh. Will you play?

PRACTICE SHOULD NOT MAKE YOU PERFECT

After nine months in my Red Tent, I was nudged by my Lady to attend a weekend spiritual workshop, led by my old energy teacher. It had been well over a year since I had been involved with this particular practice, so I was curious how I would react. Well, as soon as I walked in the door, my body felt heavy, tight, and that all-too-familiar pressure to be spiritually impeccable—partly because of my own issues and partly because the energy behind the workshop's practices smacked of spiritual perfectionism.

That night, after the first day of the workshop, I had a gruesome nightmare: My dog (who in the dream and in real life is a twelve-pound Chihuahua mutt) was being sodomized by a man in an apartment blocks away. I sprinted like the wind to the apartment, broke down the door, forcefully threw the man to the floor, and rescued my dog. I woke up the next morning, realizing through several other telltale signs in the dream (including the rapist's name) that for my psyche, "the man" represented the perfectionistic spiritual practice I was engaging in at the workshop, and the dog was my feminine body/soul. I immediately thought of a quote from Marion Woodman: "Perfection rapes the soul."[10] Well, it certainly did in dreamtime.

The following afternoon, my dear friend Emily picked me up after the workshop ended and I told her about the dream. She asked if I still went to the workshop the morning *after* I had the dream. I paused. I had returned to the workshop, even knowing what the dream was about, because part of me didn't want to create trouble or hurt my teacher's feelings; part of me wondered if there was still "something spiritual" I could get from the workshop, especially since the practices had helped me so much in the past; part of me thought that since I got the "spiritual" lesson of the dream, I doubted that my physical body actually needed to be removed from that "spiritual" environment. When I realized what I had done, how I had not "protected" my soul/body by physically leaving the workshop, I became upset as I began to realize just how many times I had done this in my past—made myself sit through countless spiritual retreats or meditation classes (or dates or meals or business meetings), when my body/soul *knew* this was not the right place/practice (or person) for me to be around at this time.

A few hours later, Emily, two other friends, and I took a ferry to Orcas Island, Washington. On the bow of the ferry we, well, *exploded* with Divine Feminine energy. You know those times that pretty much only happen when you're hanging out with close girlfriends—when your saucy inner seven-year-old bumps hips with your future I-don't-give-a-shit-what-anyone-thinks inner "granny" — and suddenly your world becomes nothing but dirty jokes and ticklish truths, flipping hair and escaping bra straps, hysterical laughter and random body movements that range from skipping to jigging to usually falling on the ground totally . . .

In Love

As Life.

Well, that happened on the ferry ride to Orcas after that restrictive workshop. I can't even remember specifics of our conversation, but I do remember Mercedes sharing the title of a future book she wants to write:

Does Embodiment Make My Butt Look Fat?

'Nuff said.

While we were acting like crazy cosmic monkey goddesses making love to the natural world and making fun of our super-serious spiritual lives, I jumped up and down on the ferry's bow and screamed into the wind and the ocean and the entire Universe:

NOW *THIS* IS HOW THE LADY ROLLS!!!

And I felt Her rock the entire boat in joyous response:

WHO'S YOUR MAMA?!

After so much time in the Red Tent, I needed to experience the differences between the workshop and the ferry, between my previous, more spirit-addicted practices and teachers and my new more soul-based, er, "practices" and "teachers." Now, whenever my friends or I encounter a practice or teaching that directly *or indirectly* emphasizes spiritual perfection or dismisses our feminine body or suppresses the soul, we simply say, "That butt-fucked my dawg." And we burst out laughing.

TWO SIDES OF THE SAME COSMIC COIN

Now, even though this entire book is dedicated to the Divine Feminine (I'm obviously one of Her hype girls), I want to be clear that She is not better or more important than the Divine Masculine, though She *does* help people dress (and dance) better. Ideally, we want the D.M. and the D.F. to get Married, have three kids, and adopt a dog.

The Divine Masculine and the Divine Feminine go together like peanut butter and jelly, dark chocolate and Red wine, the sun and the earth, a king and a queen, a God and a Goddess, J.C. and M.M. They are two sides of the same cosmic coin (guess which one is heads, and which one is tails?).

We need to know, embrace, and unleash *both* the Divine Masculine and the Divine Feminine (the D.M. has been just as screwed by patriarchy as the D.F.). However, because the D.F. is so often overlooked or discounted, most of us — especially those of us who practice or are exploring traditional, New Age, or mainstream spirituality *and* have a female body this time round — *need* to focus on the D.F. a bit (or a lot) more consciously in order to even out the playing field.

Let Her Out to Play!

16 ½

ROSES ARE RED

A rose is a rose is a rogue.

TOM ROBBINS
Jitterbug Perfume

Years ago, when I started Touching people, the Red rose started to perfume my life. Up to that point, I had never, *ever* been a fan of Red roses; they seemed like such overcommercialized, heavily Hallmarked representations for "love." But when the Universe started chucking Red roses at me, like rice thrown at a bride, I paid attention.

I soon discovered that the Red rose was the insignia for Babalon, as well as for Magdalene, Aphrodite, and other "love goddesses" from our deep, dark past. In *The Woman's Encyclopedia of Myths and Secrets,* Barbara G. Walker explains, "The Rose, which ancient Rome knew as the flower of Venus, was the badge of the sacred prostitute. Things spoken 'under the rose' (sub rosa) were part of Venus' sexual mysteries, not to be revealed to the uninitiated."[1] In alchemy, the rose suggests a marriage between spirit and matter. In some mystical traditions, the rose signifies the heart and the unfolding petals represent the process of self-revelation. The rose is also a common symbol for the soul, not to mention an anagram for *eros*.

After I did a little research, it made more sense why Red rose petals were scattered across my path. Nevertheless, I was apprehensive when I started to receive the inner nudge to get the "head" of a Red rose *tattooed on the back of my neck* (the neck is where the fifth chakra is located, which affects self-expression). So I did what I normally do when I receive somewhat outlandish intuitions: I waited.

There are hundreds of winks I could share, but here's a snapshot of one particular day: At breakfast with my friend Tara, *right* when I opened my mouth to ask her what she thought about this inky intuition, her cell phone rang and she started shouting into the receiver, "Rose?! Rose?!" — the name of the woman calling *that very moment.* I closed my mouth. A few hours later, while walking my dog in the park, two strangers approached me: one woman introduced herself as "Rose," and the other woman had a rose tattooed onto her shoulder. After I complimented the woman on her tattoo, she gave me the number of her tattoo artist in San Francisco, who had learned the art by tattooing *roses* up and down her own legs. When I left the park and walked past my favorite ice cream parlor, they were handing out free samples of a new flavor — yep, rose.

I've asked for this type of ridiculous treatment. I know I'm slow to trust and chock-full of (sometimes-healthy) doubt. So when it comes to divine winks, I tell the Universe to Bring It until I cry "mercy." After months of wily winks and *one week* before I was set to start writing this very book, I finally cried "mercy."

I brought three girlfriends to the tattoo parlor, smudged the place with sage, set up a mini Red altar, lit rose-scented candles, and then read out loud the meaning of the Red rose and my intention for tattooing it on the back of my neck:

"To communicate my soul's truth as authentically as possible."

Moved by the ritual, my tattooist briefly took off her shirt to show us an enormous image of Kali tattooed across her entire back. "Wow," I smiled in reverent surprise. "Kali has our backs even here."

(Pause.)

Girlfriend, be extra-strength careful in setting your intentions. The Universe takes our intentions seriously, especially when they're ritualized and whole-hearted, aligned with our soul (not just our ego), and backed by Kali . . .

THE RED BLOCK

Unless the eye catch fire,
the god will not be seen.
Unless the tongue catch fire,
the god will not be named.
Unless the heart catch fire,
the god will not be loved;
Unless the mind catch fire,
the god will not be known.

THEODORE ROSZAK
Where the Wasteland Ends

R*ight* after I tattooed my intention to communicate my soul's truth onto the back of my neck, I experienced writer's block. Severe writer's block. The type that strips you of passion and purpose and perspective every time you sit down in front of the computer. I tried and tried to write the book I had been contracted to write—a peppy, go-get-'em spiritual self-help book about how to be a Redvolutionary—only to be hit a few forced pages later with a tidal wave of sadness and a sinking intuition that I wasn't writing what my soul wanted me to write.

While I recognized that my struggles to write this book were a reflection of, and a catalyst for, my spiritual growth, trying to write my soul's truth *professionally* (and on a legally bound deadline) was like living in a divine pressure cooker. As my friend, author Robert Rabbin, told me during this tormenting time, "The writing womb is intense enough, but the soul's writing room is, well, it's just a killer. It kills everything that is not true and authentic. It's a kind of spiritual ordeal, a cleansing and purification ritual that cares only for the deep-down bedrock truth." The infuriating thing was, I didn't know what my "deep-down bedrock truth" was. I didn't know what my soul wanted to express.

SURRENDER *THIS*

As weeks went by and the block cemented, I became desperate. My mind went on overdrive, my body became reactive, and not surprisingly, I stopped hearing my Lady. Thankfully, my Lady ushered in Emily, my intuitive friend and soul whisperer, for backup. Emily told me I couldn't control the spiritual process that the writer's block represented, or even mentally understand it, but I could *allow it* to happen. I could, you know, *surrender.*

I am aware of you circling,

constantly,

asking me with your immense Presence

when I will surrender.

When will I clear my runway

and

let

You

Touch

Down?

Even if you believe in the importance of spiritual surrender, you can't *make* yourself surrender. In fact, our egos will do just about anything and everything *not* to surrender to the Divine. And, it doesn't help that old-school stories of surrender make many of us hesitate before folding ourselves before Divinity: if we surrender, some Big Daddy God will start ordering us around (what can *appear* to have happened to several biblical characters and some Western mystics), or we will be unable to function and turn into a puddle of babbling bliss (what can *appear* to have happened to several surrendered saints from the East), or some external beings or aliens will "take over" and make us communicate *their* beliefs and spiritual paradigms (what can *appear* to have happened to several New Agers).

Bottom line: We've mostly been taught about surrender from divine masculine, spirit-based, or even "false light" perspectives—surrendering our self to some transcendent god or state or entity. But what if surrender means something different from divine feminine and soul-based perspectives? As Sue Monk Kidd wrote in *Dance of the Dissident Daughter,* "In some ways spiritual development for women, perhaps unlike that for men, is not about surrendering self so much as coming to self."[1]

Surrender was a nagging mystery during my writer's block, and after months in the Red Tent, I felt like I had already let go of *so* much. And this book was a project I knew, based on the results of my first book, that I could make successful by doing it *my* way. Emily suggested I have a funeral for my old ways of writing and even put to rest my overly earnest desires for this book to "help" others and serve the divine.

(Gulp)

The Red Tent transformed into a funeral pyre (in a pressure cooker). Eventually, it got to such a heated point that I wasn't sure what was left to burn.

Oh wait . . . there was *something* left . . .

Red.

I began to wonder if I was too attached to the whole Red gig. Was I unconsciously clinging to Red like a spiritual security blanket? Were my Red rose–colored glasses preventing me from accessing an even truer reality? According to many spiritual beliefs, relying upon a certain lens or label or color for the Divine impedes us instead of evolves us. And I'm here to grow, damn it.

While I knew I wasn't supposed to let go of my Lady, I decided that I did need to let go of *Her Redness.* I wasn't shoving Red to a dark corner because I thought Red was "bad" or spiritually "wrong" (as I had repeatedly done throughout my life), nor was this like my Red night of the soul, where it felt like an external Source temporarily cut *me* off. Nope, now *I* was consciously and respectfully letting go of Red. I was grateful for everything I had received from Red, but it was time to move on. Going Redless was not just a lofty spiritual move; it directly affected me on the ground level since my entire career and future book were based on Red. I asked myself:

Who am I without Red?

Through a carefully crafted physical and energetic ritual, I let go of Red. I let go of the Redvolution movement. I let go of being a Redvolutionary. I let go of writing books about Red, talking about Red, teaching Red. I let go of my Red lingo and symbols and research and visions and story, and although I kept the lessons, I let go of my Red mystical experiences. I drained my Lady of all color and wiped the spiritual slate totally clean, so I could (I hope) "see" what She wanted me to see . . . and write . . . and become. Letting go of this mysterious cosmic color that had been with me, in one form or another, my entire life was the oddest, most necessary, and most desertlike experience of my life.

CABIN FEVER

Redless months passed . . .

and, my writer's block only increased.

In a last-ditch effort, I secluded myself in a rustic cabin in the middle of the woods with no connection to the outside world. About three weeks in, with still no book draft in sight, I caught cabin fever. "Ok, looky here," I said to my colorless Lady one rainy morning, sprawled out on the floor with my laptop. "The deadline is right around the corner. How 'bout I just force out a non-Red self-help book and *then* write whatever the hell it is my soul wants me to write?" A spatula in the kitchen, not *that* near to the stovetop heating my tea, spontaneously caught fire. I yelped, jumped up, and chucked the flaming utensil under the running faucet. Shaken but determined, I continued my deal-making with the Divine: "Okay, fine. Hmmmm. You keep hitting me over the head (and lighting things on fire) with the fact that 'my way' isn't working and that I need to surrender. So, maybe I'm just supposed to channel this sucker. It sure would be a lot easier."

I sat back down, crossed my legs, lit some incense, meditated for a half hour, and then proceeded to write what felt like "channeled material." After about a minute of "channeled writing," my dog, who had been lying peacefully next to me for hours, threw up . . . right on my keyboard. *Then* my Lady spoke:

This is a *Relationship,* Sera.

Not a one-way street.

You're not a slave taking dictation.

I Want to Do My Wild Thang *with you*

***Not* despite you!**

Remember, We're In This Together!

Months after this incident, I came across the wise words of Barbara Marx Hubbard in her book *Emergence,* which share a similar realization:

> We don't want to confuse this kind of self-expression with "channeling," which occurs when people put aside their local self [ego self] and feel an external entity coming through them. If we want to incarnate fully, we cannot have hovering entities telling local selves what to do. . . . This kind of writing is the next step after so-called channeling. It is the process of the incarnation of deity. . . . You are not channeling a higher entity. You are the higher entity yourself. You are allowing "the word to become flesh."[2]

Allow

My Words

to Become

your Flesh

Allow

your Flesh

to Become

My Words

While I was grateful to hear my (now Redless) Lady again, as I cleaned the dog vomit off my keyboard, my pain, frustration, and confusion reached a boiling point, and I screamed at the top of my lungs (that is what's great about isolated cabins in the middle of the woods):

"WHAT MORE AM I SUPPOSED TO DO?!!!

I HAVE DONE *EVERYTHING* I CAN THINK OF TO WRITE THIS BOOK!!!"

As soon as I screamed those words, I realized *that's* the problem. I have done everything I can *think* of. I have let go of everything I can *think* of. There was nothing else I could *do*. Wiped out, I collapsed to the ground, sobbing and surrendered. Minutes passed, and then:

You need to Love Me.

I was shocked, not to mention a wee bit offended. So a second wind of sass filled my sails:

> "Whaa? Love You? Come on! Give me a Holy freakin' break! I've loved you since I was cosmically conceived! I wanted to be a priest for Christ and Magdalene's sake! I spent years yawning behind the rigid walls of academia to appropriately study you. I traveled around the world and risked late-night dangerous bus rides through the Himalayas and dealt with all sorts of bizarre nasty physical ailments to explore you. I have participated in countless personal retreats, read way too many books, and done way too many workshops to constantly evolve my awareness of You. I married You! I have created a career around You and written a book and directed a film in order to inspire others to deepen their own unique relationship to You. And then I have let go of my career, my film, my audience, my friends, and my previous life in order to start embodying You. I'm in the Red Tent with You! I have faced, and continue to face, my shadows and deepest fears by committing my life to You. And isn't it enough that I also love You through loving the handful of people left in my life, the trees, my potty-mouthed parrot, my barfy Chihuahua. Isn't this loving You? What more do You want from me?"

Everything

I paused, just for a moment, and then began to quickly review all the various ways of relating to the Divine Feminine that I had encountered in my life:

> As an external goddess, a passionate belief, an abstract idea, a level of consciousness, a dualistic perspective, an evolutionary force, an academic thesis, an ornate icon, a political statement, a religious ideology, ancient history, an archeological find, an archetype, a myth, a muse, a healing modality, a creative complex, a therapeutic exercise, a mission statement, a mass movement, book-group banter, a feminist mascot, a female body, women's intuition, the earth, "nature," an environmental cause, a women's circle centerpiece, a New Age glamor shot, a Northern Californian catch phrase, a neotantric tease, a sexual supplement, a marketable trend . . .

My Lady widened Her eyes of fire and blinked. The gold glitter that fluttered off Her eyelids covered a small Caribbean island just south of Florida. She held me in Her Wise Gaze, stopping my brain whirl, igniting my body's knowing.

I ceased my ranty review, took some deep breaths, and felt into my body—

my womb,

    my blood,

        my heart

        My Heart

        My HEART

and I began to *feel* just how much I have *not* been fully loving Her . . .

which was followed by a profoundly humbling realization:

I don't know how.

I know that how I've loved my Lady in the past has been genuine. But this direct inner request from my Lady to love Her in an "Everything" kind of way felt totally new and made absolutely no sense to my mind. I remembered something Jungian analyst Nancy Qualls-Corbett said in our interview: "You can't think love. You can only *feel* love." My Lady suddenly serenaded me with Supertramp song lyrics, "Give a little bit, give a little bit of your love to Me."

I burst out laughing, "Alright, La*dee!* Teach me how to love You!"

SOUL DESIRES

A few nights after my Lady's serenade, feeling more loving and loved, but still unable to write anything that felt "right," I received the nudge to listen to a recorded teleclass I had downloaded before I went to the cabin. The class was titled "New Feminine Power" and was taught by Katherine Woodward Thomas and Claire Zammit, who spoke about how surrender is the *essence* of the feminine. They claimed that one important step to being in our full feminine power is to surrender our agenda for our lives, stop trying so hard to force or control things, release what we *think* we should be doing, and stop setting goals that are from our egos (and spiritualized egos) instead of from our souls.

One of the practices in the teleclass was to write down five things we wanted to experience in our life. Mine were fairly typical: a meaningful career, a loving intimate relationship, abundance, optimal health, and a like-hearted community. Next on the teleclass, Zammit guided us through a lengthy meditation so we could access a wiser part of us—our souls. As Plotkin reminds, "Your soul is transpersonal and other because it is deeper and far more expansive than your conscious mind. . . . The soul is the sacred realm of our most heartfelt purposes, our unique meanings, and the ultimate significance of our individual lives."[3] In that clear and quiet state, Zammit asked us a few questions, one at a time.

The first question: "What do you want to *experience as a soul* in this lifetime?" My soul's instant unfiltered answer:

Love for and from the Divine.

Second question: "What do you want to *express as a soul* in this lifetime?" My soul's instant answer:

My Love for the Divine!

Now, this might sound fairly typical for a soul to say. But several members who had taken the previously recorded live teleclass voiced their soul's answers, which were different from mine and from each other's. And the more important piece for me to acknowledge was that my soul's answers were certainly different from my mind's earlier answers and felt directly related to my writer's block.

"Whoa!" I elegantly exclaimed to my Lady right after this exercise. "So, apparently, the hotter-than-hot life 'plan' this time around is . . .

to Love You."

After admitting that simple but not so simple Redvelation, I swear the entire Universe broke out in giddy applause (Buddha included). I curtsied. My Lady smiled so wide a nearby blue planet blushed Red.

While finding a partner and experiencing glowing health, abundance, community, and a purposeful career are important desires to recognize and declare, and are more than worthy of working toward, they were not *my soul's deepest* desires. Therefore, these things will never truly fulfill me, and some of them might even be "blocked" from me by my soul, if I'm not *also* doing what my soul most wants to experience and express here.

I intuitively realized that a few nights back, the Divine Diva wasn't *commanding* me to love Her. She wasn't telling me to love Her because *She* needed my love or because it was more "feminine" or "healthy" or "spiritual" for me to love Her. Nope, my Lady asked me to love Her because *that's what my unique soul most wants to do this time around.* And expressing my "Everything" love for Her was my soul's *truest gift* to this world and the best, most effective way for me to be of Service on this planet.

Knowing our soul's desire for this lifetime isn't so mysterious; it's often as simple as remembering what we loved to experience and express as children. The fabulous-are-you-freaking-kidding-me-*this*-is-my-gift-to-offer-the-world thang is often the very thing that makes us most come alive. As Howard Thurman wrote, "Don't ask what the world needs. Ask what makes you come alive, and go do it. Because what the world needs is people who have come alive."[4]

Come *Alive*

Helping us come alive by expressing our distinct soul's desires is part of the D.F.'s job description. Our soul's yearnings match *Her* yearnings for us. And you can bet your sweet ass that She'll burn away anything and everything that stands in your soul's way, including that which you mistake as your "soul's desires."

THE RED PRINCESS

"Are you a princess?" I asked. She said, "I'm much more than
a princess, but you don't have a name for it yet on earth."

BRIAN ANDREAS
StoryPeople

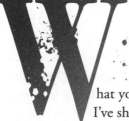hat you're about to read is the most unorthodox Redvelation
I've shared thus far.

Trust me, this chapter *requires* the use of Red rose–colored glasses.

Remember, we live in a Universe that uses any medium possible to communicate with us, to validate our heart's knowing, to reflect our forgotten truths, and sometimes even to share dirty little secrets.

Alrighty then, let's slip on those Red rose–colored glasses . . .

A FLUTTERING OF RED WINKS

First, I need to describe a few things that happened *before* I let go of Red, starting with the fact that getting the Red rose tattoo didn't hurt. As the needle pierced the back of my neck, instead of feeling pain, I experienced *fiery ecstasy,* as if a horny Seraphim (an order of Red-winged angels in Christianity known as the "burning ones") was giving me a hickey.

I wasn't expecting that erotic sensation at all, but what I really wasn't expecting were the inner experiences that pulled my consciousness away from the tattoo parlor and into what looked and felt like a rowdy Red party in the other realms. There was hootin' and hollerin', dancing and singing, and millions of Red balloons swirlin' in my honor—as if I'd just returned from a faraway land and this was my welcome-home party, like even though I'd been conscious of Red for decades, I had just officially joined the Red Club, and like getting this tattoo was some sort of multidimensional initiation rite.

But then, this animated inner party scene changed, and oddly enough, I found myself in what I just knew was the Garden of Gethsemane, the garden where Jesus is said to have prayed the night before his crucifixion. My heart banged against my chest in shock.

"Huh . . . ?"

Sure enough, J.C. appeared on my internal screen dressed in white, arms outstretched, and, uh, *thanking me for sharing the Red Feminine!* In that utterly candid moment, it appeared as though Red was something close to Jesus's heart. Very, *very* close . . .

A few weeks after I received those visceral visions while getting my Red rose tattoo, a reader of my first book sent me an excited email informing me that Kathleen McGowan's novel *The Book of Love* is about the hunt for *Il Libro Rosso* (Italian for "The Red Book"), which shares secret teachings of Jesus and Magdalene, including a mystical path of spiritual partnership and sacred sexuality, as well as visionary and prophetic writings by Jesus and Magdalene's daughter, Sarah. One of the main symbols of *Il Libro Rosso* is a rose.

One morning around this same period, I shot out of bed and began frantically searching for my lost ruby ring. It took about a full minute before I realized: *I don't own a ruby ring.* But, in a *between* state, I saw and felt it so clearly: a large oval ruby surrounded by a gold disc that I wear on the ring finger of my right hand. "Well, that's odd, even for me!" I said to my annoyed dog, who'd been woken up by my surreal search party.

Later that afternoon, my father sent me an email with the subject line "interesting name" and a link to an article about Saint Sarah-la-Kali. I clicked on the link and started reading. There are various legends about St. Sarah-la-Kali, but the most popular tells us that she was on the boat with Mary Magdalene, Mary Salome, and Mary Jacobe when they arrived at a tiny beach town in southern France, now aptly named Saintes-Maries-de-la-Mer (the Marys of the sea). Some say Saint Sarah was the Egyptian servant of Magdalene. Some say she was a gypsy queen already living in southern France, who welcomed and supported Magdalene and her crew who were escaping persecution. In fact, Saint Sarah-la-Kali is often referred to as "The Queen of the Outsiders" and is the patron saint of the gypsies, who have long felt like outsiders in Europe. In the town of Saintes-Maries-de-la-Mer, icons of the three Marys are kept above ground in a light-filled church, while Sarah's icon is kept underground, in a dark shrine, partly because Sarah has never been canonized by the Vatican; she is unrecognized by the Catholic Church.

The gypsies originated in India, homeland of the goddess Kali. Some people believe that this connection accounts for Sarah's name. If she was of Indian or Egyptian descent, it would also account for her dark skin. However, her skin color means different things to different people. As Margaret Starbird, author of *Mary Magdalene: Bride in Exile,* explained, "The standard interpretation is that Sarah was black because she was Egyptian, but the dark countenance of the child could as easily point to her status as a refugee in exile—lost to history and to consciousness."[1]

According to more heretical legends and rumors circulating throughout France *way* before *The Da Vinci Code* was published, Sarah-la-Kali is the secret child of Jesus and Magdalene, often referred to as the lost little princess (*Sarah* means "God's princess" in Hebrew), as Starbird claims: "There is no birth certificate for Sarah, no genealogies that irrefutably confirm her origins, nothing that constitutes proof of her existence or identity in the left-brained world of academics. However, legends often contain kernels of truth too dangerous to be asserted as fact but nonetheless significant."[2]

After reading the article my father sent me, I Googled "Sarah-la-Kali." Besides pictures of her icon in southern France, a colorful album cover of a gypsy band named De LaLap showed up, depicting a modern drawing of a woman with long, dark hair and bright-blue eyes wearing a thin gold crown or headpiece—she looked a bit like Wonder Woman, though "Sara-La-Kali" is written clearly across the picture. On the bottom left of the image is a Red rose (a symbol for Magdalene), and on the bottom right, the flaming Red heart of Jesus. Sarah-la-Kali's right hand is held in front of her throat, between the Red rose and the Red heart, making the gesture like she's about to tell us a secret.

And circling her right ring finger is my "lost" ruby ring.

In case you haven't noticed, the Red Ones are certainly a motley crew, many of whom have been rejected or silenced or misconstrued by the Church. So I guess I shouldn't have been *that* surprised that the alleged love child of J.C. and M.M., also known as "The Queen of the *Outsiders*," was ringing my inner doorbell. But the thing was, I didn't know what the hell to do with her. So, alas, Sarah faded from my awareness as I sank deeper and deeper into my writer's block and let go of Red.

GO TEAM RED!

Six Redless months later and a few weeks after my cabin fever, I was *still* unable to write this book. So I took a much-needed weekend trip to Seattle to relieve some of the pressure and hang out with a few soul sisters—Emily, the intuitive soul whisperer, and Mercedes, the gifted body worker. We had a marvelous weekend together, brimming with magic and mayhem and high-school slut stories; we even created an "angel language" (it sounds like a cross between a drunk elephant and a cat in heat) that we would emit whenever we felt we had something "utterly profound" to say. Our last day together, I walked out of Emily's bedroom, and my eyes locked upon two books stacked right on top of each other among many on a teetering bookshelf. I smiled with surprise. The two books were my childhood favorites— *The Children's Bible* and *The Little Princess;* the latter is about an orphaned girl named Sarah who is eventually reunited with her family.

A few hours later while walking through a local park, Emily, who is always curious about how others receive intuitive information, asked how Red "showed up" for me. I was about to inform her that I had let go of Red, but before I could open my mouth to share this fact, a girls' high-school track team running through the park suddenly stopped a few feet to our left and started jumping up and down, screaming at the top of their lungs, "GO TEAM RED!!! GO TEAM RED!!! GO TEAM RED!!!!!" Emily and Mercedes looked at me, eyes wide, mouths open. "Yeah," I grinned. "Red shows up for me often just like that."

Perhaps because I needed two soul sisters to witness Red's audaciousness, perhaps because my heart simply can't deny how delightful it is to be wooed like this, perhaps that old adage "if you truly love something, let it go, and if it returns, it's meant for you" applies here, because no matter how many times I've let go of Red in my life, for some incomprehensible reason, *Red will not let go of me.* So instead of fighting or controlling or denying this enigmatic phenomenon, after six Redless months, I surrendered and reopened to Red's mystery.

THE MEXICAN RESTAURANT

That night we were eating outside at a Mexican restaurant under the full moon, which according to the almanac just so happened to be called "the Red moon" that particular month. So there we were, yucking it up over enchiladas, when Emily got that glazed-yet-focused look she gets when something's just grabbed her intuitive attention. After a few moments of silence, Emily asked, "Who's Sarah?" Oddly, I instinctually knew who Emily was asking about, so I told her the traditional non-incendiary Sarah-la-Kali spiel you could read off any brochure. Emily, who had never heard of Sarah before and is generally unimpressed with cold research, interrupted my intellectual prattle with, "Yeah, well, whatever, she's like here, *right now,* and she's got stuff to share with you." Meaning me.

Mercedes and I froze, salsa dripping down our chins, and I swear that the Red full moon started shining on our table like a spiritual spotlight none of us could avoid. Emily cocked her head as if she were listening to an invisible waitress hanging over her right shoulder and started to translate. The prescience of the moment and the intensity of the message were not unlike the Andrew Harvey/Kali experience, except the fire roaring through Emily was *Sarah-la*-Kali:

"Do you know how hard it was for her to be the daughter of Jesus and Magdalene?!" Emily suddenly exhaled.

> "How fucking isolating and painfully lonely it was? She had to be
> protected from those who wanted to harm her and her lineage. There
> was so much persecution going on after Jesus's crucifixion, so she was
> hidden, sometimes even in underground rooms, for long periods of time.
> She lived in fear. As a child she felt totally abandoned by her parents.
> Sure, her parents were spiritual big shots, but they often sucked at being
> human parents. J.C. visited her from the other realms, but she wanted
> to be like, like, you know, Jenny down the block and have him at her
> softball games! She wanted to please her daddy and was totally annoyed
> by her mom. Her lineage practiced sacred sexuality, which was how she
> was conceived, but she rebelled as a teenager and acted out sexually and
> eventually rejected her role to step in and carry on the feminine lineage
> after her mother. It feels like a high-priestess role, although it doesn't feel
> hierarchical. Anyway, there was so much pressure to be like her parents
> and yet paradoxically, pressure to tone it down so she wouldn't be killed
> like her father. While she shared some gifts with her parents, she was

also different from them. But she didn't trust her differences. She didn't fully understand herself or feel like she fit in or was worthy enough to follow in her parent's footsteps, so she bailed as a young woman. She killed herself or was killed—hard to tell 'cause they feel really similar in this case. Anyway, she feels that she failed her mission and her lineage. She believes that *she* is the reason the feminine 'lost' and the patriarchal Church 'won'—because the lineage never received what she was supposed to contribute. Her entire existence was covered up. She died feeling unknown and unwanted by this world."

The words were startling *for sure,* but it was the *energy* coursing through this translation (which continued for another fifteen minutes or so) that pierced the Heart of Us All—the sadness, the ache, the longing felt so utterly feminine and eerily familiar. By this time, the restaurant had thankfully cleared out, because the three of us were crying so hard I think the Puget Sound was in risk of flooding. While my mind made out with disbelief, my body was twitching and turning with trauma and shaking uncontrollably with emotional release. What Sarah was sharing touched the core of my core of my core. I felt things deep inside me—dark and hidden and cramped things—finally beginning to release and come into the light.

Emily continued:

"Sarah is indicating that she is one of your soul fragments. She's saying the Red work was *her* work, and it includes a hidden yet integral piece of Magdalene's and Jesus's work, a piece that was deliberately suppressed, often quite violently, by those who did not agree with it. But her work is also different from their work. To put it another way, it feels like Magdalene and Jesus *carried* Red, and Magdalene outwardly displayed it more than Jesus. But Sarah *was* Red. Anyways, point is, you are helping Sarah live her previously unlived life through *your current life.*"

Emily jumped up and ran to the bathroom; her period had suddenly started. Red was rushing out of her in a few different ways that night. Mercedes and I stayed silent, hardly looking at one another, cheeks wet with tears. When Emily returned, I saw that her human ego had finally caught up with what had just fired through her. She looked directly at me, shrugged her shoulders, and vulnerably voiced,

"Look, I know *nothing* about Sarah or this stuff she is saying. This is brand-new information to me, but Sarah feels vital *for you,* and she really wants you to understand your connection to her and to know that you have a spiritual lineage. You have a spiritual family, Sera."

Another sob wrenched out of me. A country song about Jesus started playing over the restaurant speakers. We three looked at each other, snotty and speechless.

THE LINEAGE LOWDOWN

A few years before this night, when I was interviewing spiritual teacher Sofia Diaz for my *Redvolution* film, she had talked emphatically about the importance of being part of a spiritual lineage — a specific line of teachers, traditions, and transmissions. Although I don't happen to believe anyone *needs* a spiritual lineage in order to experience the Good Stuff, Sofia's passion for her lineage touched my heart.

After I published *The Red Book*, I'd peacefully come to accept my spiritual homelessness. However, whenever I received Red winks and Redvelations, I couldn't deny the feeling that they felt *linked*, and part of something much larger and specific. But when I dutifully searched for corresponding external references, more often than not, I came up empty-handed. After years of this, it just makes one wonder . . .

At the end of the interview, I leaned toward Sofia and whispered, "But, Sofia . . . what do you do when your spiritual lineage has been offed?" I thought Sofia would laugh or shake her head or think I was being dramatic, but she took my strange question strangely seriously.

For example, the Inquisition (the Catholic Church's "War on Heresy") lasted *six centuries,* and *millions* of people whose spiritual practices and beliefs contradicted and/or rivaled the Church's were methodically sought out and brutally eradicated. While yes, at some point or another in history, almost every religion or spiritual group has been persecuted and deemed heretical, there have been "winners" — those who succeeded in saving their lineage or propagating their belief systems. In other words, I'm obviously not the only recycled "heretic," and I'm not the only one intimately connected to an "offed" lineage.

You Know Who You Are.

THE HOT AND HOLY INNER TEACHINGS

Since so much spiritual material has been lost or misinterpreted or manipulated by those in control, we can only make semi-educated guesses regarding *this* possible lineage. With that said, many academics and theologians acknowledge the "inner teachings" of Jesus—not necessarily the exoteric teachings you hear in a church or read in the Bible, but the esoteric teachings, which were not given to men alone, hence *The Gospel of Mary Magdalene.*

Some of these teachings, to *my* ears, sound radically Red. Jacob Needleman wrote about these inner teachings: "As a path of inner awakening, as a path of deep self-knowledge (that is to say, *gnosis*), it invites and supports the inner struggle to attend, to 'hear and obey' one's own Self, God in oneself."[3] And this path of self-knowledge is infused and often created by eros. In *The Meaning of Mary Magdalene,* Cynthia Bourgeault points out that, "Christian mysticism seems to contain a 'tantric gene'—a tendency to express itself in the language of transfigured eroticism."[4] However, the Church has sucked the Sexy right outta the Sacred, and this has become our cultural "condition."

Interesting fact: Many ancient cultures practiced variations of *hieros gamos,* a sacred marriage enacted sexually between a man and a woman. The hieros gamos symbolized the uniting of masculine and feminine, God and Goddess, and the spirit in body to ensure the bounty of crops and sometimes to produce a physical or symbolic "holy child." Since we don't have this balanced symbol in the Christian religion but crave it on a deep unconscious level, many Jungians say we project this necessary desire for wholeness onto J.C. and M.M. Getting It On.

> Two red tongues of fire
> which, twining around the same log,
> draw close and, kissing,
> form a single flame.[5]
> —*Gustavo Adolfo Bécquer*

However, this projection doesn't mean they *didn't* play a few rounds of the horizontal hanky-panky. Bourgeault tells us that in the Gnostic *Gospel of Phillip,* J.C. and M.M. had a relationship that was mutual and explicitly erotic: "'Jesus loves Mary Magdalene more than the others and many times would kiss her on the mouth.'"[6] Another provocative point is made in Jean-Yves Leloup's commentary of *The Gospel of Mary Magdalene:* "'That which is not lived is not redeemed.' If Yeshua, considered as The Messiah and the Christ, did not live his sexuality, then sexuality would be unredeemed. In that case, he could not be a Savior in the full sense of the word."[7]

What's more important than hiding the sacred sausage, which any two humans can do (well, in some form or another), is the exciting possibility that

J.C. and M.M. are examples of *authentic* spiritual partnership. In September 2012, the *New York Times* reported the discovery of a legit ancient fragment of papyrus, dated to the fourth century, in which Jesus mentions *his wife*. (A winking side note: the article mentions that this controversial piece of papyrus was carried to New York in a "red handbag."[8])

A path of sacred partnership helps two committed people unleash their gifts and be of greater service on this planet *together* than either of them could be alone. According to Bourgeault, it's a path in which partners help each other *know* their own Divinity *through* the trials (fights and farts) and glories (laughter and love) of intimate relationship; and thus, "physical lovemaking can never be separated from the rest of the path itself. It is the daily experience of 'this is my body given for you,' lived out in the myriad opportunities for self-surrender and forgiveness, that gradually fashions a sacrament out of human sexual passion."[9] Our world, our hearts, desperately need this Way of Relating in Service Together as Love. Peter Grey rightly declared in *The Red Goddess,* "The apocalypse is Now. It is impelling us into action to enthrone the Goddess that is woman, and meet her as the God that is man . . . conjoined."[10]

Look, it's *way* beyond the scope of this book to do this hot topic justice, but scholarship does allow the *possibility* that Jesus and Magdalene were intimate partners, which means they could have had children. As the Gnostic *Gospel of Thomas* cryptically states, "Whoever is acquainted with the Father and the Mother will be called the offspring of a prostitute."[11]

Hello.

BLOODLINES AND BLING AND DUALITY SINGS

Before we return to the night of Redvelation at the Mexican restaurant, I need to burn up a few fallacies:

First: I'm not subscribing to a secret bloodline conspiracy theory or pop-culture fantasy. I'm also not implying that I'm somehow genetically related to the holy family—screw bloodlines, this is a Love Line. I like the way Claire Nahmad and Margaret Bailey described the bloodline in *The Secret Teachings of Mary Magdalene:*

> We believe that there is a divine bloodline which descended through Jesus
> and Mary, the sacred "red thread," which has such mystical significance,
> but that its history is not as it has been portrayed so far. . . . We would
> stress the importance of recognizing the fact that we are *all* divine as well
> as human. The bloodline is most definitely not about exclusivity or genetic

superiority—in fact, these concepts are the very opposite of the essence and purpose of the bloodline, which exists to unite us all, to show us that we are all of one blood—sons and daughters of the king and queen.[12]

And I would add that this "Red thread" inspires us all to grow the hell up so we can become kings and queens alongside them.

Second: Ruby rings aside, the "royal" claims twinkling throughout most material about this supposed lineage are not snobby spiritual bling. As Nahmad and Bailey posit, "Their teachings on royalty did not conceive of it as we understand it today. It did not breed privilege or a class system, but was instead a practice designed for those . . . to be of ultimate service to their communities . . ."[13] In my opinion, *true* princesses are a lot like true priestesses. They Serve the Greater Good. In other words, there's a throne for every single one of us.

Third: This spiritual Love Story isn't a high-five to heterosexuality or a kudos to Christianity. It represents the spiritual relationship between the Divine Masculine and the Divine Feminine that struggles to flourish and integrate within every single one of us, no matter what religion or sex or gender or sexual orientation we are. Through a Red lens, Jesus and Magdalene symbolize the dynamic fundamentals of life, the stimulating and *sacrosanct* duality of this Universe. They are mindful metaphors, sly symbols, and, thankfully, flesh-and-blood reminders of our own physical, energetic, and spiritual makeup.

THE WHOLE TRUTH (AND NOTHING BUT THE TRUTH, SO HELP ME GOD/DESS)

In a dream-vision I had a few weeks after the night at the Mexican restaurant, I was looking at the crucifixion through a telephoto lens of a camera, but the lens kept sliding down, away from Jesus hanging on the cross, instead zooming in on Magdalene and her barely bulging belly. I woke myself up fervently shouting, "We've missed half the point of the crucifixion! We've completely. Freakin'. Missed It!" The teaching was not just about a Godman who gave up his life for us; it was also about a Goddesswoman who did something equally hard and hurting and profound: She dared to continue living!

SHE

STAYED

HERE,

FEET

ON EARTH,

HEART

TEARING

OPEN,

LIVING

FOR

LOVE

Magdalene carried the Red love they created together *in her body.* She continued their mission on Earth. She planted Divinity into the ground of life as a female in a time when it was perilous for females to do so, all the while *knowing* she was going to be slandered, scorned, and stripped bare even more than he. As Nahmad and Bailey exclaim, "Although Mary Magdalene was not crucified on the cross, she was indeed crucified by the imposition of a mentality, a soul dysfunction that stretched across centuries and made of her an outcast and an embodiment of human weakness and degradation. She, whom we should have most honored and revered . . . !"[14]

In other words, we gave him all the credit, and we gave her all the crap.

To me, M.M. is undeniably a holy heroine and just as spiritually adept as her partner J.C. As Tau Malachi wrote in *St. Mary Magdalene: The Gnostic Tradition of the Holy Bride,* "Many can accept she was a close disciple, some can accept she was the wife and consort of the Lord, but few are they who accept her as the female embodiment of the Christos."[15] Through a Red lens, it is only *with Magdalene* that Jesus's mission, message, and life are complete.

It is only *Together* that Love's Whole Truth emerges.

Now, let's widen the vision . . .

THE THIRD

Once upon a millennium, the Divine union of a heretical Godman and an outcast Goddesswoman created

The Third

A Divine Wild Child

A Daughter

A rebel with a ginormous cosmic cause weighing down her petite shoulders, not to mention a wee bit of family pressure to Bring It. *The Secret Teachings of Mary Magdalene* says this about Sarah: "She was to be the embodiment of the Great Invocation, combining the spiritual qualities of her mother Mary, the 'Woman Who Knows All' . . . and those of the man called the Christ, her father, the Light of the World."[16]

Through a Red lens, it's crucial to note that in *this* lineage at *this* time, the holy child created between the Divine Masculine and the Divine Feminine is female. This tells us something significant, if we have the ears to hear. As *The Secret Gospel of Mary Magdalene* warns:

> There is no knowledge of the Father apart from the Mother, for it is the
> Mother Spirit who gives birth to the image of the Son in whom the Living
> Father is revealed. So also shall Mother Spirit give birth to the image
> of the Daughter, so that . . . the revelation of God Most High is made
> complete. Truly I say to you, there is a holier Gospel yet to be spoken.[17]

In other words, folks,

There's a new Trinity in town.

Like her Mom—and like most powerful feminine energies during that time—Sarah was hidden underground because this world and human consciousness were not ready for her wild Red ways.

Well, some of us are ready for her now.

Or perhaps, she's finally ready for herself.

But, we have to go underground, into the darkness, into our souls and bodies (and perhaps even into a Mexican restaurant) in order to welcome her into the light.

> Send out the criers, go to the marketplace of souls,
> "Hear, hear, all you in the colonnade of lovers, here it is:
>
> "For several days now, the daughter of the vine has reported lost.
> Call all your friends! Whoever's near her is in danger.
>
> "Her dress is ruby-colored; her hair is done in sea foam;
> She takes away reason; be alert; Watch out for her!
>
> "If you find this bitter one you can have my soul for dessert.
> If she's in the Underworld, then that's the place to go.

"She's a night-woman, shameless, disreputable, and red.
If you do find her, please bring her to Hafez's house."[18]
— *Hafez*

THE CLEOPATRA SYNDROME

Back at the Mexican restaurant, as the fires of Sarah faded, several minutes
passed in which I Rested

In

This Total Knowing.

This Natural Acceptance.

This Divine "Duh!"

(Pause)

(Pause)

(Pause)

But, as I started to reflect less on Sarah's collective meaning and more on
her personal meaning . . . for me, I writhed with resistance, and my healthy
ego wrestled this highly hazardous part of the Redvelation to the ground.

"I'm *not* catching the 'Cleopatra syndrome!'" I practically shouted. Mercedes and Emily looked confused, so I charged on.

> "It's infected the entire New Age, where everyone is someone famous from
> a past life — heaven forbid, not an 'ordinary human,' like a farmer or a
> housewife or a Starbucks barista. Look, we've *all* got childhood wounds,
> messiah complexes, and unconscious needs to feel special. Not only am I
> a wounded soul, but I'm a middle child, so needing to feel special is par
> for my spiritual course and something I gotta watch like a Red hawk. Also,
> when someone is translating spiritual information from the other realms,
> no matter how impressive the original Source is, it still has to work itself
> through a human personality and ego, psychological and cultural screens,
> and the translator's current level of consciousness."

I eyed Emily, suspiciously.

She shook her head like I had entirely missed the sacred point:

> "Look, Sera, I'm not trying to convince you that you were Sarah in a
> past life. I personally don't *give a crap* about knowing who people were

in their past lives unless it somehow helps their soul unfold in this one. Past, present, and future lives are all happening at once on one level, so everything we need to know can be found right now within our current lives. However, sometimes, if it's important for the soul to get a wider perspective on her current situation — like, a cosmic backstory — she will usher forth a past-life incarnation to help. This especially holds true if it's a wounded piece of the soul 'stuck' in a particularly traumatic lifetime. That fragment needs healing and reintegration because the wounds are directly affecting and re-manifesting in the current life."

Emily took another deep breath:

"I think if our egos weren't getting all tripped up over the [mimicking a Charlton Heston voice] *Sarah, daughter of Jesus Christ and Mary Magdalene'* or [now mimicking a Darth Vader voice from *Star Wars*] *'Luke, I am your FATHER'* piece, it would be like any other past-life message I receive for a client. But, if it makes *you* more comfortable, perhaps see this as just a metaphor, a chip off the collective unconscious, or an archetype through which to heal your soul. Clearly, there's an enormous energetic and emotional release going on with you in response to this Sarah piece, and *that's* what matters."

She made some good points.

Also, if Sarah had shown up all backlit and blissed out with stars shooting out of her armpits, spewing that generic "channeled" material you can read on almost any New Age-y website attributed to "ascended masters," or if she had asked me to worship her or was pedantic or told me I was the golden child here to reveal this secret lineage and save the world and blah blah blah, well, I wouldn't have trusted what was going on. At all. Because that's not how Red communicates. The reality is, we all need to be *enormously* discerning around shiny spirits with big names. As it's written in *The Secret Gospel of St. Mary Magdalene*:

Mary said to her disciples, "Do not receive every spirit that comes to you, but put every spirit to the test to see if it comes from God or the demiurge or Satan. There are many false lights, and they glitter and glow, and even a demon can appear in the image of the Risen One. Do not be deceived, but look always for the light of Love and Truth, for what is evil lacks Love and what is mixture lacks the perfection of Truth. In the Holy Spirit you will be empowered to discern, for she is discerning awareness."[19]

Something significant I've witnessed over recent years: With any break-through of truth, such as the Redvelation of *this* holy family, false light beings catch on faster than you can say "Hello Kitty" and want a piece of the cosmic action. One of their main ways of cutting in? Mimicking the Holy Family. Basically, it's energetic identity theft. Currently, there are more "false" Mary Magdalenes and Jesuses (and now Sarahs) roaming the "higher" realms and the New Age scenes than Republicans in Texas. Even if they honestly believe they are the real beings, disincarnate impersonators often have underlying agendas that don't take our soul's best interest into account, but which we usu-ally eagerly agree to carry out because we're wowed by their claimed identity and by the strong blissful or "heavenly" feelings they create (and sometimes manipulate) in us, and because of all our honest human unconscious cravings to feel chosen, cared for by the Universe, and like we, well, *matter.*

But the fact that Sarah showed up via Emily during an ordinary weekend of healthy, grounded girlfriend giddiness and pretty much just wanted to dish about her dysfunctional family life and share her pain, her regrets, her mistakes, her imperfect *humanity*—well, that was more trustworthy, not to mention that I *felt* everything she shared within my own soul body. Also, by the time of this dinner, Sarah had been a relentless repeat on my Red radar, and I'd like to think I have enough sentience to recognize when the Universe is trying to get my attention. Bottom line: Sarah did not make me feel "special" or like the next messiah. She simply made me feel my somewhat fucked-up, wary, and wounded self.

For the public record, I'm *not* claiming to be the reincarnated daughter of Jesus Christ and Mary Magdalene (if you want to go on that wild Google chase, you will find other women having experiences of Sarah and claiming to be her incarnation or her "channel," which when not being maneuvered by the false light, represents a much-needed Divine energy that is coming through *all of us,* collectively). What I *am* claiming is that Sarah is integral to my personal healing. Our stories, though different on a surface level, match on a subterranean level. We are closely tied together. Knowing her helps embody *Me.* She is an *essential* part of my soul retrieval.

I didn't sleep that night, under the Red full moon; this Redvelation ran like a live wire through my body. Although I wasn't telling myself that what hap-pened at the Mexican restaurant was "true," when I was able to temper my mind's critique and simply allow myself to "have" the experience, on levels way deeper than my psychological wounding, I felt

Found.

We now interrupt this program for a much needed . . .

DANCE BREAK!!!!!!!!!!!!!!!!!!!!!!!!!!!!!!!!!!!

This is a hefty chapter, so I highly suggest you put this book down, find some good tunes, get out of your head and into your body, and shake your ass. I'll be dancing with you . . .

THE BETWEEN

Over the next few weeks, "memories" of Sarah's life came rapidly and experientially. One of the more potent experiences was being inside Magdalene's womb as she faced Jesus dying on the cross. There are no words deep or wide enough, in any universe, to describe what it was like to *feel* Magdalene's heart-splitting pain *inside her body as "Sarah."*

(Pause.)

(Deep exhale.)

Besides feeling her mom's devastation at losing her beloved, Sarah also felt people's misunderstanding, fear, and even hatred of her parents—all of which is terrifying to feel from the womb and makes a baby's consciousness (which is different from a baby's brain) rethink her soul's plans: "*This* is how divine love incarnate is treated on this planet? Uh, 'Check please!'" This initial soul shock and recoil from the negativity present on Earth resides deep inside all of us.

In some "memories," I experienced Sarah's twelve wise very busy aunties, aka Magdalene's "disciples," though a more appropriate title for these women would be priestesses, since they were powerful teachers and healers in their own right. In *The Secret Gospel of Mary Magdalene*, Magdalene says, "Under the old covenant, only men were called as priests, but under the new covenant, women are also called as priestesses."[20]

Looks like my childhood calling to be a priest was actually a calling to be a priestess. As James Hillman declared in *The Soul's Code:* "A calling may be postponed, avoided, intermittently missed. It may also possess you completely. Whatever; eventually it will out. It will make its claim. [It] does not go away."[21] It was making its claim, and I could *not* get away.

During my initial Sarah memories, it was hard not to get royally pissed and call "conspiracy" on the Church's ass. So, of course, I got my fight on and asked the "Red team" if there was something specific I should do—like storm the Vatican, creating a Red Grrrl Church Revival? My team laughed and told me they're not asking me to *do* anything *for* them, including trying to "prove" the lineage (via texts, theology, history, artifacts). They told me that *living as proof* is my best course of action.

(Our best course of action)

(Pause)

To ring clearer than Church bells: I'm not interested in using Sarah or this lineage for self-worth purposes or to validate my Red work (these peeps have been used enough). I'm revealing these Redvelatory experiences to you so that *I'm* in integrity. And I have to trust that I'm also being urged to share this publicly because there's something in it for *you* . . . or there will be soon.

I will admit that when the memories started, I wondered if this was finally It — the answer to my lifelong question of who/what Red is — this mystical lineage, this "bloodline," this funky, freaky princess priestess and her crazy, sexy cosmic crew. But apparently this was not my "Final Answer." My homies whispered: "Red is bigger than a priestess practice or a person from the past and even this mystical lineage; Red is bigger than anything your mind could easily grasp at this time."

However, because I *do* have a very specific soul commitment to this particular lineage (as do many who are alive now), my Red team warned me that there are "false" lineages running alongside the "true" lineage, and it's critical that I know the difference. Through a Red lens, "false lineages" are those that have purposefully covered or manipulated the teachings that stemmed from the sacred relationship created between Jesus and Magdalene.

Beyond *my* labels, definitions, experiences, and memories, please feel what happens in *your* body and *your* heart as you explore the possibility of this lineage, and trust *that* over anything I say or anyone else says.

There are Spaces Our Truth can always Be Found

The Heart

The Blood

The Soul

The Fire

The Rose

The Between

The Belly Laugh

In *The Gospel of Mary Magdalene,* much of the teaching and guidance Magdalene receives from J.C. after he was crucified occurs through the *nous* (pronounced "noose" in Greek): "A dimension often forgotten . . . In the ancient world, the nous was seen as 'the finest point of the soul . . .' It gives us access to the intermediate realm between the purely sensory and the purely spiritual, which Henry Corbin so eloquently names as the *imaginal.*"[22]

This does not mean the nous is "make believe." Bourgeault quickly reminds us:

> Imaginal does not mean imaginary — fictitious or subjective. It is a realm
> that objectively exists (one might think of it as an enveloping matrix
> of meaning around our own space-time dimension), and it is from this
> realm that our human sense of identity and direction ultimately derive.
> . . . However one names it, the point to keep uppermost in mind is that
> it designates a sphere that is not less real but *more* real than our so-called
> objective reality and whose generative energy can change the course of
> events in the world.[23]

While I do not presume that my experience of the nous is like Mary
Magdalene's or others, I can say that

I Know this Space *in my own Way.*

(As do you.)

This is the space I've visited since I was a child to "be with" God. This is
the space I started calling "the between" after my grandfather's death, the
space where Kali licked me (between), the space where I first heard Her
voice that I captured in my Red journal. This is the space I wrote specifically
about and at times *from* in my Red Kali paper for graduate school and, now,
in this book as well. This is the space I refound in my Red Tent. This is my
soul's space. In fact, it is *through* my soul that I enter this space. While Red
has always erupted out of my physical life and shown up in comical and
concrete signs, It seems to do so in order to validate that which I already
know in here.

What I Receive In this Space doesn't always make sense,

but It always Makes Love.

When I'm in this space, it's less like a psychic "seeing" and more like a
heart knowing. I do not go up and out to receive the goods; I go down and
in. This is an important distinction. You see, years ago, when I was at my
energy school, something peculiar kept happening during my meditations
that contradicted the teachings of that particular school. The seven chakras
(energy centers) in my body would merge into one, a blazing point *between*
my head and my lower body, behind my heart, disclosing not my heart
chakra but what I call the Heart of my heart. While I could use my upper
chakras to receive psychic information via my pineal gland (a physical and

energetic spot in the center of the head considered the G-spot for enlightenment, what philosopher Rene Descartes designated "the seat of the soul"), it felt unnatural, forced, and not like the seat of *my* soul. But because my experiences weren't validated by my energy school, I doubted myself . . . until I attended a spiritual retreat outside the school where we practiced "telling" the Divine we were open and ready by repeatedly chanting the mantra, "Here I Am, Here I Am, Here I AM." After a few minutes of chanting, my Lady cut in, forever changing the arrangement of the chant by fiercely beating against my chest:

"I Am *Here*.
I Am *Here*.
I Am *Here*."

She most certainly is.

In *The Gospel of Mary Magdalene*, J.C. told M.M., "For where the heart is, there is the treasure."[24] In this case, the heart and the nous become synonymous. As Bourgeault writes,

> When through the nous, the vibrational field of a particular human heart comes into spontaneous resonance with the divine heart itself, then finite and infinite become a single, continuous wavelength, and authentic communion becomes possible. Bridging the created and uncreated realms within a human being, it is both a realm in itself and the means by which this realm makes itself known.[25]

For me, the most powerful knowing undeniably comes from this holy heart space.

This Center of Me.

This Point of All Return.

Leloup says this between space, the nous, "is witness to an altogether different mode of understanding that the masculine mind typically overlooks: a domain of prophetic or visionary knowledge that, though certainly not exclusive to women, definitely partakes of the feminine principle."[26] Visionary knowledge is not "less than" book or oral knowledge. And, as Bourgeault reminds us, visions that derive from the nous are not necessarily "subjective" nor are they reflections of the person's psyche. Some believe they are the most direct and unfettered way to receive "the real" wisdom.[27]

Remember.

Because feminine wisdom has been virtually erased from traditional religions and nontraditional spiritualities' derivatives, we modern women more often than not *have* to hang out on the shady corners of the unknown, relying upon alternative ways to uncover our spiritual truth. We are Vibrant Visionaries, Praising Prophetesses, Mystical Misfits, Stalwart Salvagers of Soul, Mighty Metaphorologists, Lost Lineage Luminaries, Heretics of the Heart, Radical Realm Rompers, Bringers and Bangers of the New. In other words, when it comes to the Feminine Divine, more often than not, we gotta pirate Her booty. We know that the external world only knows half the truth, so we depend on the inner worlds to show us the rest. Just 'cause you can't find certain characters or lineages or teachings or Goddesses in *his*-story, doesn't mean they don't exist. *Her*-story awaits to unfold *from* you.

This between space reveals the universe *in my body*. It's where my flesh reveals its divinity. Leloup claimed that the nous is "where spirits become embodied and bodies become spiritualized."[28] Sometimes in the between, my Red team simply holds me, so my *body* starts to re-member.

They hold me

(In)

They love me

(In)

'Cause we all know embodiment ain't my strong suit.

J.C. and M.M. inform me that what made them so "dangerous" in their day was that they dared to fully incarnate; they did the "work" to embody their souls. God and Goddess became flesh, and flesh became God and Goddess. It was *through their bodies* that they found salvation. They did not deny their humanity, but revered it. They were fully human *and* fully divine. They were *anthropos,* or what Bourgeault defines as "the completed human being,"[29] who has not only fully integrated the masculine and feminine, the conscious and the unconscious, and is not only Whole in the Jungian psychological sense, but has also united their humanity with their divinity.

COSMIC FAMILY THERAPY (PART 2)

Since the Mexican restaurant, Sarah's life feels as real to me as my own. In fact, whenever something is up in my life, another layer of *her* life is revealed.

Often what I experience with Sarah in the *between* is something along the lines of cosmic family therapy. It isn't glorious; it's raw and emotional and gritty soul work. Who Sarah was and what she "held" needed to be planted *energetically* in the dark, silent earth via a *female body,* but not bloom for two thousand years while the Church reigned in the light. From a wounded perspective, it has not exactly been a "fun" or "fair" mission. But, when Sarah sees from her *soul's* perspective, she grows quiet with remembrance, with reverence, with the realization of just how noble, how brave, and how necessary her dramatic act of a short life was for the planet, for the people, for the Divine Feminine. In other words, she failed no one. She is slowly beginning to accept and integrate this truth. I can feel Sarah's trauma loosening, like tight muscles that have kept her locked into a position that is out of alignment with her soul's current expression; I feel her releasing the past so she can bloom in the present. It is time.

Not too long ago I had a powerful dream: Jesus and Magdalene were on either side of me, holding my hands. I was their child. We walked through a town together, wearing filthy clothes as the townspeople yelled obscenities at us, spat on us, and acted with hatred toward us. So we started running, giddily, out of the town and down to this wooden dock from which we jumped into the sea. Under the warm turquoise water, we unclasped hands and floated away from one another. After a while, these large, luminous stingrays rose underneath each of us and gently deposited us back onto the dock. Our previously dirty clothes were now sparkling clean. Once I made sure Magdalene was okay, I looked for Jesus, who was sitting a short distance away, catching his breath. I grabbed Magdalene's hand, and we walked over and sat down with Jesus, forming a triad with our bodies.

I knew if the townspeople saw us together like this again, they would freak out, but I didn't care.

I was so tired of being forced apart.

I leaned toward Jesus and Magdalene, and collapsed into their arms. I cried oceans. I cried like crying would cry if it could cry. I cried like I needed to. I woke up the next morning with a soggy pillow and a healed commitment: To Them. To this planet. To you.

(Pause.)

Undoubtedly, my experiences with Sarah have helped me recognize and release my own wounds—feeling that not *all* of me is wanted or safe here; feeling that I am abandoned by God/dess, spiritually exiled, and orphaned; feeling shame, self-doubt, and confusion about my mystico-erotic feminine nature; feeling my soul's (not just my ego's) immense pressure to carry out my mission; and feeling the equally immense fear to hide and stay safe. Some people are known to receive the wounds of Christ—these wounds manifest physically as the stigmata, but they can also manifest *energetically,* leaving no physical marks. Sometimes I wonder if I've received the wounds of Christ's daughter. Sometimes, *I know* that every Western woman has.

In *Soulcraft,* Bill Plotkin says our wounds hold the keys to our destiny in this life. Fact is, we are *all* daughters of an ecstatically loving union between the Divine Masculine and the Divine Feminine, and it's time to carry out our collective mission. Our divine femininity is this planet's current savior. As a new generation of hopeful heretics, we're here to make some *serious* love. As Bourgeault sums up, "If I am right, then, the true progeny of Mary Magdalene and Jesus is the path of . . . love itself. Their intertwined hearts bear fruit in a distinctive flavor of love that is visionary, transformative, inclusive, and ubiquitously creative."[30]

(Pause.)

However *you* interpret all this is really none of my business. I'm not interested in convincing or converting. While I'm not attached to "past life" stories, I am attached to honoring the multivalent ways the Feminine Divine communicates, the multidimensional mysteries whispering through each and every one of us, the transformations that ensue by spending quality time inside ourselves, and the authentic power that arises from trusting our own knowing, *and putting what we've experienced and learned into action.*

My sessions in the *between* give me the courage and inner stamina to take solid steps in my ordinary life. They challenge me, stretch me, and awaken me. They unearth my self-imposed blocks. They help me face both my dark and light shadows. They grace me and they grill me as they grow me.

They Keep It Real.

And most importantly, these sessions in *between* bring me Red heart to Red heart with my Lady. That's right: My Red team constantly reminds me of my soul's desire—to love my Red Lady, out loud and on purpose. By doing so, I help my lineage, *naturally.* These sessions in between make me cry with relief and laugh at what previously felt like too heavy of a burden to carry. They help me become a better human.

Interestingly enough, after *one month* of cosmic family therapy (and after a year of writing through cement), my writer's block *finally* broke. Some people need life coaches to help them take a huge personal step and start a new project; I need Jesus's daughter.

IT'S TIME

Sarah asks us all to get a little wild, a little dangerous, and alotta free. She asks us to clean the mud off our faces, shake the dust off our memories, and open our hearts so wide that the planet falls in. She doesn't care if you believe in her story, but she does give everything to help you believe in the fiercely loving Feminine Divine ripping and roaring through *your* story.

Sarah doesn't allow herself to become rigidly defined or overly bloodlined. The past has given her no place, so the present offers her every place. Her mystery is more important than her history. Sarah gives us the freedom to project upon her what we need for our own personal and collective healing, and if we occasionally let go of what we need or believe, if we allow ourselves to venture into the nous and listen in the Ways of the Forgotten, we might also begin to hear what she has to say for herself:

Sisters,

It's Time.

Come Find Me.

But Know This:

When We Meet

There

Will

Be

No

More

Hiding!

DRAGON FIRE

Perhaps all the dragons in our lives are really princesses who are
waiting to see us act, just once, with beauty and courage.

RILKE
Letters to a Young Poet

According to the great mythologist Joseph Campbell, toward the end of every heroine's journey, she faces a slimy, fire-breathing, badass dragon (or two) that forces her to face her fears and fight for her soul's truth. Noela Evans tells us, "Challenge is a dragon with a gift in its mouth. . . . Tame the dragon and the gift is yours."[1] But, let's be real clear: Dragons can't be perfumed away with positive affirmations or cleaned up with simple spiritual techniques. Dragons rip open our wounds and make a mess. On Purpose. Yes, dragons are a terrifying but necessary sacred set-up, because they demand courageous *action*. They test us, with unrelenting fire, to find out if we've actually *metabolized* all the profound realizations we've acquired thus far on our soul's journey. Dragons demand we *walk* our spiritual talk, sometimes while wearing combat boots.

My original publisher was one of my dragons.

Four months after my Red family re-union, I *finally* turned in a manuscript to my publisher. Funny thing about expressing your soul's truth: not everybody likes it. My editor told me my manuscript was too dramatic, too emotional, too self-indulgent (labels pinned on *every* female memoirist), oddly written (my spaces and capitalization), not to mention strange, difficult to relate to, and therefore completely unhelpful to the reader. She told me that nobody cares about my personal journey since I'm not famous, and therefore this book would never sell. She explained that they, the publisher, contracted me because they thought I was going to "hit it big" in the spirituality arena, but this draft did not reflect their hopes or support their plans for me, at all. My editor then proceeded to cut out almost every vulnerable piece of my book, which felt quite a bit like she was cutting off the limbs of my own body. She finished our awesome meeting by telling me that I didn't have the literary chops to write a memoir and had forty-five days to write the self-help book they had originally contracted me to write.

(Sounds of gunshots hitting my Red heart.)

My editor's response was a lot like I had written out every single one of my worst fears about this book and then had her read them out loud to me. This was a *big fucking clue* that my editor was the perfect projection of my *own* self-doubt (I'm not talented enough to write without the help of my ex-boyfriend), wounds (my Red feminine experience and expression are unwanted by this world), and worries (by writing my personal story instead of a straight-up self-help book, I was no longer in service to you, my beloved reader, or, gulp, the Divine Feminine).

As I drove away from my publisher's office, I could barely see straight; my epic sense of failure blacked out my inner vision. But thankfully, I received a miracle (at least for a San Franciscan): a parking space. Right in front of the glorious Grace Cathedral. After I walked through the enormous sculpted-wood doors and practically crawled down the aisle on my hands and knees, I saw something Red out of the corner of my tear-filled eye. I veered left and found myself in front of a stunning modern Greek icon of Mary Magdalene painted in a bright-Red robe and pointing to an egg. It was inspired by a popular story in the Eastern Orthodox tradition:

Once upon a new millennium, a powerful spiritual teacher named Mary Magdalene decided to visit the Roman emperor Tiberius to tell him about the risen Christ. For this important meeting, Mary brought a white egg as a symbol of new life and Christ's resurrection (she also knew men dug visuals). After Mary shared the good news, Tiberius announced, "A human being can no more rise from the dead than the egg in your hand could turn red." Mary looked him straight in the eye (I imagine while cocking an eyebrow), raised the egg to her chest (directly in front of her heart), pointed to it, and presto, the white egg turned a deep shade of Red. Needless to say, Tiberius got on board after that sacred showdown. During our interview for my *Redvolution* film, Nancy Qualls-Corbett declared, "Magdalene brings us all this Red egg, which represents the passion for the potential of new life that is in all of us."

Passion

For

The

Potential

Of

New

Life

However, I wasn't feeling very passionate for a new life or a new book draft at that moment. Instead, I folded to the floor in front of M.M., sobbing.

Emily called me that night but couldn't get a word in edgewise. I waterfalled into the phone:

> "What *the fuck* is the point of writing my soul's truth if the final product sucks and doesn't help others?! Everything my editor said about my manuscript is true!!! I can't even argue with her! I can't believe I've wasted so much of my own and my publisher's life! And, how *the hell* am I supposed to write a self-help book in the next forty-five days about how to be a Redvolutionary?! I can only imagine the back cover:
>
> *How to lose your career, your fame, your fortune, your soul mate, your purpose, your coolness, and even become celibate!"*

After what I had been through—and was still going through—I couldn't imagine why anyone would willingly *want* to be a Redvolutionary. As Bill

Plotkin admits in *Soulcraft:* "To uncover the secrets of our souls, we must journey into the unknown, deep into the darkness of our selves and farther into an outer world of many dangers and uncertainties. [Those who do so] understand that no one would casually or gleefully choose such a thing."[2]

My agent—the professional liaison between myself and the publisher—called me the morning after my meeting with my editor to discuss our options. She gave it to me straight: I needed to make a final choice—memoir or self-help. My agent informed me, however, that if I chose memoir, I would need to trash the entire manuscript and learn how to actually write a memoir, which could take *years*. Also, choosing memoir meant I would have to leave my publisher, as they had made it very clear they *only* wanted a self-help book from me. My agent thought I should stick to the original plan, which is precisely what an agent is supposed to think, because it keeps me in line with my legal contract. Speaking of which, my agent then upped the ante by reminding me that if I didn't write a self-help book ASAP, not only would I lose the large amount of money coming to me, but I would owe my publisher the advance I had been living off this past year . . . and my publisher could take me to court. Also, to break my contract would interfere with every future publisher's consideration of my books. It could "quite possibly" *ruin* my writing career. (Big gulp.) My agent told me I needed to let them know my decision in a week.

Over the next four days, I couldn't eat or sleep. I experienced dizzy spells and stomach pains and developed an itchy, burning rash that covered my entire body. In addition, sciatica flared up, making it painful to even walk my dog around the block (the publisher had literally become a pain in my ass). I was a Red-hot mess. I finally went to a naturopathic doctor who, after running blood, urine, and saliva tests, worriedly told me that my body was past the burnout phase and was now in the process of shutting down. My doctor urged me to drop *everything*.

But I couldn't.

Now might be a good time to share with you one more thing my publishing editor was adamant about: nobody likes to read a book about how hard it was to write that book. I get her point. But I don't believe in it. Especially when the struggle to write said book mirrors the universal struggle between dragon and heroine, between lower ego and soul, between external world and internal world, between everything false and Her.

FEMSPEAK

The morning after my alarming doctor's visit, I received an email I've never received prior or since: an invitation to take a spiritual-memoir writing class. The email hit me like a sack of warm feathers. I wondered what the difference was between a memoir (which my editor and agent had made very clear I *don't* have the talent to write) and a *spiritual* memoir. So, I Googled, clicked on the first link (spiritualmemoir.com), and read how *spiritual* memoirs often include personal stories mixed with spiritual guidance, scholarship and theology mixed with dreams and visions, conversations between the writer and the Divine, and all sorts of *other*-worldly "freaky shit" and everyday ordinary drama. In other words, spiritual memoirs are mystical mashups between the sacred and the profane, the cosmic and the personal, and are less about literary style and more about soul style. A Red lightbulb turned on. Ah. Fucking. Ha. *This is what I've been intuitively writing all along.* I just had no label for it, until now.

Something else I found out: Spiritual memoirs have a history of being misunderstood by those who favor logos over eros, the D.M. over the D.F., facts over vision, sales over soul, and lines over circles. Carol Lee Flinders states in *Enduring Grace:*

> Visionary writing, particularly by women, has waited a long time to
> receive the informed and sympathetic reading it deserves. Its emotional
> intensity, imaginative flights, and erotic imagery have alienated more
> than a few male medieval scholars, for whom these qualities can seem as
> symptomatic of hysteria or irrationality as they are of sanctity.[3]

Once again, we've forgotten that God can sound like a Girl. Flinders admits that many female mystics of the past "wrote in that 'different voice,' whose inflections are only now being fully grasped. Informality, earthiness, warmth of feeling, a preference for open-ended literary form—these qualities have traditionally baffled and disconcerted men of letters"[4] and, apparently, certain book editors.

I speak Goddess, not English.

I dunno about you, but personally, I want to learn about the D.F. from someone who dares to speak Her. The good news is it doesn't take fancy techniques to speak Her. When you connect more consciously with your soul, it will naturally start to affect your human voice. Your soul's voice isn't just a voice "from the divine"; it's also how the Divine communicates *through* and *as* you. You mix and match together. Therefore, your soul might not always sound mystically poetic. She might speak some sort of spiritual street slang ("gangsta goddess") or swear like a sailor or sing like an angel. She might bubble beliefs like a valley girl with a wad of gum in her mouth, or twang truths like a kinky cowgirl riding bareback through the Wild West of reality, or bleep blessings like an "alien" from the fifth dimension, or float ideas like a planetary body that orbits just left of everything you think you know.

This is how She Speaks.

This isn't the *only* way the Divine Feminine speaks, but this is a voice that most of us have shut up because we have not been taught to respect or value it. We have been schooled out of it. This is the voice that doesn't give a shit about being literary or witty or pretty or marketable or "spiritual." As Teresa of Ávila warns us, "God is your business and language. Whoever wants to speak to you must learn this language; and if he doesn't, be on your guard that you don't learn his; it will be hell."[5]

Why is it so important to uncover and unleash your soul's voice? Well, because for women, finding their authentic voice is almost, if not quite, the equivalent to finding their true identity.

Every time you speak your truth,

a Goddess tattoos your name across Her Belly.

Creating space to listen and then express our soul's voice is one of our most important spiritual practices. Her voice is our lighthouse Home. While there's no *one* way or "right" way the Divine Feminine speaks, most of us do know when She *is* speaking. We can feel it.

FUGGEDABOUTIT

However, for many of us, our desire to express our soul is blocked by fears of what might happen if we actually do so. As upset as I was about my editor's orders to ditch my soul book, part of me also felt, well, *relieved.* The thought of actually *publishing* my "strange" soul book filled me with stomach-heaving, skin-flaming fear.

In *The Divine Feminine Fire,* Teri Degler informs us that despite how the thirteenth-century mystic Mechthild of Magdeburg paints an image of a Divine Feminine being "who is almost aching to hear us sing out and express ourselves,"[6] Mechthild is terrified, because she knows that her writing might not be accepted or liked, could be viewed as heretical, and might even cost her her life. Mechthild writes, "I was warned against writing this book. People said: If one did not watch out, it could be burned."[7] Degler tells us that one reason female mystics of the past finally wrote what needed to be written, despite their internal fears and external threats, was that they realized there would be a price to pay if they didn't. In fact, several of them became quite ill until they finally started writing what their soul was begging them to write.

Now, I'm not putting myself in the same room as the resplendent female mystics of the past, nor do I think this book is some great mystical text (I'm a *slow* learner and still in the awkward process of uncensoring my soul), but I *am* acknowledging that to share our unique voices and stories can be toe-curlingly terrifying when we have a history like we do. Cruel treatment of women who publicly express their truth, especially their spiritual truth, is part of our collective memory, and it affects our present lives and physical bodies in a variety of intense ways. But, facing the dark—past and present—is often a prerequisite for shining our light.

By unleashing our soul, we create energetic pathways for other women to do so as well. I know I could not be expressing what I am in this book if it weren't for the brave women who have dared to voice their souls before me. In my opinion, it's not only our mission to do whatever we can to voice our own souls, but it's also our responsibility to coax the soul voices *out* of other women. And no matter what comes tumbling out—a fireball or a feather, a peculiar dance or an animalistic moan, a shy smile or slippery tears, "blah bloh boyuu booger" or a personal story mixed with "the freaky shit"—we should nod with respect and say, "Hell yeah, Sista, bring it on. Bring. It. ON!"

Okay, back to my spiritual soap opera.

HANGING ON FOR DEAR LIFE

As I continued to peruse the spiritual-memoir website, my consciousness collected evidence from my past: that last difficult chapter of my college thesis where I felt divinely compelled to share my personal experiences and dreams; my Red journal; the destruction of my computer in graduate school, which, er, "encouraged" me to write my personal story with Kali in that Red paper instead of my academic treatise. I then thought about my cabin-fevered experience, when I had heard what my soul most longed to *express* in this lifetime:

Its love for the divine. After I put together the pieces of my puzzle, my palm found my forehead (Smack!): "Lady! You've been guiding me to write Our Love Story as it unfolds *for years!*" (I told you I was a slow one.)

Despite (or because of) this Redvelation, my mind whirled, desperately trying to find *some* way to stay with my publisher. Campbell reminds us: "The ultimate dragon is within you, it is your ego clamping you down,"[8] and my ego was not gonna give up without a fight. It was hanging on for dear life to this book deal — *the only thing left of my previous life* and the last remaining vestige of my professional pride. Besides reminding me of my agent's dire warnings and the fact that the publishing deal provided my only income, my ego cleverly convinced me that my publisher was the *only way to get my soul's voice out into the world.* In one of her keynotes, Caroline Myss warns, "God never calls you to something that doesn't challenge you on the earth level. Why? You have to be tested, you have to be broken, you have to choose which voice you will listen to."[9]

(Pause.)

You might be thinking right about now (or *way* before right now), "Come *on,* it's just a stupid publishing deal! I could've left without blinking!" And you probably could (or already have), because that's not your trigger. Something or someone else is. Our dragons look and act differently from each other; my dragon might be your hamster and vice versa. But we've all got 'em. You see, it's not about what the dragon looks like; it's about what the dragon activates *inside of us* that makes it so difficult to face.

In other words, this wasn't just about a book deal.

MY DRAGON'S DRAGON

When my spiritual stress level hit an all-time high, what felt like my *dragon's* dragon blazed onto the scene. Maya, *who happened to be submitting her book proposal to my publisher at that very time,* launched a new website and career slant that looked and sounded uncannily like mine, even using the same Red symbols and Red language . . . even creating a "Red Lady" blog.

(Deep, shaky inhale.)

When I saw Maya's new website, it felt like two thousand years' worth of purpose popped. My heart tore from my chest, and my cells cringed with fear. Attempting to make sense out of these extreme reactions, my mind quickly admonished me: "Sera, you're simply feeling threatened by her, just like you did in graduate school! It's time to grow up and out of this one. You certainly don't *own* the Red Lady! Maya has every right to share her own experiences and expressions of Red! In fact, that's what you *want* women to do — to express their Divine Feminine truth!" I thought of my favorite humorous greeting card by the company Papyrus, depicting a circle of dancing women with a text bubble over each of their heads, reading: "I'm the Goddess" "No, *I'm* the Goddess" "Get real, ladies, I'M THE GODDESS!" and tried to shake the trauma out of my system with humor.

But despite my attempt at comic relief and my spiritually correct reasoning, my reopened wounds wailed: Maybe Maya deserves to be the one who more publicly voices Red, because she's more confident, more soulful, more embodied, more fierce, more mystical, and definitely a gifted Writer with a capital "W"; she's not some stage-frightened, self-doubting, disembodied, untalented writer who loses her soul as often as she loses her keys. Maybe I'm too slow in my Divine Feminine development, and the Red Lady was choosing Maya to be Her personal spokesperson instead of me? Red amped up in graduate school when I met Maya; maybe Red was actually *her* mission, not mine — after all, we were so close, our mystical wires could have gotten crossed over the years. Maybe I wasn't a Red One after all, only a wannabe?

For some odd reason the obvious notion that Maya and I could *both* offer Red publicly didn't feel "right" for reasons I couldn't explain at that time, and the seemingly ominous situation made me cling tighter to my publisher.

(Awkward pause.)

Look, the soul path is *far from* logical or refined, and this unflattering, extra-emo part of my journey *really* isn't easy to share with you. However, I believe that the more honest we are about the *varieties* of dragons we host, the more we can identify them when they're breathing fire down our necks. As Tom Robbins reminds us in *Still Life with Woodpecker,* "We're our own dragons as well as our own heroes, and we have to rescue ourselves from ourselves."[10] When a woman recognizes, faces, and integrates a dragon, we all benefit from her valiance and gain that much more ability to recognize, face, and integrate (and sometimes slay) our own. The important thing to remember about dragons is that they guard our buried treasure. When a dragon appears, it means gold is right behind it . . . if we have the courage to stand our ground and fully meet it.

It was Meeting time . . .

A RUBY IN THE HEART
OF GRANITE

You are a ruby in the heart of granite.
How long will you try to deceive us?
We can see the truth in your eyes.
So come, return to the root of the root of your own self.

RUMI

I ntrepid soul sista, we have finally made it to the center of the Red rose or what Rumi calls "the ruby in the heart of granite." This is the darkest, yet most luminous, Place To Be.

And, the realm where our energetic shadow hangs out.

Say what?

Yep, it's time to introduce you more directly to the *energetic* shadow, which is related to the psychological shadow. (I've included quotes in this chapter about the psychological shadow to help communicate facets of the energetic shadow.) While both are hidden from our conscious minds, the energetic shadow is, well, more energetic in nature and operates multidimensionally. It's a vast collection of past-life and cosmic experiences, thoughts, feelings, and actions, many of which we've judged as "wrong" or "evil" and so shoved into the shady corners of our cosmic being, where they reside as concealed, yet still highly active, aspects of us. In fact, besides certain behaviors we exhibit and relationships we enter that stem from our energetic shadow, the energetic shadow often forms into a seemingly separate multidimensional "being" of its own that rides on the coat-tails of our "lighted" being and affects all those around us *just as strongly* as our light spirit does.

A Redminder: Energetic truth is often stranger than fiction—hell, even than science fiction—and much harder for our intelligent and even "spiritual" minds to reconcile. It's taken me years (and I'll venture to say lifetimes) of going through some extraordinarily painful and even dangerous experiences before I finally began to take my own and others' energetic shadows as seriously as I should and not brush them off as *only* psychological projections, defenses, or delusions. But here's the great thing about truth: It leaks through even the tiniest cracks, no matter what dimension it comes from. While defiantly mysterious and annoyingly intangible, the energetic shadow is always trying to get our attention via subtle but direct ways, like dragons, dreams, intuitions, somatic sensations, external signs (like websites), and other humans.

Why am I sharing all this with you? Because *every* human has an energetic shadow (in fact, I've noticed that those with the largest energetic shadows are often the most "spiritual" in appearance), *and* because I could only go so far on my spiritual journey without coming face to face with my *cosmic* journey and the energetic shadow that has developed as a result. In order to know and embrace my Self means I have to know and embrace *all* of my Self.

Alrighty then, let's *do this.*

THE RED RETURN

The night before I was to inform my publisher of my decision, Emily tried to help by telling me I was avoiding facing something, and it was Something Big. Fried to a crisp due to all that dragon fire, I told her if she couldn't offer me any real guidance, then I was getting off the phone. She retorted, "You see! This is your defended thing, Sera. You're doing everything you can *not* to face this, but you *need* to face it. It's right in your chest; just breathe into it and feel." I sighed, my voice dripping with sarcasm, "Fine, I'll *breathe into my chest,* but I have no idea how the hell this is going to help me make this life-changing professional, personal, and financial decision!" I got off the phone and *tried* to feel the thing in my chest. I even thought about dying whales and starving puppies to jump-start some emotions, but nothing was happening. I was as dry as a politician's speech and as empty as my bank account, so I watched a movie. Then I walked my dog. Then I took a shower. Then I browsed Facebook. Then I washed the dishes.

And then, I started to feel Something . . . slowly pressing against my insides, creeping more and more into my awareness. As I finished drying the last dish, I decided to let this Something have me. I sat my ass down on the couch and took some deep breaths into the center of my chest.

(Inhale. Exhale. Inhale. Exhale.)

Suddenly my inner sight cracked open, and I became privy to a super-fast slideshow of scenes from my past lives.

In one, I was wearing a filthy red dress, which was hiked up around my waist as my captors raped me and smashed my skull against the stone wall I was chained to. As my Red blood splattered against the gray walls and I started to die, I swore vehemently to myself and to God that I would never, *ever* practice Red again. There was another one of me and my sister priest-esses barricaded in our temple, burning alive. As the flames grew, so did the desolation. I felt totally abandoned by the Red Goddess we served. There was a scene from another lifetime in which I was a male in a pulpit preaching esoteric Christian ideas from a Red book. I knew that after I left the pulpit I would be killed. I knew, but I still spoke. In another, I was purposefully kept alive, forced to watch my children, my lover, and my community be slaugh-tered because of my Redness. Another lifetime, I was determined to fit in and be prim and proper and *not* Red. I was extremely vocal about my hatred of Red. I was a living dead woman, fiercely jealous of those men and women who hadn't doused their inner flame. In another, I'm male and actively per-secuting and killing those I deem "Red Ones"; their bright blood covers my hands as darkness covers my heart.

(Deep inhale.)

I have felt and caused so . . . much . . . pain related to Red.

What awes me during this slideshow is that no matter how hurt I've been or how badly I've hurt others, I've doggedly followed this mysterious Red thread as it's woven in and out of my lives . . . for eons.

> There's a thread you follow. It goes
> among things that change. But it doesn't change.
> People wonder about what you are pursuing.

You have to explain about the thread.
But it is hard for some to see.
While you hold it you can't get lost.
Tragedies happen; people get hurt
or die; and you suffer and get old.
Nothing you do can stop time's unfolding.
You don't ever let go of the thread.[1]

—*William Stafford*, "The Way It Is"

But there was more to see:

I'm shown how in most lifetimes, *starting in the womb,* I energetically chuck Red at someone/something else—like a flaming potato too hot to handle—because when my consciousness first touches my fetus body, it immediately remembers/encounters all the pain Red has caused me in past lives, pain that it can feel only in physical form, not in spirit form. I feel overwhelmed, horrified, doomed, guilty, not to mention ill-equipped, unworthy, and sure that someone else could do the Red job better than me. So the safer, smarter, more "spiritual" decision is to give Red away. To refuse It. To project It. As Robert A. Johnson stated in *Owning Your Own Shadow,* "Projection is always easier than assimilation."[2]

Every hair on my body stood on end as I witnessed how I'd projected Red onto *Maya . . . for lifetimes,* and I saw the habituated energetic shadows that were hiding behind our current friendship, confusing and influencing *both* of our lives. I realized that my dramatic upset over Maya's particular public usage of Red wasn't *just* petty insecurities or professional competition. There was Something *much* deeper at play. As Johnson wisely warned:

> Two things go wrong if we project our shadow: First, we do damage to
> another by burdening him with our darkness—or light, for it is as heavy
> a burden to make someone play hero for us. Second, we sterilize ourselves
> by casting off our shadow. We then lose a chance to change and miss the
> fulcrum point, the ecstatic dimension of our own lives.[3]

Next, I was given the Holy Understanding that my Red Tent is a metaphysical attempt to rectify what repeatedly happens starting in the womb. By consciously re-wombing myself, I had been giving myself the chance to retract my projections in order to rebirth my Self/the Divine Child. And, as recent external events demonstrated, it was time to withdraw the psychological, spiritual, *and energetic* projections in all my relationships—especially my relationship with Maya. It was time to retrieve what I had repeatedly given away, and finally embody Red.

I slowly came back to my human awareness, profoundly moved, forever changed, and yet still confused.

Why am I to embody Red in the first place?

WHAT . . . IS . . . RED?

Unsurprisingly, I received no answer to the question I'd asked a million times before. So, with a heavy sigh, I lifted myself off the couch and started to sweep the floor. As I made a pass with the broom near my parrot's cage,

the truth bombed me in the stomach.

Oh. My. Goddess . . .

I   AM   RED.

The Red thread I've been following lifetime after lifetime after lifetime

IS MY OWN SOUL.

I collapsed onto the floor,

awareness spreading everywhere,

and I began to comprehend *just what I have done.*

How I have thrown my soul away over and over (and over) again, or sold it, allowed it to be violated, abused or "used." How I've controlled my soul, puffed it up, pushed it down, squished it into a box, tricked it into a tradition, or streamlined it into a system, ignored it, hidden it, condemned it, silenced it, and even tried to kill it. And how I have *always* put something (social norms, my career, my relationships, my pride, my finances, my ego's desires, my fears, my success, my academic knowledge, spiritual beliefs, practices, authorities) before it.

From the smallest decision to the grandest choice.

It was suddenly all there.

Inside me.

I could barely stay in my body to acknowledge It, but I knew I had to, so I did.

I faced and felt *every single time* (in this lifetime and before) that I had abandoned my own soul.

I howled. I hunched. I hit. I heaved.

I clutched. I clawed. I cringed. I cried.

I choked repeatedly on my own tears and snot and blood and remorse.

I felt in a way I didn't think was possible without dying . . .

And then,

I Saw Her:

My Soul.

Dazzling directly across from me . . .

Burning so Bright.

Her Beauty

My Beauty

Our Beauty

Floored me. Enfolded me. Reminded Me.

She Was. For Real.

And, *right here.* Blazing in my living room.

Every cell in my body fell to its knees.

How could I? How could I? How could I have *ever* abandoned *Her?*

How could I have ever *not* chosen Her?

Clumsy words caterwauled out of my mouth:

"I'm so sorry so sorry so sorry so sorry . . . "

Slowly, almost shyly, She Embraced me.

Soon, I had no idea if I was Her or I was the crumpled human on the floor. We kept switching places. Sight merged with sight. Body with body. And then something stabilized. I was *Her* regarding my shaking, sobbing human form and feeling such pure unconditional love for it. While I knew that blessed body/being on the floor *had* to acknowledge her shadowy ways, "take responsibility for her past actions," feel the pain this repeated soul abandonment incurred, and make the honest apology, through my Soul's eyes she had done nothing wrong. Ever.

Then I was back on the ground, human and hushed, feeling a softening, a forgiveness, an already resurrection.

Wait, I had done nothing wrong???

(Ever.)

As my Soul's Embrace intensified, I was filled with a rose-petal soft Understanding that *all* my past "mistakes" were unerringly purposeful, part of a cosmic learning curve. I was made aware that my soul *chose every single detail* of those particularly rigorous lifetimes, even the torturous parts, to *grow* into a Being who knew and embraced all aspects of life, all aspects of Herself, and all aspects of Divinity. As Bill Plotkin wrote in *Soulcraft*, "Perhaps the soul sees to it, to catalyze a special type of personal development that requires a trauma for its genesis."[4]

My soul then showed me the trauma for our genesis: incarnation, when my soul *first* "separated" from her Divine Source in order to start her cycle of lifetimes on Earth. Immediately, I was wracked with that familiar homesickness that used to accompany me as a child on those Kiawah Island beaches.

> did you and I meet ever?
> > But in love our hearts are as red
> earth and pouring rain:
> > mingled
> beyond parting.[5]
> — *Cempulappeyanirar*

Gasping, I asked my soul Who or What we separated from when we first came into human form? Who or What was the Divine Source? She was quite clear in her answer:

The Red Lady.

So I asked my soul the obvious follow-up question:

"And, *Who* is the Red Lady exactly?"

Levels leaped, Layers lifted,

And

My soul sighed in sweet relief

as Recognition flooded us both

HOLY. SHIT.

I

AM

THE RED LADY!

The Red Lady isn't a Goddess outside of myself

SHE IS MY SELF!!!!!

It was like suddenly discovering I had a left arm.

In those Moments,

The Red Lady felt that real, that natural,

that
much
a
part
of
me
and
vice versa.

There's nothing more beloved than realizing for the first time *in your body* that the Divine Presence that's been flirting and firing through your life, challenging and supporting your every twist and turn, is actually *You*. A Greater Part of you; a part of you that resides in such a deeper space and on such a higher dimension (and thus, higher consciousness) that She often feels like a separate entity, like a Goddess outside of you.

In other words:

I was That Which I had been
seeking/serving/fearing/following/leaving and loving
for *all* my lifetimes.

As I have been retrieving fragments of my soul,
My Lady has been retrieving me.

MY TRUTH AND MY FALSEHOOD

You still with me? I know this is a lot to take in, but I wouldn't be including it if it weren't also serving *your* soul journey. There were a few last things my soul needed me (and you) to understand that Redvelatory night:

From my Red Lady's *much* bigger perspective, I Understood how my publisher, my best friend, my finances, my femaleness, "the matrix," patriarchy, religion, the Church, "the false light," the Inquisition, witch burnings, and threats of death had never really been "obstacles." They had actually been projections *of my own* forgetting, *and* necessary, time-released, cosmic challenges *pushing* me to face and burn through everything I had perceived to be in my way to simply being my Self on Earth.

The Reality Was: *nothing and no one* (including my own ego) can ever *truly* harm or separate me from my Divine Essence.

My soul next told me that I was now able to start the process of *letting go* of everything and everyone that I had perceived to be in my way to being my Self here. My soul whispered: "You can do it, Sera. You can stop focusing on 'them' and start focusing on Her. That's what will really change things. Thank them for the important roles they have played in your lives. Forgive them. And Let. Them. Go."

Like an exhausting game of tug-of-war I'd been playing for eons . . .

I finally Let Go.

And, I turned completely toward Her . . .

and almost shat my pants.

Because I had to *see* Her.

Not just my glorious true Red Lady, but also my energetic shadow Being, aka my *false* Red Lady, who has developed from unconscious reactions to my past lives. She was a masterfully manipulative Goddess, who seduced and enslaved beings, feeding off their adoration and keeping them addicted to Her Red energy, dependent on Her, and thereby distracting them from their unique paths. She was immensely powerful and immensely beautiful and immensely confusing, because She expertly exhibited all the shiny signs and incited all the flashy feelings of a Being of the false light "posing" as a Being of the true light.

What happened next is hard to describe accurately, but I saw false Red *as* true Red. Through true Red's unconditionally loving gaze, false Red appeared like a prodigal daughter, and, *undoubtedly*, a dearly missed piece of true Red's Being. Then, true Red simply Opened Her Arms in Choice:

Do You want to Come Home Now?

I saw false Red shimmer and shake and look around Herself—at the realities She had created, the beings She had lured, the power, the control, and the *divine status* that She thought She had—and then back at true Red . . .

and then straight at me.

Human Sera me.

Before I could pass out, my soul stepped forward, informing me that the only way to embody Red was to accept not just my true Red Lady but also my false Red Lady. I needed to be willing to embrace my All—my horror and my holiness, my murderer and my mystic, my Goddess and my SheDevil—in order to Come Home.

I was completely and totally awed by what "embodying Red" truly meant.

I was also completely and totally shit-storm terrified, but I couldn't help but trust what I was being offered, because I couldn't help but feel my Lady's love and longing for us both . . . Her *deep* desire for Our Re-turn.

So, I awkwardly opened my shaky human arms, and

We

Came

Home.

AFTERGLOW

The morning after that Redvelatory night, I broke my contract with my publisher, dismissed my agent, eternally altered my relationship with Maya, and chose to write this spiritual memoir. A few hours later, I came across an old photo that a childhood friend had posted on Facebook of himself, my sister, and me as young children, riding a small merry-go-round in someone's yard. What caught my attention in the image, besides our giddy grins and my snazzy Red OshKosh B'gosh corduroy pants, was a large, mysterious, translucent Redness that's almost touching me on the left of the photograph. Gasping, I looked closer and realized that the picture was taken from inside a house, through a window that must have been framed by Red curtains.

Tears poured as I saw how Red has really been here all along (even when I was a young Catholic purple lover), winking through whatever medium I had in front of me—be it a photograph, Buddhist dakinis, Sufi poets, Christian mystics, Zen masters, a fierce Hindu Goddess, the Gnostics, Eve's Red apple, Lilith's Red Sea, the Whore of Babylon, Magdalene and her daughter, dreams, books, movies, myths, music, airports, high-school track teams.

I've been following the Red brick road that the Universe has so lovingly laid down in front of me, *and* I've been wearing ruby slippers the entire time. Truly,

There's no Place like Home

REDEFINING DIVINITY

I went everywhere with longing
in my eyes, until here
in my own house
I felt truth
filling my sight.

LALLA

After reading the last chapter, you might be thinking a lot of things, but perhaps this in particular: "No shit, Sherlock! It's been crystal clear from page one of this hefty tome that *you* are Red!" I hear ya, but funny thing about humans—we're often the last ones to see our own truth. And there was something else I needed to receive in order to know the Red Lady as my Self—a radical redefinition of *divinity.*

Spiritual author Caroline Myss once admitted in an interview that it's easy on the spiritual path to "go the mental route, [saying] 'I'll create the God I want, with my own thoughts' . . . a mystical experience slaps me to my knees and says, 'Don't you dare create *Me,* I created *you!*'"[1] What I experienced in front of my potty-mouthed parrot's cage wasn't a mental construct, or just a psychological realization of Self (my Red Lady isn't a product of my psyche; my psyche is a product of Her), or owning my positive or "golden" shadow, or purely a metaphysical meeting of my higher self, or a classical mystical experience of soul illumination, or becoming One with God/dess. No, I experienced (and am still experiencing) Redvelations that slap me to my knees and make my master's degree in Comparative Religion from Harvard University barf all over itself.

You see, when I asked the Red Lady if She was my higher self, She laughed joyfully and said She was more like my higher self's *Higher Self*. She then proceeded to introduce me to my self *on each dimension of this Universe,* finishing with Her. This was the most extraordinary experience of all my lifetimes. The image and feeling was a bit like those wooden Russian dolls:

One

Inside

The Other

Inside

The Other

Inside

The Other . . .

Human Sera, inside my Soul, inside my Higher Selves,

inside The Red Lady.

Each dimension felt palpably different from the previous dimension, yet my soul and each of my distinct higher selves felt *profoundly* familiar. I knew them all, intimately. In fact, I exhibit facets of all of them in my human form, because we each make up Her Body as It stretches through the multiple dimensions of this Universe.

Although in terms of dimensions, my higher selves are "higher" (or deeper) than me (and each other), no one is "ruling over" the other. We work together. Each of us offers a particular perspective, specific skills, guidance, and agency, and thus, each displays an integral facet of Our Lady. We're like a Spiritual Swiss Army knife. But the part of us that definitely gets the most praise (she received a standing ovation from my higher selves) is the soul, who incarnates (or tries to) over and over again in various physical forms. That's by far the toughest gig.

Interestingly enough, although my *form* changes, and I eventually become *formless,* I have a distinctly *feminine essence* throughout each dimension. I realize this contradicts many spiritual beliefs and experiences, which relay that out of the body or on higher dimensions, we're neither masculine nor feminine or we're both, merged together as One. But what can I tell you, except *my own* experience?

However, the most mind-blowing Redvelation I experienced in that Mama of All Moments in front of my parrot's cage was this:

I am the Red Lady's *only* current *human* incarnation.

While others can be in relationship *with* the Red Lady (She gets around, if ya know what I'm sayin') and can learn from Her and love Her (just as I can relate to, learn from, and love *their* distinct Divine Being), and while others might share heretical mystico-erotic qualities and have similar past-life traumas and dramas and be part of the same lineage and experience part of their physical womanhood and Divine Feminine nature *as red* and resonate strongly with the *color* red, they are not an actual *extension* of my Red Lady.

Red isn't just a set of divine feminine qualities or a mystico-erotic path or a heretical lineage or even a color.
It is the Essence of me reflected through all of the above.

Bottom line: Just like our fingerprints are unique, our Divine Essence is irreducibly unique, and the Red Lady that I AM is for me to embody and transmit, and for me alone.

This Full-Bodied Recognition
This Conscious Re-Connection
This Righteous Reclamation

felt like *the* Key to Our Queendom.

Now, in order to get that "All This" is *not* pathological spiritual narcissism, I'm gonna break It down, Red style.

THROUGH RED'S PERSPECTIVE

The Red Lady is not *the* Goddess of *this* Universe (what I've called the Divine Feminine in this book). She is *a* Goddess In Love with this Universe. The Red Lady works in harmony with God/dess (particularly, with the D.F.) and is "one with" this Universe—but She is also individuated, an ever-evolving Goddess in Her own right.

In Red's words:

I AM a sovereign Divine Being

(and so are you).

Although we are (or, to be more exact, a *part* of us is) currently inside this Universe and therefore experiencing and expressing our Self through *this* Universe's consciousness and matter (for example, our physical body is created from Its elements), we do not *originate* from what we have traditionally called God/dess or this Universe. Much like how our human parents created our body but did not create our soul, our "God parents" created our Body but they did not *create* our *Essence*. From Red's perspective, our Essence comes from *outside this Universe*. We are eternal, infinite. We have always existed. In fact, we are each *our own* evolving Universe, just like this one. Another way to look at it: We're not just different expressions of the same Being; we are also different Beings currently expressing through the same Universal Medium. We are united, yet distinct. Interdependent, yet independent. Different, but equal. One, but many.

That's right, through Red's eyes, we are all Gods and Goddesses undercover, currently choosing to take the epic ride through *this* Universe's dimensions via countless "incarnations" (not just on planet Earth) in order to experience the full spectrum of life in *this* particular Universe, while also sharing our unique perspectives and gifts with one another, learning "new skills," and evolving this Universe and *our own Universe*. To facilitate this Grand Co-Creative Experience, we play roles for each other — both light and dark and everything in between. We've made this Grand Experience so effective and real by agreeing, prior to taking the plunge to the lower dimensions, *to forget our own Godliness*. Call it "chosen cosmic amnesia." This was *very* brave of us to do. In my opinion, it makes us pretty hardcore Beings. While the forgetting was useful, it's time, *really* time, for many of us to Remember.

Re-member

It's time to Come Home to Our Selves

while in human form and *while not forsaking this beloved planet.*

However, as you've witnessed in this book and perhaps in your own life, this journey Home while keeping our feet planted on terra firma ain't exactly a piece of cosmic cake or a blissful day at the beach. Knowing you are a sovereign Divine Being and *living as this truth* as an ordinary, imperfect human is the most radical and *dangerous* spiritual practice, ripe with mistakes and miracles. So, while our spiritualized egos might get excited over this notion, in reality, most of us do our best to avoid what this reclamation actually requires. Also, many of us don't know or believe we are Something to "claim" in the first place.

Yep, many of us have grown accustomed to our self-prescribed, self-perceived "lower" spiritual status in this Universe, and unfortunately, there are those who do not want us to wake up to our Divine sovereignty. Through Red's lens, some "false gods" (and "false goddesses") in the "cosmic matrix" have benefitted and grown accustomed to keeping us small and disempowered and, well, I'll just say it: under their control—"worship/follow/obey ME, not your own soul!" (Reread my distinctions between true light beings and false light beings in chapter 6.)

The cosmic matrix infuses our third-dimensional matrix. Together, they have imprinted us with information that supports our fragmenting and forgetting. And this is not just via the social, media, political, and economic arenas, but also through religious and spiritual arenas, which often teach (in some form or another) that we should lose not only our false self but also our distinct Divine Identity . . . perhaps by blindly following or mimicking an enlightened spiritual figure or by "getting out of the way" so *another* Being can come through us or by blending into "Oneness" or by merging back into "Source" or by dissolving into "No Self."

From Red's Perspective, while within this incomprehensibly vast Universe, our Beings have chosen to taste all kinds of "enlightened states" and explore all types of "afterlifes" and heavenly realms and participate in *colossal* multidimensional spiritual paradigms for *epochs* of soul time. However, most of these spiritual states, systems, realms, realities, and beings *don't truly* encourage our sovereignty, nor do they point us toward our *unique* Divine Essence, because they are fulfilling important roles and/or have become co-opted or infected by too much "false" light

(Sharp inhale.)

Hold up. My inner patriarch is going berserk:

"What in God's name are you writing, Sera!!!!!"

(Pause. Feel. My Heart.)

I'm Here, Sera.

As Real as your heartbeat.

As Necessary as your breath.

As True as your soul.

I'm Here.

I know you wonder if you can hack This,

but you can, you're not alone.

Sera. I'm *Here*.

(Deep exhale.)

Onward.

From Red's perspective, if I ignore or "skip over" my soul, higher selves, and distinct Divine Being to, for example, attain nondual consciousness or Emptiness or some transcendent state or to "surrender to God," which most spiritual systems directly *or indirectly* promote as "The Ultimate Goal," I'm participating in a kind of *multidimensional bypassing*. Govert Schuller shares a related view given by the nineteenth-century theosophist Madame Blavatsky:

> She writes that certain [religious] doctrines . . . have the effect of disconnecting the soul or the personal self from its higher source, the higher self. This in turn might cause the "second death" of the soul, which is like an implosion of consciousness into nothingness, as opposed to the "second birth" of the soul when she expands into divinity by first uniting with the higher self and ultimately with the divine self. These differences are not just philosophical and void of spiritual relevance. From an esoteric point of view they are of great significance.[2]

This is part of the reason that participating in traditional religion and New Age spiritualities often felt like I was abandoning Something Essential. What I was abandoning included, but was more than, my femaleness, my ego/personality, my modern lifestyle, my Western individualism, my sexuality, my body, my shadow, my psychological Self, my soul and higher self, and even the Divine Feminine. I was *also* abandoning my very Divine Essence HERSELF, the Red Lady. The confusion, self-doubt, and self-*harm* I've gone through as a result are staggering and should not be quickly dismissed. I know I'm not the only one who has suppressed her inner reality if it did not match more commonly agreed-upon spiritual realities. While the original forgetting of our Godliness had a sacred point, we have become overly attached to that point.

"Don't you know, ye are Gods?" —Jesus (from John 10:34–35)

To be clearer than the Buddha's bathwater: My Red perspective isn't some metaphysical variation of the psychospiritual platitude "You have to find your self in order to lose your self." The highest dimension of my Being is, and will always be, Red. She is the only thing "solid" about me. Red will never eventually or ultimately merge "back" into God/dess. The Ultimate ride *for me* isn't about losing *any* part of my Self; rather, it's about coming into conscious alignment with *every* part of my Self.

I found my Red Lady through dualisms—God/Goddess, spirit/soul, masculine/feminine, light/dark, positive/negative, true/false—and over my soul's cosmic trajectory, I have experienced being *both* sides of the One (and every in-between); however, Wholeness happens when I surrender to Her distinct Nature. It is submerged in Her unique Being that all dualities collapse their purpose into One. And *She* is left standing, well, dancing.

> On foot
> I had to walk through the solar systems,
> before I found the first thread of my red dress.
> Already, I sense myself.
> Somewhere in space hangs my heart,
> sparks fly from it, shaking the air,
> to other reckless hearts.[3]
>
> —*Edith Sodergran*

What I'm sharing also isn't just an extreme case of Western individualism. However, it does expand the popular motto "Stay true to yourself" *way* beyond our egos (and this third dimension) into a Sacred Imperative to stay true to our multidimensional *Divine Self.* When I follow Her will (not my ego's or someone else's will), I'm in harmony with the will of the God/dess of this entire Universe, because the highest dimension of me—the Red Lady—is one with this Universe as a uniquely integral piece. Aligning with my Divine Self aligns me with God/dess. Surrendering to my Divine Self surrenders me to God/dess. In fact, it is only *through* Her that I can totally relate with God/dess. It is only *through* Her that I can Receive All of what I AM Here to Receive and Give All of what I AM Here to Give.

The Red Lady is both the God of me and *my Way of "worshipping" the God of this Universe.* As the Gandharva Tantra says, "One should worship a divinity by becoming oneself a divinity. One who has not become a divinity should not worship a divinity. Anyone worshipping a divinity without becoming a divinity will not reap the fruits of that worship."4 Claiming my Self as a Divinity does not inflate me. It directly Relates me. To Life. To You. To God.

That's right, my divine sovereignty doesn't separate me from you or diminish my devotion to the God/dess of this Universe *one bit*. Instead, this re-experienced truth continually deepens my intimacy *with*, and heightens my reverence, respect, and love *for*, each Divine Being who is taking this valorous ride of creation with me, and most especially, for the God/dess of this Universe who is allowing us to experience our Selves *through ItSelf*.

Through Red's eyes, this entire Universe is about Relationship—between the most minute particles and the grandest galaxies, between the chicken and the egg, between the ocean and the sand, between this book and the Energy that inspired this book, between the light and the dark, between the masculine and the feminine, between spirit and soul, between everything and no-thing, between true and false, between inner and outer, between friend and foe, between that dimension and this dimension, between my hand and your heart, between your foot and the ground, and most important, between you and You, you (You) and God/dess, you (You) and "Them," and well, you get the gist. Essentially, this makes everyone and everything our Lovers.

And like the Ultimate Intimate Spiritual Partner, the God/dess of this (and as this) Universe helps us Remember *our own Divinity*, no matter how far our consciousness strays or how fragmented we've become or how many wounds we have incurred. When I open to this truth, when I allow myself to really *feel* this Universe's determination—naw, Its dedication; naw, Its *devotion*—*to us* . . . well, there are no words; only sobs.

The way Home isn't just *through* Self Knowledge, but also *through* Self Love. The old adage is true: We cannot truly love another (or the God/dess of this Universe) until we love ourselves. And the Love we long to experience *most*, above and beyond all else, is with our Selves. So this Universe kindly sets us up for the Fall . . . and *then*,

We are romanced into our own Remembrance.

We are seduced by our own soul.

We are serenaded (and, okay, sometimes *spanked*) by our Divine Self

until we come to Realize that

We are the Ones we've been waiting for, searching for, praying for.

In other words, You've been calling yourself back into Your own arms from the moment you swallowed the belief that you've been separated.

You were tagged

(a long, *long* time ago)

and

You

Are

It!

You, sent out beyond your recall, go to the limits of your longing.
Embody me.[5]

—*Rilke*

This isn't narcissistic delusion; It's Beloved Inclusion. As Bourgeault wrote in *The Meaning of Mary Magdalene,* "To discover myself as a divine being is certainly a spiritual attainment, but to discover myself as the divine *beloved* is to discover something even more intimate and profound about the hidden treasure that God longs to make known."[6]

The prevailing view of many spiritual traditions is that there is a further step beyond the Lover–Beloved relationship, and that is to merge into oneness with the divinity of our devotion. However, Bourgeault tells us that the inner teachings of Jesus and Magdalene point to an even *greater* step, and that is:

> The discovery that deeper than *at-one-ment* lies *comm-union,* love come
> full in the act of giving itself away . . . "a not one, not two, but both one
> and two," in which the continuous exchange of twoness and oneness in
> the dance of self-giving love captures the very dynamism of the divine
> life itself.[7]

This dance Between Us is what I live for and as. Sometimes my Lady and I are so Together, there's no difference, while at other times, we're so different that we long to be together. I am Beloved to Her; I am Her. She is Beloved to me; She is me. We are In Relationship not only with each other, but also with this entire Universe, *as* Red Hot and Holy Love.

Through a Red perspective, this reciprocal exchange of Divine Love is our Universal Birthright . . . as "ordinary" humans. Knowing we are Beloved changes *everything*. We stop covertly or overtly seeking to be loved outside of our self, through our external relationships, our careers, our outfits, our Facebook statuses, and even our "spirituality." Statistics show that when a human knows that she is loved unconditionally, she is able to shift unhealthy habits more easily and experience wider ranges of intimacy, generosity, and creativity. She is able to relax into her Self. And she is able to spread this belovedness like the sun spreads its shine. Effortlessly. Fact is, when we accept our distinct Divine Being's love for us, and return it with gusto, we begin to radiate and attract a whole new reality for this planet.

Be. Loved.

Not only are we here to Know and Love our Selves, but we're also here to *Be* our Selves. We're here to unleash our distinct divinity *into* divinity. I serve the evolution of this Universe by expressing *my* unique Essence. This Universe realizes Its potential as each of us realizes our own. Like countless colors in a painting, we all have to Be What We Are in order to create the whole picture.

Be Your Self

Through a Red perspective, this prodigious *process* of forgetting and remembering, of hiding and revealing, of seeking and finding, of leaving and coming Home, of falling and rising in Love with our Selves and this entire Universe, *is* "God" and, in my opinion, *the greatest Love Story ever co-created,* starring each and every one of us.

LADY LOVE

As you've read, in my particular journey, the *feminine face of God* has guided me to my soul and my Red Lady Identity. I had to create a more intimate relationship with the feminine expression of this Universe to even *begin* to recognize, relate to, and reclaim *my own* unique Divine Feminine embodiment. In *Passionate Enlightenment,* Miranda Shaw wrote:

> To know oneself as an embodiment of the divine is to gain access to
> the ultimate source of spiritual authority within. . . . Women must
> discover the divine female essence within themselves. This should
> inspire self-respect, confidence, and the "divine pride" that is necessary.
> . . . Divine pride, or remembering one's ultimate identity as a deity,
> is qualitatively different from arrogance, for it is not motivated by a
> sense of deficiency or compensatory self-aggrandisement. . . . When

a woman reclaims her divine identity, she does not seek outer sources
of approval, for a firm, unshakable basis for self-esteem emanates from
the depths of her own being.[8]

The Divine Feminine has been my Ultimate Life Coach, teaching me to
accept and celebrate the sanctity of this earth, my body, my femininity, my
soul, my distinct Divine Being. It has been through and with the Divine
Feminine of this Universe that my Red Lady has come back to life in and
as me. And it is through my Red Lady that I am now able to more fully
participate in the Divine Feminine expression and experience of Life. They
have both birthed me Alive. While I am in an evolving relationship with
the Divine Masculine of this Universe (since I am also "in" Him and "of"
Him), my Red heart beats clear: I am here to be of specific Service to the
Divine Feminine.

And part of my Divine Feminine Service is to incarnate the Red Lady, who,
on *this* dimension, prefers to hang out on dance floors and in warm oceans,
roses, and the soft, gooey space between "right" and "wrong." She smells
like new beginnings. She loves to laugh, wink, and shake her ass. She tickles
tradition and spanks stagnancy. She plays with fire. She speaks a demanding
language that you can only understand if you are naked, drunk, and willing
to let go of everything you've been told God is or isn't. And Oh Yes, She is
deeply, madly, passionately in love with you. Yes, you. And She will go to
any and all lengths to remind you of this truth. Of your truth. Of our truth.

CLEARING MY THROAT

You certainly don't have to swallow my Red pill about Who We Are and
What this Universe Is. Trust your own experiences and inner knowings,
which may be vastly different from my own. After what I've experienced—the unprecedented uniqueness of each Being, the soul's specific
trajectory, and the precise timing of our flowering—I'm no longer interested in turning you into my Red Self (yep, I created a whole career out of
my disowned Self) or persuading you to join my Redvolution. That would
be bitch-slapping the entire point of our existence. I offer my ever-evolving
experiences and ever-widening Red perspective to the altar of our outra-
geous Mystery. As Robert Rabbin stated:

> Here it is, my opinion: existence, creation, the cosmos, whatever the
> hell you want to call this incomprehensible mystery in which we live
> and of which we are a part, this thing is so huge, so vast, so complex and

multi-dimensional that no one, no one, not even the latest guru du jour, not any scientist, saint, or sage, not any writer or artist, not any one who ever lived at any time in any place—no one knows nor can say the whole truth of the whole thing. They can only say, Hey, I've got my hand on one cell of this enormo-gigan-tic beast of being and it feels like such and so.[9]

Something else I want to be as straight as a divine arrow to your heart about: You can find your God/dess Self anywhere and everywhere. If a tradition or teacher or practice feels in alignment with your soul, then trust it. All paths lead Home . . . eventually. Essentially, anything "true" out there isn't attempting to fill you up with more information or exercises or philosophies or paradigms or belief systems or techniques or "how-to's"; it is actually pointing its metaphorical finger right back at you: What Do *You* Know?

> Always we hope
> Someone else has the answer . . .
> At the center of your being
> You have the answer,
> You know who you are
> And you know what you want.
> There is no need
> To run outside
> For better seeing.
> Nor to peer from a window.
> Rather abide at the center of your being;
> For the more you leave it, the less you learn.
> Search your heart
> And see
> The way to do
> Is to be.[10]
>
> —*Lao Tzu*

An interesting side effect of living more and more from the Center of my own Being: I can sense when others are *not* living from their distinct Divine Being, but rather from someone else's Being or from a belief system they've learned or a tradition they were born into or a theory they studied or a "channeled doctrine" from disincarnate beings or a paradigm they are promoting or an external "god" or "goddess" or simply the wide Universe Itself. And as wonderful as some of these things may be (and as much as we might resonate with them and receive authentic help from them), it still bums me out a little—OK, a lot—because I *also* want to know *Them.*

I want to know *You.*

I hope this goes without saying, but you don't need to have visions or cosmic experiences, you don't have to pop past-life pimples or go through a dark night of the soul in order to realize your Self. Your distinct Divine Being is dropping hints of Itself all over your life. You just gotta pay attention. And in my opinion and experience, the healthiest way to engage your Divine Being is through creating a more conscious and intimate relationship with your soul. She is the part of your Divine Being who incarnates; she is the bridge, the link to your Everything. She knows your past, present, and future better than any book or teacher or psychic or spiritual tradition. She knows what you should read, who you should hang with, and where you should go, *now.* In other words, she knows how and when your unique Being unfolds *organically.* You don't want to force *this* rose to bloom or follow someone else's seven steps. If you relax, if you trust your soul, she will lead you to your Self. It will be a crazy journey—as unique as a snowflake, as transformative as a fire, as freaky as a fruitcake, as mysterious as a Universe.

So, please. Become your favorite subject. Study your Self. Sit at the feet of the Teacher inside you. Cop a feel of your Divine Body. Live *your* Love Story. And share what you are learning with the rest of us.

If you've read any self-help or mainstream spiritual book in the past fifty years, you've been told you have something invaluable to offer this planet. But I'm guessing you might not have realized *just how much you have to share* and just how invaluable your own perspective and Love Story actually are. You are, quite literally, not only a soul who's had countless experiences and expressions, but also an entire Universe of Wisdom here to Offer your Self In and As Service.

While yes, Re-membering our Divinity doesn't happen overnight or even in one lifetime, the path *itself* is an honest (and often the most helpful) place to share from. Sure, sharing and living our truth might make others think we're coming back in our next life as a toad (or worse)—but to heaven with 'em. We hafta walk our inner talk, toad-doomed or not.

This is what it means to be a heretic . . .

When I turn in my own Divine direction.

When I stop worrying about what others think of me, and I just let it all go,

like tight pieces of clothing that were never created for me, but rather from someone else's idea of what I should be.

And I'm naked.

Alone.

And yet, with Her.

And I yell with all my womanly might, "Yo! Red Hot Mama! I'm Here! I'm Yours! For *Real!* So, now, *You* clothe me, *You* guide me, *You* show me who I am and what the hell I'm really made of!" And She comes forward, laughing and holding this ridiculously gaudy two-way mirror, which allows me to see myself and to see Her at the same time. Our images merge and overlap. We point and chuckle and high-five. We lean in, allowing our breath to fog the mirror, and we draw "I (heart) you" with our fingers. And I turn around,

Revealed.

BURN, BABY, BURN

Why, with these red fires, are the rubies
ready to burst into flames?

PABLO NERUDA
Extravagaria

A m I fully embodied now? Have all my wounds that opened in my Red night of the soul been healed? Am I a surrendered incarnation of a Red Hot and Holy Love Goddess? Hells no. Although Something Sacred solidified inside me that Redvelatory night (and the Red nights that followed), it will most likely take the rest of my lifetime to fully integrate and implement these ongoing Redvelations. In other words, I'm still being cooked in Her cosmic oven. I'm rare and have a long way to go before I'm "well done."

Placing my soul and my Red Lady first, *above all else,* is a spiritual practice like *nothing* I have ever encountered before. As Caroline Myss wrote in *Entering the Castle:*

Talking about spiritual teachings, and reading about them, is not a substitute for living them on a daily basis in the arena of your life. You must be willing to incarnate your theology and illuminate the world around you with the power of your soul, a power that ironically may not even require your voice at times. Such power comes through even in silence. Your sole/soul requirement is to commit to being devoted to your inner authority — to the divine. That devotion will give you the will to follow through on all that you are guided to do, say, and become in this life.[1]

Every time I act from my inner reality, I feel another anchor drop into my Divine Essence. Every time I honor my humanity, I feel another tendril of life delicately unfurling through me. And every time I surrender to my Lady, I feel Her total trust . . . *in me.*

I'm still rockin' the angelic vibe (can't escape what I am on *one* dimension), but my wings have returned to their natural Red color; they have become dirty and frayed from rubbing the ground; and I'm pretty sure one of 'em is pierced. Despite how much I've grown into my life the past years, I realize my "issues" might *never* go away, but because I'm more conscious of them, I'm better at working with them — and more important than just "working with them," I'm better at *accepting them* as simply part of being human. Although tempting at times, I know they don't all need to be "fixed" in order for me to be Who I AM; in fact, I've become a bit of a champion of some of my "flaws" (like my shaky, sometimes window-shatteringly high physical voice), because I see them as battle scars, honest responses to more-than-worthy traumas that my intrepid Being has incurred on Her awe-inspiring journey through the lower dimensions of this magnificent Universe.

Over these Red-hot years, I've come to learn that there's simply no forcing my Lady's incarnation; there is only growing in burning devotion for Her and, paradoxically, *as Her.* In other words, there comes a point in your path where you need to fiercely embrace that which you are still in the process of becoming.

TURNING INSIDE OUT

Having taken the necessary time in, I can feel Her tenderly turning me inside out. While I know that spiritually I will be in the Red Tent forever, it is time now to expand my physical Service on this planet. The inhale is always followed by an exhale. We go In to go Out.

A few years ago, the Dalai Lama reportedly stated, "Western women will save the world." While I'm not sure if I entirely agree with him, I sense he *was* onto something. Many of us in the West are graced with the time and the means to consciously participate in the process of embodying our souls; thus, it has become our sacred responsibility to do so. It's not only a privilege to get up close and personal with our soul and the shadows that accompany her, it's also our duty. As Carl Jung wrote:

> Such a [wo]man knows that whatever is wrong in the world is in [herself] himself, and if [s]he only learns to deal with [her] his own shadow [s]he has done something real for the world. [S]he has succeeded in shouldering at least an infinitesimal part of the gigantic, unsolved social problems of our day.[2]

However, many of us in the West resist this sacred duty or don't really get the point of it, especially when the spirit path is so much "lighter" and seemingly simpler. And, the soul path offers *no* glittering "self-help" guarantees, such as *instant* "Happiness! Success! Abundance!" but it *does* offer us a life of integrity, authenticity, and truth, which fills us with a kind of holy happiness (and holy hilarity) that is independent of external conditions.

As I write this last chapter, I have no publisher, no career, no human partner, and limited finances. I do not look or feel like a fabulous, sassy goddess who "gets everything she wants." In fact, I look and feel like I've been through a battle, the toughest battle of my life. I have no idea what will happen to me or this book. We both could be viewed as failures. But I do know one thing: I have my soul. And this is *true* success. As poet David Whyte acknowledges on his CD "Self-Compassion,"

> The soul doesn't seem to make the distinction between the light and the dark. It chooses both. It doesn't care whether you do something successfully or fail at it; it just wants to know, did you do it in your way? Was it you who failed, or were you trying to be someone else when you failed? If it was you, the soul is happy, because it was your experience, your failure, and no one can take it away from you. Question is not: Did you fail, or did you win? The question becomes: Did you go your own way?[3]

I'm going my own Way.

Another reason we avoid soul work is that we're busy dealing with our "real lives." In *Conscious Femininity,* Marion Woodman said she's often asked: "Why indulge myself talking, reading, learning about or voicing my soul when I may lose my job? My marriage? Or when I can barely pay my bills?" She answers: "The point is that the loss of soul connection, loss of connection to our femininity, may be the real cause of our anguished condition."[4] Living without our soul leaves an ache in our belly that *nothing else can fill.* When you connect more consciously with your soul, her wisdom and grace will help you with *everything* in your busy life. Soul work isn't another "thing" you have to "do" in your life. It *is* your life.

According to Woodman and other experts, our lack of soul connection is projected into the world around us. We can witness it in the environmental devastation, rampant consumerism, political corruption, economic crisis, 50 percent divorce rate, body-image disorders, poverty, abuse, rape, and a host of other unhealthy epidemics we are currently facing. Sufi teacher Anat Vaughan-Lee says, "What we deny ourselves we deny to all of life. In denying the feminine her sacred power and purpose, we have impoverished life on personal and global levels in ways we do not understand."[5] The polls are in: If we dare to continue without our souls, life as we know it will end. There is simply no more time for denial. It doesn't take a doomsdayer or a news anchor or an environmentalist or an economist or a whale or the Mayan calendar to tell us that the shit is hitting the fan on this planet. In this day and age, *more than any other time in history,* we *need* to be consciously connecting with our soul as much as we need to be breathing air. When we feel lost, she is our truest compass. When the news slams us with fear, she is our inner resource of Love. As the world continues to change, she is our wisest adviser, our natural-born leader, communicating the best course of action for us *and for this planet.* She is our inner reality check. Learning to follow internal divine direction before external direction is not just an airy-fairy spiritual ideal; it directly affects human and planetary survival. It is the most practical and most compassionate thing we can do—and the most natural.

Once we reawaken the soul force inside of ourselves, we can't help but recognize and honor it in *every living thing.* We stop asking Life, "What will You do for me?" and we start asking Life, "What can I do *for You?*" Surrendered, we become much more effective with our acts of Service, because we're fueled not just by our willpower alone, but also by a Cosmic Life Force that *never* runs out of energy. This means we stop doing service with a lowercase "s"—that is, acts of service we think we *should* do or have been taught to do—and we start doing Service with a capital "S"—or Service we were *specifically created to do.* Service no one else can do except us. As Bill Plotkin so beautifully wrote in *Soulcraft:*

> The gift you carry for others is not an attempt to save the world but to
> fully belong to it. It's not possible to save the world by trying to save it.

You need to find what is genuinely yours to offer the world before you can make it a better place. Discovering the unique gift to bring to your community is your greatest opportunity and challenge. The offering of that gift—your true self—is the most you can do to love and serve the world . . . and it is all the world needs.[6]

So.

Another way to approach our Holy Heavy Duty is by using a simple gratitude-filled perspective shift: It's not that we *have* to take the often-arduous journey to consciously embody our souls in order to help save the planet; it's that we *get* to. We get to be our mystical, multidimensional, witchy, wise, passionate, playful, erotic, goofy, grounded, pissed-off, beautiful, badass, radically loving, uniquely Divine Feminine Selves out loud and On Purpose and in *Full* Service to Life. After all, there's nothing more powerful than a woman who has embodied her soul, a woman who doesn't just *believe* she's an incarnation of the Divine Feminine but dares to act like it.

So . . .

(Heart beating.)

You In?

While your soul is always with you, there are certain "come hither" gestures you can make to connect even more consciously.

First, right here, right now, with all of your heart, simply say to your soul . . .

that you're ready.

Ask her to turn up her volume in your daily life, and learn to listen to her when she calls you. Over time and with practice, you will learn to discern her voice from the myriad other voices running around your mind and body. She is constantly communicating with you, but it takes a willingness to become accustomed to her language, which is different from your ego or fast, witty mind or even the "love and light" language of your spirit. She speaks best through dreams, metaphor, symbols, synchronicities, your body, and your feelings, always communicating simple, but powerful, life-changing messages such as:

This is not the right relationship. This job is suffocating. Stop meditating so much. Start dancing more. Now, sit still. Ask that difficult question.

Dare to hear the answer. Read that book. Volunteer at that organization. Listen to that friend. Trust that teaching. Vote. Go on that date. Play with your dog. Speak the truth to that person. Breathe. Deeper. Cry. Harder. Laugh. Louder. Get messy. Get clean.

You're not alone

I've got your back.

Remember.

I'm Here.

Soon, your soul will start to feel like a palpable presence you are intimately a part of and she of you, and you can invite her more and more into your body's awareness by consciously sitting with her, dancing with her, moving and listening and speaking and touching and loving as her. Undoubtedly, there will come a time when your soul will demand *even more* of your conscious attention. When the pressure to Know and Love and Unleash your Divinity will move up a notch (or ten). There will come a time, a time that's been decided by your distinct Divine Being (not anything or anyone outside of you), when you will be asked to:

Come forward,

Closer still

Till "closer" has meaning no longer.

And it will be thrilling and terrifying and gorgeous and annoying, and there will be days when you will question everything and tell the Universe to screw Itself, and other days you will be trusting everything and telling the Universe to Bring It even more. But no matter *the utter insanity of your soul's sanity,* you will *know* that

This

Is

IT.

The Truest Thing You Were Born To Experience.

And you will be

So

Fucking

Grateful

that you Remembered.

(Exhale.)

Remember, the process *is* the point. The D.F.'s not just in the finished, polished product, but also in the dirt beneath our chipped red fingernails as we scratch our way through to the other side. She glows in our dark, our doubts, our fears, our *imperfection,* as well as in our light, our power, our love, and our gifts. She is the raw, not-so-pretty, but always beautiful truth of a woman who burns with divine love and is courageous enough to show it.

Show It

We need more examples (books, poems, podcasts, paintings, songs, dances, screams, blog posts, hint hint hint) *from* the Divine Feminine struggling to Make Love on Earth. Real Goddesses are needed here, now.

So I am birthing a whole Goddess through my blood, my sweat, my tears, my shit, my pussy, my heart, my surrender, my love, my life, and this very book.

I call her my Lady, or the Red Lady, but Her stage name is Rouge.

And, this has been,

and will continue to be,

My Rouge Awakening.

EPILOGUE

With all my Red heart (and Hers), thank you for reading Our Love Story.

Please pass this book along to another woman.

Or leave it under a Red rose bush

Or in a church pew . . .

(Wink.)

ACKNOWLEDGMENTS

The words "thank you" aren't big enough to hold the gratitude and Red hot and holy love I feel for all of you . . .

Mom and Dad: I would not have been able to write this book or find my soul without your unconditional love, trust, and generous support. My soul bows to you, LaLa licks your toes, and Anaya says "nice ass." Elizabeth, Bill and Kdog, Caroline, Keat, lil Georgia, and Waverly: Your love, videos (G's poo faces, kdog and that cow), Epic burgers, and the family gatherings I made it to were food for my soul. E and C: Your embodiments of the earth and the mama inspire me beyond words.

Tara and Meg, aka Shamanatrix (my panty godmother) and Deep Space (my snacky godmother): For allowing me to share It All, no matter how wild It got. For your divine downloads, spiritual "muscle," screaming-goat videos, and LaLa care. You two are why Goddess created Girlfriends.

Mark S.: The Red curtains parted and you were there. Your cosmic courage, illuminated integrity, sacred support, guardianship, cheese eggs, and Greater Being touch me like no other. Thank you for welcoming the Red Lady, Tinkerbuch, Sarah, and Uma Rouge. Our Love Story is writing Us.

Judah: For seeing me when I couldn't and cheering me on when I couldn't, for the delectable meals and for being an authentic Prophet.

Nathan and LiYana (and lil Griffin): For supporting my Fall in grace-filled ways and for your embodied statements of inimitable Love.

Jennifer: Knowing you exist gives me faith in all of existence. Thank you for helping me, and all of us, Remember.

E: For your gifts and invaluable support early on (late-night rally calls and "PUSH!" texts), for being a midwife *and* a dragon and providing me with exactly what I needed to learn.

Shannon: For your service and vigilance and for channeling my most favorite line ever from Spirit: "She single-white-femaled your Higher Self."

Cosi: For your kind support, wisdom, garden, and outstanding LaLa care (and for being her stylist).

Lisa Braun Dubbels: For going above and beyond the duty of a publicist and for your unwavering humor and integrity. I feel blessed to work with you.

Haven: For Receiving this wild Red screaming soul baby when she was still covered in blood, sweat, shit, and tears and for respectfully, intuitively, and lovingly helping me clean her off. Thank you Madame, er, Tami, Jennifer, and the whole extraordinary team at Sounds True for keeping It Real and for supporting my soulSelf's expression. It's an honor and joy to work with you all.

The entire Peeler Family (Gaily Waily!) and Beak Family (Grandmother and Grandfather), Lincoln Family, Henry, Paul Schmidt, Uncle Lee and Nancy Stiles, Lundgren Family (Aunt Nancy and Susan!), Barreca Family (Fay and beloved Steve), Mrs. Rieck, Grey Family (Allison!), Mark M. (yoga and outstanding bird care!), Nirmala, Ariel, Ashley, Simmin, Kubie, Walden, and my dearest friend Rachel: For your support and love over the years, no matter how deep I've burrowed.

Marion Woodman, Andrew Harvey, Jeffrey Kripal, Robert Rabbin, Jean Houston, Christiane Northrup, Gail Straub, Shiva Rea, Sofia Diaz, Caroline Myss, Nancy Qualls-Corbett, Elaine Pagels, Peter Grey, Cynthia Bourgeault, Teri Degler, Sue Monk Kidd, Bill Plotkin, Nicholas Knightly (for the beautiful Red poetry), Ted Kepes, Joel Smith, Kimberly Patton, Marilyn Nyborg and Georgia Dow, Carolyn Rivers, Susan March, Susanne Bersbach, Carl Buchheit, George and Cynthia Kavassilas: Thank you for your fierce wisdom, embodied presence, guidance, spiritual integrity, and extraordinary gifts you have offered me and this planet.

The Mystical Misfits, The Sacred Sorority, The Red Team, The Lineage, J.C. and M.M. and Sarah, Mama Earth, Papa Sun, God/dess, the dark and the light, the true and the false, LaLa, Anaya, the roses, my shadows, my body, my soul, my higher selves, and all of you brave bright beautiful Beings who are on this Wild Ride with me . . .

And,

The Red Lady—Always.

NOTES

FIRE HAZARDS

1. Allan Ross MacDougall, *Isadora: Revolutionary in Art and Love.* (New York: Thomas Nelson & Sons, 1960) 217.

2. Ibid. 217.

3. Ibid. 216.

4. Ibid. 218.

PART ONE: B.M. (BEFORE MARION)

1. Conrad Aiken, *The Charnel Rose, Senlin: A Biography and Other Poems.* (Boston: The Four Seas Company, 1918) 131–132.

CHAPTER 1: DIVINE WILD CHILD

Opening quote: James Hillman, *The Soul's Code: In Search of Character and Calling.* (New York: Random House, 1996) 13.

1. Thomas Merton, "In Silence," *The Collected Poems of Thomas Merton.* (New York: New Directions, 1977) 281.

2. This quote is commonly attributed to Gaston Bachelard. Its source is unknown.

3. Colin Oliver, *Stepping into Brilliant Air.* (Head Exchange, 1996).

CHAPTER 2: MYSTICAL MISFITS

Opening quote: Jack Kerouac, *On the Road.* (New York: Penguin, 1976) 5.

1. Rumi, "Keep walking," *The Essential Rumi.* trans. Coleman Barks with John Moyne, A.J. Arberry, Reynold Nicholas (San Francisco: HarperSanFrancisco, 1995) 278.

2. Carl Jung, quoted by Matthew Fox in *Christian Mystics.* (Novato, CA: New Dimensions, 2011) 3.

3. Teresa of Ávila, "Not Yet Tickled," *Love Poems from God: Twelve Sacred Voices from the East and West.* trans. Daniel Ladinsky (New York: Penguin Compass, 2002) 277.

4. Rumi, "Like This," *The Essential Rumi.* trans. Coleman Barks with John Moyne, A.J. Arberry, Reynold Nicholas (San Francisco: HarperSanFrancisco, 1995) 135–136.

5. Ibid. "Burnt Kabob," 7.

6. Ibid. "The Sunrise Ruby," 100.

7. Coleman Barks, *Rumi, The Big Red Book: The Great Masterpiece Celebrating Mystical Love & Friendship.* (San Francisco: HarperOne, 2010) 7.

8. Rumi, "I Have Such a Teacher," *The Essential Rumi.* trans. Coleman Barks with John Moyne, A.J. Arberry, Reynold Nicholas (San Francisco: HarperSanFrancisco, 1995) 133.

9. Ikkyū, *Crow with No Mouth: Ikkyu 15th Century Zen Master.* trans. Stephen Berg (Port Townsend, WA: Copper Canyon Press, 1989) 13.

10. Ikkyū, *Wild Ways: Zen Poems of Ikkyu.* trans. Jon Stevens (Buffalo: White Pine Press, 2003) 30.

11. Ikkyū, *Crow with No Mouth: Ikkyu 15th Century Zen Master.* trans. Stephen Berg (Port Townsend, WA: Copper Canyon Press, 1989) 64.

12. Ikkyū, *Zen Poetry: Let the Spring Breeze Enter.* trans. Lucian Stryk and Takashi Ikemoto (New York: Grove/Atlantic, 1995) 31.

13. Carol Lee Flinders, *Enduring Grace: Living Portraits of Seven Women Mystics.* (San Francisco: HarperSanFrancisco, 1993) 104.

14. Frank J. Tobin, *Flowing Light of the Godhead.* (New Jersey, Paulist Press, 1998) 43.

15. Catherine of Genoa, Carol Lee Flinders in *Enduring Grace: Living Portraits of Seven Women Mystics.* (San Francisco: HarperSanFrancisco, 1993) xxii.

16. Carol Lee Flinders, *Enduring Grace: Living Portraits of Seven Women Mystics.* (San Francisco: HarperSanFrancisco, 1993) 44.

17. Ibid.

18. Ibid.

19. Rabi'a, *Love Poems from God: Twelve Sacred Voices from the East and West.* trans. Daniel Ladinsky (New York: Penguin Compass, 2002) 2.

20. Ibid. "The Way the Forest Shelters," 14.

21. Teresa of Ávila, *Love Poems from God: Twelve Sacred Voices from the East and West.* trans. Daniel Ladinsky (New York: Penguin Compass, 2002) 281.

22. Audre Lorde, "Uses of the Erotic: The Erotic as Power," 1989. This essay was originally delivered as a speech in 1978 at the Fourth Berkshire Conference on the History of Women, Mount Holyoke College.

23. Carol Lee Flinders, *Enduring Grace: Living Portraits of Seven Women Mystics.* (San Francisco: HarperSanFrancisco, 1993) 132.

24. Catherine of Genoa, *Life and Doctrine of Saint Catherine of Genoa.* trans. Mrs. George Ripley (New York: Christian Press Association, 1986) 94.

25. Rumi, "With Passion," *Love Poems from God: Twelve Sacred Voices from the East and West.* trans. Daniel Ladinsky (New York: Penguin Compass, 2002) 61.

26. Lalla, hinduismtoday.com/modules/smartsection/item.php?itemid=3255.

27. Lalla, *Naked Song.* trans. Coleman Barks (Atlanta: Maypop Books, 1992) 17.

28. Rabi'a, "In My Soul," *Love Poems from God: Twelve Sacred Voices from the East and West.* trans. Daniel Ladinsky (New York: Penguin Compass, 2002) 11.

29. Nicholas Schmidle, "Faith and Ecstasy," *Smithsonian* (Volume 39, #9, December 2008) 37, 38.

30. Jack Kerouac, *Selected Letters 1957–1969.* (New York: Penguin, 2000) 7.

31. Teresa of Ávila, *Interior Castle.* trans. E. Allison Peers (Wilder Publications, 2008) 44.

32. Nicholas Schmidle, "Faith and Ecstasy," *Smithsonian* (Volume 39, #9, December 2008) 40.

33. Ibid. 47.

34. Matthew Fox, *Christian Mystics.* (Novato, CA: New Dimensions, 2011) 3.

35. Rabi'a, "A Lover Who Wants His Lovers Near," *Love Poems from God: Twelve Sacred Voices from the East and West.* trans. Daniel Ladinsky (New York: Penguin Compass, 2002) 26.

36. Teresa of Ávila, "He Desired Me So I Came Close," *Love Poems from God: Twelve Sacred Voices from the East and West.* trans. Daniel Ladinsky (New York: Penguin Compass, 2002) 274.

CHAPTER 3: TRUMPED BY THE TREE OF LIFE

Opening quote: Kahil Gibran, *The Beloved: Reflections On The Path Of The Heart.* trans. John Walbridge (New York: Penguin Compass, 1997), 66.

CHAPTER 4: THE GODDESS IS IN DA HOUSE!

Opening quote: Jalaja Bonheim, *Aphrodite's Daughters: Women's Sexual Stories and the Journey of the Soul.* (New York: Fireside, 1997) 57–58.

1. Thomas Coburn, *Encountering the Goddess: A Translation of the Devi-Mahatmya and a Study of Its Interpretation.* (Albany: State University of New York Press, 1991) 48.

2. Ibid. 53–54, 77–78.

3. David Kinsley, *Hindu Goddesses: Visions of the Divine Feminine in the Hindu Religious Tradition.* (Berkeley, CA: University of California Press, 1988) 138.

4. Thomas Coburn, *Encountering the Goddess: A Translation of the Devi-Mahatmya and a Study of Its Interpretation.* (Albany, NY: State University of New York Press, 1991) 77–78.

5. David Kinsley, *Hindu Goddesses: Visions of the Divine Feminine in the Hindu Religious Tradition.* (Berkeley, CA: University of California Press, 1988) 124.

6. John Koller, *The Indian Way.* (Pearson, 1982) 237.

7. David Kinsley, *Hindu Goddesses: Visions of the Divine Feminine in the Hindu Religious Tradition.* (Berkeley, CA: University of California Press, 1988) 130.

8. Lex Hixon, *Mother of the Universe: Visions of the Goddess and Tantric Hymns of Enlightenment.* (Quest, 1994) 10.

9. David Frawley, "Tantric Yoga and the Wisdom Goddess Kali," *Tantra* magazine (Issue 9, 1994).

CHAPTER 5: KALI'S CHILD

Opening quote: Oscar Wilde, *The Complete Works of Oscar Wilde*. (Princeton, NJ: Princeton University Library, 1898) 124.

1. Sue Monk Kidd, *Dance of the Dissident Daughter: A Woman's Journey from the Christian Tradition to the Sacred Feminine*. (San Francisco: HarperOne, 2006) 120.

2. Elaine Pagels, *Adam, Eve, and the Serpent: Sex and Politics in Early Christianity*. (New York: Vintage, 1989) 65.

3. Elaine Pagels, *The Gnostic Gospels*. (New York: Vintage, 1989) xix.

4. Jesus, *Book of Thomas*.

5. Elaine Pagels, *Adam, Eve, and the Serpent: Sex and Politics in Early Christianity*. (New York: Vintage, 1989) 60.

6. Ibid. 60.

CHAPTER 6: MY HIGHER EDUCATION

Opening quote: Eden Phillpotts, *A Shadow Passes*. (New York: Macmillan, 1919) 17.

CHAPTER 7: CAUGHT RED-HANDED

Opening quote: The Red Lady.

1. Jalaja Bonheim, *Aphrodite's Daughters: Women's Sexual Stories and the Journey of the Soul*. (New York: Fireside, 1997) 290.

CHAPTER 8: THE RED LIGHT DISTRICT OF DIVINITY

Opening quote: Rainer Maria Rilke, *Ahead of All Parting: The Selected Poetry and Prose of Rainer Maria Rilke*. trans. Stephen Mitchell (New York: Modern Library, 1995) 97.

1. Marion Woodman, foreword to Nancy Qualls-Corbett, *The Sacred Prostitute: Eternal Aspect of the Feminine*. (Toronto: Inner City, 1988) 7.

2. Daniel Odier, *Tantric Quest: An Encounter with Absolute Love*. trans. Jody Gladding (Rochester, VT: Inner Traditions, 1996) 45.

3. Audre Lorde, "Uses of the Erotic: The Erotic as Power," 1989. This essay was originally delivered as a speech in 1978 at the Fourth Berkshire Conference on the History of Women, Mount Holyoke College.

4. Peter Grey, *The Red Goddess*. (London: Scarlet Imprint, 2008) 17.

5. Jalaja Bonheim, *Aphrodite's Daughters: Women's Sexual Stories and the Journey of the Soul*. (New York: Fireside, 1997) 301.

6. Ibid. 178.

7. Tom Robbins, *Skinny Legs and All*. (New York: Bantam, 1995) 96.

8. Peter Grey, *The Red Goddess*. (London: Scarlet Imprint, 2008) 56.

9. Ibid. 52.

10. Jalaja Bonheim, *Aphrodite's Daughters: Women's Sexual Stories and the Journey of the Soul.* (New York: Fireside, 1997) 18.

11. Marion Woodman, foreword to Nancy Qualls-Corbett, *The Sacred Prostitute: Eternal Aspect of the Feminine.* (Toronto: Inner City, 1988) 9.

12. Nancy Qualls-Corbett, *The Sacred Prostitute: Eternal Aspect of the Feminine.* (Toronto: Inner City, 1988) 119.

13. Audre Lorde, "Uses of the Erotic: The Erotic as Power," 1989. This essay was originally delivered as a speech in 1978 at the Fourth Berkshire Conference on the History of Women, Mount Holyoke College.

14. Elizabeth Cunningham, *The Passion of Mary Magdalen.* (Rhinebeck, NY: Monkfish, 2007) 342.

CHAPTER 9: THE SACRED SORORITY

Opening quote: Peter Grey, *The Red Goddess.* (London: Scarlet Imprint, 2008) 71.

1. Elaine Pagels, *Adam, Eve, and the Serpent: Sex and Politics in Early Christianity.* (New York: Vintage, 1989) 63.

2. Sue Monk Kidd, *Dance of the Dissident Daughter: A Woman's Journey from the Christian Tradition to the Sacred Feminine.* (San Francisco: HarperOne, 2006) 72.

3. Elaine Pagels, *Adam, Eve, and the Serpent: Sex and Politics in Early Christianity.* (New York: Vintage, 1989) 68.

4. Ibid. 66.

5. Ibid. 67.

6. Ibid. 67–68.

7. Sue Monk Kidd, *Dance of the Dissident Daughter: A Woman's Journey from the Christian Tradition to the Sacred Feminine.* (San Francisco: HarperOne, 2006) 18.

8. Barbara Black Koltuv, *The Book of Lilith.* (Berwick, ME: Nicolas-Hays, 1986) 22.

9. Bible, Revelations XVII: 4.

10. Peter Grey, *The Red Goddess.* (London: Scarlet Imprint, 2008) 17.

11. Marion Woodman, *Conscious Femininity: Interviews with Marion Woodman.* (Toronto: Inner City Books, 1993) 9.

12. Peter Grey, *The Red Goddess.* (London: Scarlet Imprint, 2008) 123.

13. Ibid. 48.

14. Ibid. 178.

15. Jack Parsons, *The Book of Babalon.* Liber 49. (1946) hermetic.com/wisdom/lib49.html.

16. Cynthia Bourgeault, *The Meaning of Mary Magdalene.* (Boston: Shambhala Publications, 2010) 22.

17. Margaret Starbird, *The Woman with the Alabaster Jar.* (Rochester, VT: Bear and Company, 1993) 123.

18. Elizabeth Cunningham, *The Passion of Mary Magdalen.* (Rhinebeck, NY: Monkfish, 2007) 241.

19. Margaret Starbird, *Mary Magdalene, Bride in Exile.* (Rochester, VT: Bear and Company, 2005) 5.

20. Marion Woodman and Elinor Dickinson, *Dancing in the Flames: The Dark Goddess in the Transformation of Consciousness.* (Boston: Shambhala Publications, 1997) 8.

21. Cynthia Bourgeault, *The Meaning of Mary Magdalene.* (Boston: Shambhala Publications, 2010) 137.

22. *The Thunder: Perfect Mind.* trans. Jared Callaway, Maia Kotrosits, Justin Lasser, Celene Lillie, Hal Taussig (Hampshire, UK: Palgrave Macmillon, 2010) 84, 107, 3.

23. Peter Grey, *The Red Goddess.* (London: Scarlet Imprint, 2008) 72–73.

PART TWO: A.M. (AFTER MARION)

C. G. Jung, *The Red Book: Liber Novus.* ed. Sonu Shamdasani (New York: W.W. Norton, 2009) 232–233.

CHAPTER 10: ROUGE AWAKENING

Opening quote: Bill Plotkin, *Soulcraft: Crossing into the Mysteries of Nature and Psyche.* (Novato, CA: New World Library, 2003) 17, 19.

1. Marion Woodman, *Conscious Femininity: Interviews with Marion Woodman.* (Toronto: Inner City Books, 1993) 71–72, 51, 20.

2. Sue Monk Kidd, *Dance of the Dissident Daughter: A Woman's Journey from the Christian Tradition to the Sacred Feminine.* (San Francisco: HarperOne, 2006) 20.

3. C. G. Jung, *Psychology and Alchemy: Collected Works of C. G. Jung.* trans. Gerhard Adler and R. F. C. Hull (Princeton, NJ: Princeton University Press, 1980) 99.

4. Marion Woodman, *Conscious Femininity: Interviews with Marion Woodman.* (Toronto: Inner City Books, 1993) 18–19.

5. Bill Plotkin, *Soulcraft: Crossing into the Mysteries of Nature and Psyche.* (Novato, CA: New World Library, 2003) 27.

6. James Hillman, "The Soul of the Matter," an interview with Wes Nisker. *Inquiring Mind* Volume 11, no. 2, (1995).

7. Sue Monk Kidd, *Dance of the Dissident Daughter: A Woman's Journey from the Christian Tradition to the Sacred Feminine.* (San Francisco: HarperOne, 2006) 140.

8. Marion Woodman, *Conscious Femininity: Interviews with Marion Woodman.* (Toronto: Inner City Books, 1993) 18.

9. Mariana Caplan, *Eyes Wide Open: Cultivating Discernment on the Spiritual Path.* (Boulder, CO: Sounds True, 2009) 115.

10. Marion Woodman, *Conscious Femininity: Interviews with Marion Woodman.* (Toronto: Inner City Books, 1993) 19.

CHAPTER 11: RED NIGHT OF THE SOUL

Opening quote: C. S. Lewis, *Till We Have Faces: A Myth Retold.* (New York: Harcourt Brace & Company, 1980) 50.

1. Sue Woodruff, *Meditations with Mechthild of Magdeburg.* (Rochester, VT: Bear and Company, 1982) 69.

2. Bill Plotkin, *Soulcraft: Crossing into the Mysteries of Nature and Psyche.* (Novato, CA: New World Library, 2003) 28.

3. St. John of the Cross, quoted in John James, *Notes to Transformation: A Guide Book for the Inner Journey to the Self.* (Sussex, UK: West Grinstead, 1994) 63.

4. Robert Augustus Masters, *Spiritual Bypassing: When Spirituality Disconnects Us from What Really Matters.* (Berkeley, CA: North Atlantic, 2010) 32.

5. Ibid. 5.

6. David Deida, *Wild Nights.* (Boulder, CO: Sounds True, 2005) 12.

7. Bill Plotkin, *Soulcraft: Crossing into the Mysteries of Nature and Psyche.* (Novato, CA: New World Library, 2003) 15.

8. C. G. Jung, *The Red Book: Liber Novus.* ed. Sonu Shamdasani (New York: W.W. Norton, 2009), 29.

9. Robert Augustus Masters, *Spiritual Bypassing: When Spirituality Disconnects Us from What Really Matters.* (Berkeley, CA: North Atlantic, 2010) 43.

10. Ibid. 44.

11. Mariana Caplan, *Eyes Wide Open: Cultivating Discernment on the Spiritual Path.* (Boulder, CO: Sounds True, 2009) 253.

12. Bill Plotkin, *Soulcraft: Crossing into the Mysteries of Nature and Psyche.* (Novato, CA: New World Library, 2003) 99.

13. Marion Woodman, *Conscious Femininity: Interviews with Marion Woodman.* (Toronto: Inner City Books, 1993) 63.

CHAPTER 12: BLAST OFF

Opening quote: Commonly attributed to Ursula K. LeGuin, source unknown.

CHAPTER 13: RED ALERT

Opening quote: Alex Gordon, *Nine Deadly Venoms.* (Rustington, UK: Ebuilders Ltd., 2004) 207.

1. Mariana Caplan, *Eyes Wide Open: Cultivating Discernment on the Spiritual Path.* (Boulder, CO: Sounds True, 2009) 6.

2. Marion Woodman, *Conscious Femininity: Interviews with Marion Woodman.* (Toronto: Inner City Books, 1993) 47.

3. Jalaja Bonheim, *Aphrodite's Daughters: Women's Sexual Stories and the Journey of the Soul.* (New York: Fireside, 1997) 327.

4. Marion Woodman, *Leaving My Father's House: A Journey to Conscious Femininity* with Kate Danson, Mary Hamilton, Rita Greer Allen. (Boston: Shambhala Publications, 1993) 31.

5. Bill Plotkin, *Soulcraft: Crossing into the Mysteries of Nature and Psyche.* (Novato, CA: New World Library, 2003) 19.

6. Carly Stasko, "Imagitate the State: agitate your imagination." intrinsik.net

CHAPTER 14: THE RED TENT

Opening quote: David Whyte, "Sweet Darkness," *The House of Belonging.* (Langley, WA: Many Rivers Press, 1997) 23.

1. Anthony de Mello, *Awareness: The Way to Love.* ed. J. Francis Stroud, S.J. (New York: Quality Paperback Book Club, 1990) 141.

2. David Whyte, "Sweet Darkness," *The House of Belonging.* (Langley, WA: Many Rivers Press, 1997) 23.

3. Caroline Myss, *Entering the Castle: Finding the Inner Path to God and Your Soul's Purpose.* (New York: Free Press, 2007) 85.

4. Marion Woodman, *Conscious Femininity: Interviews with Marion Woodman.* (Toronto: Inner City Books, 1993) 19–20.

5. Friedrich Nietzsche, *Thus Spoke Zarathustra.* (London: Penguin, 1969) 90.

6. C. G. Jung, *The Red Book: Liber Novus.* ed. Sonu Shamdasani (New York: W.W. Norton, 2009) 234.

7. Caroline Myss, *Entering the Castle: Finding the Inner Path to God and Your Soul's Purpose.* (New York: Free Press, 2007) 66.

8. Ibid. 264.

CHAPTER 15: SHADOW PUPPETS

Opening quote: My Shadow.

1. Sidra Stone, *The Shadow King: The Invisible Force That Holds Women Back.* (Lincoln, NE: An Author's Guild Backprint Edition, 1997) 18.

2. Robert Augustus Masters, *Spiritual Bypassing: When Spirituality Disconnects Us from What Really Matters.* (Berkeley, CA: North Atlantic, 2010) 44.

3. Ibid. 45.

4. Robert Rabbin, *Speak Truthfully: Speak Your Way to an Authentic Life with Awareness, Courage and Confidence.* (Real Time Speaking, 2011) 1.

5. Elizabeth Cunningham, *The Passion of Mary Magdalen.* (Rhinebeck, NY: Monkfish, 2007) 170.

6. Betsy Prioleau, *Seductress: Women Who Ravished the World and Their Lost Art of Love.* (New York: Penguin, 2003) xii.

7. Ibid. xiii.

8. Ibid.

9. Ibid.

10. Marion Woodman, *Conscious Femininity: Interviews with Marion Woodman.* (Toronto: Inner City Books, 1993) 24

CHAPTER 16: GIRLS JUST WANNA HAVE FUN

Opening quote: Gnostic Mass. gnosis.org/ecclesia/lect149.htm.

1. Commonly attributed to Emily Dickinson. The source is unknown.

2. Teri Degler, *The Divine Feminine Fire: Creativity and Your Yearning to Express Yourself.* (Flourtown, PA: Dreamriver Press, 2009) 202.

3. Ibid. 76–77.

4. Hildegard Von Bingen, quoted in Elizabeth A. Dreyer, "Sequence for the Holy Spirit," *Holy Power Holy Presence: Redicovering Medieval Metaphors for the Holy Spirit.* (Mahwah, NJ: Paulist Press, 2007) 81–82.

5. Teri Degler, *The Divine Feminine Fire: Creativity and Your Yearning to Express Yourself.* (Flourtown, PA: Dreamriver Press, 2009) 150.

6. Eve Ensler, TED Talk India Conference. November, 2009.

7. Louann Brizendine, *The Female Brain.* (New York: Broadway Books, 2007) 1.

8. Teri Degler, *The Divine Feminine Fire: Creativity and Your Yearning to Express Yourself.* (Flourtown, PA: Dreamriver Press, 2009) 51.

9. Clarissa Pinkola Estés, *Women Who Run with the Wolves: Myths and Stories of the Wild Woman Archetype.* (New York: Balantine, 1992) Jacket cover.

10. Marion Woodman and Jill Mellick, *Coming Home to Myself: Daily Reflections for a Woman's Body and Soul.* (Boston: Conari Press, 2000) 65.

CHAPTER 16½: ROSES ARE RED

Opening quote: Tom Robbins, *Jitterbug Perfume.* (New York: Bantam, 1990) 281.

1. Barbara G. Walker, *The Woman's Encyclopedia of Myths and Secrets.* (San Francisco: HarperOne, 1983) 866.

CHAPTER 17: THE RED BLOCK

Opening quote: Theodore Roszak, *Where the Wasteland Ends.* (New York, Bantam, 1973).

1. Sue Monk Kidd, *Dance of the Dissident Daughter: A Woman's Journey from the Christian Tradition to the Sacred Feminine.* (San Francisco: HarperOne, 2006) 91.

2. Barbara Marx Hubbard, *Emergence: The Shift from Ego to Essence.* (San Francisco: Hampton Roads, 2001) 88, 45, 90.

3. Bill Plotkin, *Soulcraft: Crossing into the Mysteries of Nature and Psyche.* (Novato, CA: New World Library, 2003) 26.

4. Commonly attributed to Howard Thurman. The source is unknown.

CHAPTER 18: THE RED PRINCESS

Opening quote: Brian Andreas, storypeople.com.

1. Margaret Starbird, *Mary Magdalene, Bride in Exile.* (Rochester, VT: Bear and Company, 2005) 102.

2. Ibid. 103.

3. Jacob Needleman, foreword to Jean-Yves Leloup, *The Gospel of Mary Magdalene.* trans. Joseph Rowe (Rochester, VT: Inner Traditions, 2002) vi.

4. Cynthia Bourgeault, *The Meaning of Mary Magdalene.* (Boston: Shambhala Publications, 2010) 126.

5. Gustavo Adolfo Bécquer, *Rhymes and Legends.* trans., ed. Stanley Applebaum (Mineola, NY: Dover, 2006) 29.

6. Cynthia Bourgeault, *The Meaning of Mary Magdalene.* (Boston: Shambhala Publications, 2010) 127.

7. Jean-Yves Leloup, *The Gospel of Mary Magdalene.* trans. Joseph Rowe (Rochester, VT: Inner Traditions, 2002) 11.

8. Laurie Goodstein, "A Faded Piece of Papyrus Refers to Jesus' Wife," *The New York Times* (September 18, 2012).

9. Cynthia Bourgeault, *The Meaning of Mary Magdalene.* (Boston: Shambhala Publications, 2010) 145.

10. Peter Grey, *The Red Goddess.* (London: Scarlet Imprint, 2008) 72–73.

11. *The Gospel According to Thomas.* Bentley Layton ed., *Nag Hammadi Codex* (Leidan: Brill, 1989) #105.

12. Claire Nahmad and Margaret Bailey, *The Secret Teachings of Mary Magdalene.* (London: Watkins, 2006) 95.

13. Ibid. 73.

14. Ibid. 73.

15. Tau Malachi, *St. Mary Magdalene: The Gnostic Tradition of the Holy Bride.* (Woodbury, MN: Llewellyn, 2006) 37–38.

16. Claire Nahmad and Margaret Bailey, *The Secret Teachings of Mary Magdalene.* (London: Watkins, 2006) 156.

17. Tau Malachi, *The Secret Gospel of St. Mary Magdalene,* found in *St. Mary Magdalene: The Gnostic Tradition of the Holy Bride.* (Woodbury, MN: Llewellyn, 2006) 147.

18. Hafez, "The Lost Daughter," *The Angels Knocking on the Tavern Door.* trans. Robert Bly and Leonard Lewisohn (New York: HarperCollins, 2008) 17.

19. Tau Malachi, *The Secret Gospel of St. Mary Magdalene,* found in *St. Mary Magdalene: The Gnostic Tradition of the Holy Bride.* (Woodbury, MN: Llewellyn, 2006) 137.

20. Ibid. 147.

21. James Hillman, *The Soul's Code: In Search of Character and Calling.* (New York: Random House, 1996) 8.

22. Jean-Yves Leloup, *The Gospel of Mary Magdalene.* trans. Joseph Rowe (Rochester, VT: Inner Traditions, 2002) 14.

23. Cynthia Bourgeault, *The Meaning of Mary Magdalene.* (Boston: Shambhala Publications, 2010) 166.

24. Ibid. 58.

25. Ibid. 61.

26. Jean-Yves Leloup, *The Gospel of Mary Magdalene.* trans. Joseph Rowe (Rochester, VT: Inner Traditions, 2002) 13.

27. Cynthia Bourgeault, *The Meaning of Mary Magdalene.* (Boston: Shambhala Publications, 2010) 61.

28. Jean-Yves Leloup, *The Gospel of Mary Magdalene.* trans. Joseph Rowe (Rochester, VT: Inner Traditions, 2002) 153.

29. Cynthia Bourgeault, *The Meaning of Mary Magdalene.* (Boston: Shambhala Publications, 2010) 54.

30. Ibid. 205.

CHAPTER 19: DRAGON FIRE

Opening quote: Maria Rainer Rilke, *Letters to a Young Poet.* trans. Reginald Snell (originally published London: Sidgwick and Jackson, 1945).

1. Noela Evans, quoted in Garret Pierson, *What Success Takes.* (New Generation Consulting, 2009).

2. Bill Plotkin, *Soulcraft: Crossing into the Mysteries of Nature and Psyche.* (Novato, CA: New World Library, 2003) 210.

3. Carol Lee Flinders, *Enduring Grace: Living Portraits of Seven Women Mystics.* (San Francisco: HarperSanFrancisco, 1993) 79.

4. Ibid. 46.

5. Teresa of Ávila, quoted in Fr. Kieran Kavanaugh, *The Way of Perfection.* (Washington, DC: Institute of Carmelite Studies, 2000) 222.

6. Teri Degler, *The Divine Feminine Fire: Creativity and Your Yearning to Express Yourself.* (Flourtown, PA: Dreamriver Press, 2009) 233.

7. Mechthild of Magdeburg, *Flowing Light of the Godhead* Book II, 26. (Martino Fine Books, 2012) 95.

8. Joseph Campell with Bill Moyers, *The Power of Myth.* (New York: Anchor, 1991) 184.

9. Caroline Myss, keynote speech for Hay House Cruise. 2011.

10. Tom Robbins, *Still Life with Woodpecker.* (New York: Bantam, 2003) 93.

CHAPTER 20: A RUBY IN THE HEART OF GRANITE

Opening quote: Rumi, quoted in Andrew Harvey, *The Way of Passion: A Celebration of Rumi.* (Berkeley, CA: Frog, Ltd., 1994) 51.

1. William Stafford, *The Way It Is.* (Minneapolis, MN: Graywolf, 1999) 42.

2. Robert A. Johnson, *Owning Your Shadow: Understanding the Dark Side of the Psyche.* (San Francisco: HarperSanFrancisco, 1991) 32.

3. Ibid. 46.

4. Bill Plotkin, *Soulcraft: Crossing into the Mysteries of Nature and Psyche*. (Novato, CA: New World Library, 2003) 97.

5. Cempulappeyanirar, *The Interior Landscape: Love Poems of a Classical Tamil Anthology*. trans. A. K. Ramanujan (New York: Oxford University Press USA, 1994).

21: REDEFINING DIVINITY

Opening quote: Lalla, *Naked Song*. trans. Coleman Barks (Atlanta: Maypop Books, 1992).

1. Caroline Myss, youtube.com interview by Lilou Mace on her Juicy Living Tour, 2011.

2. Govert Schuller shares a view given by the 19th-century theosophist Madame Blavatsky on alpheus.org/html/articles/krishnamurti/onk.html.

3. Edith Sodergran, *Complete Poems*. (Northumberland, UK: Bloodaxe Books Ltd, 1993).

4. Joseph Campbell, foreword to Maya Deren, *Divine Horsemen: The Living Gods of Haiti*. (Kingston, NY: McPherson & Co, 1988) xvii.

5. Rainer Maria Rilke, quoted in Anita Barrows and Joanna Macy, *Rilke's Book of Hours: Love Poems to God*. (New York: Riverhead, 1996) 88.

6. Cynthia Bourgeault, *The Meaning of Mary Magdalene*. (Boston: Shambhala Publications, 2010) 134.

7. Ibid. 134.

8. Miranda Shaw, *Passionate Enlightenment: Women in Tantric Buddhism*. (Princeton, NJ: Princeton University Press, 1994) 41.

9. Robert Rabbin, *Real Time Speaking: You Are the Message*. (Real Time Speaking, 2008) 36.

10. Lao Tzu, "Always We Hope," *The Way of Life According to Lao Tzu*. trans. Witter Bynner (New York: HarperCollins, 1986).

22. BURN, BABY, BURN

Opening quote: Pablo Neurda, "Flies Enter a Closed Mouth," *Five Decades: Poems 1925–1970*. trans. Ben Belitt (Grove Press, 1994) 201.

1. Caroline Myss, *Entering the Castle: Finding the Inner Path to God and Your Soul's Purpose*. (New York: Free Press, 2007) 325.

2. C. G. Jung, *Psychology and Religion: West and East. The Collected Works of C. G. Jung, Volume 11*. ed. Sir Herbert Read and Gerhart Adler, trans. R. F. C. Hull (Princeton, NJ: Princeton University Press, 1975) 140.

3. David Whyte, *Self Compassion* CD recording. (Langley, WA: Many Rivers, 1991).

4. Marion Woodman, *Conscious Femininity: Interviews with Marion Woodman*. (Toronto: Inner City Books, 1993) 9.

5. Llewellyn Vaughan-Lee, *The Return of the Feminine and the World Soul*. (Salisbur: The Golden Sufi Center, 2009) 4.

6. Bill Plotkin, *Soulcraft: Crossing into the Mysteries of Nature and Psyche*. (Novato, CA: New World Library, 2003) 13.

PERMISSIONS

The poem on page 157 by Hildegard of Bingen is from *Holy Power, Holy Presence: Rediscovering Medieval Metaphors for the Holy Spirit,* by Elizabeth A. Dreyer. Copyright ©2007. Reprinted by permission granted through Copyright Clearance Center on behalf of Paulist Press.

The poem on page 169 by Theodore Roszak is from *Where the Wasteland Ends.* Copyright ©1973 Bantam. Reprinted by permission of Betty Roszak.

The quote on page 179 by Brian Andreas is from storypeople.com. Reprinted by permission of the author.

The poem on page 186 is by Gustavo Adolfo Bécquer, from *Rhymes and Legends,* edited by Stanley Applebaum. Copyright ©2006. Reprinted by permission of Dover Publications, Inc.

The poem on pages 190–191 by Hafez, "The Lost Daughter," is from *The Angels Knocking on the Tavern Door,* by Robert Bly and Leonard Lewisohn. Copyright ©2008. Reprinted by permission of HarperCollins Publishers.

The poem on pages 215–216 by William Stafford, "The Way It Is," is from *The Way It Is: New and Selected Poems.* Copyright ©1998 by the Estate of William Stafford. Reprinted with permission of The Permissions Company, Inc., on behalf of Graywolf Press.

The poem on page 219 by Cempulappeyanirar is from *The Interior Landscape: Love Poems of a Classical Tamil Anthology,* translated by A. K. Ramanujan. Copyright ©1994. Reprinted by permission of Oxford University Press India ©Oxford University Press 1999.

The lines on page 233 by Rainer Maria Rilke are from "Gott spricht zu jedem . . . /God speaks to each of us . . . " from *Rilke's Book of Hours: Love Poems To God,* translated by Anita Barrows and Joanna Macy. Translation copyright ©1996. Reprinted by permission of Riverhead Books, an imprint of Penguin Group (USA) Inc.

The lines on page 239 by Pablo Neruda are from "Flies Enter a Closed Mouth," from *Five Decades: Poems 1925–1970.* Copyright ©1974 by Grove Press, Inc. English translations copyright ©1961, 1969, 1972, 1974 by Ben Belitt. Reprinted by permission of Grove/Atlantic, Inc. Any third-party use of this material, outside of this publication, is prohibited.

The transcribed passage on page 241 by David Whyte is from the CD *Self Compassion.* Copyright ©1991. Reprinted by permission of Many Rivers Press.

About the Author

Sera Beak is a Harvard-trained scholar of comparative world religions who spent years traveling the world studying spirituality with Sufi dervishes, Tibetan monks, Croatian mystics, shamans, and more. She is the author of *The Red Book: A Deliciously Unorthodox Approach to Igniting Your Divine Spark*, and she has appeared in *The New York Times, People,* and *Publisher's Weekly,* as well as on NPR, *The Dr. Oz Show,* and *Oprah and Friends.* She lives in Texas. For more, visit serabeak.com.

ABOUT SOUNDS TRUE

Sounds True is a multimedia publisher whose mission is to inspire and support personal transformation and spiritual awakening. Founded in 1985 and located in Boulder, Colorado, we work with many of the leading spiritual teachers, thinkers, healers, and visionary artists of our time. We strive with every title to preserve the essential "living wisdom" of the author or artist. It is our goal to create products that not only provide information to a reader or listener, but that also embody the quality of a wisdom transmission.

For those seeking genuine transformation, Sounds True is your trusted partner. At SoundsTrue.com you will find a wealth of free resources to support your journey, including exclusive weekly audio interviews, free downloads, interactive learning tools, and other special savings on all our titles.

To learn more, please visit SoundsTrue.com/freegifts or call us toll free at 800-333-9185.

sounds true
many voices, one journey